I'LL TELL ME MA

By the same author

NON-FICTION

An Evil Cradling
Between Extremes: A Journey Beyond Imagination
(with John McCarthy)
Four Quarters of Light: An Alaskan Journey

FICTION

Turlough

Brian Keenan

I'LL TELL ME MA

JONATHAN CAPE
LONDON

Published by Jonathan Cape 2009

2 4 6 8 10 9 7 5 3 1

Copyright © Brian Keenan 2009

Brian Keenan has asserted his right under the Copyright, Designs
and Patents Act 1988 to be identified as the author of this work

This book is a work of non-fiction based on the life, experiences and
recollections of the author. In some limited cases names of people,
places, dates, sequences or the detail of events have been changed
solely to protect the privacy of others. The author has stated to the
publishers that, except in such minor respects not affecting the
substantial accuracy of the work, the contents of this book are true.

First published in Great Britain in 2009 by
Jonathan Cape
Random House, 20 Vauxhall Bridge Road,
London SW1V 2SA

www.rbooks.co.uk

Addresses for companies within The Random House Group Limited
can be found at: www.randomhouse.co.uk/offices.htm

The Random House Group Limited Reg. No. 954009

A CIP catalogue record for this book is available from the British Library

ISBN 9780224062169

The Random House Group Limited supports The Forest Stewardship
Council (FSC), the leading international forest certification organisation.
All our titles that are printed on Greenpeace approved FSC certified paper
carry the FSC logo. Our paper procurement policy can be found at
www.rbooks.co.uk/environment

Typeset in Minion by Palimpsest Book Production Limited,
Grangemouth, Stirlingshire

This bookproof printed and bound in Great Britain by
CPI Antony Rowe, Chippenham, Wiltshire

To my parents, whose ghostly shades looked over my shoulder

CONTENTS

AUTHOR'S NOTE

WHEN I SET OUT ON THIS JOURNEY, I DIDN'T KNOW WHERE TO BEGIN. I was sure there was much I could not remember. My past seemed to have been extinguished in a big black abyss. I was convinced that memory would fail me. At times I stared in panic at the blank page. It had become another abyss. It took some time for me to realize that it was because I was trying to move between them like a bird. It was only when I stopped trying to see what I wanted to see, and began to understand the difference between memory and history, that the past revealed itself: when I stopped chasing after history's dubious record and let memory come to me like returning radar signals.

Memory is like a bat rather than a bird. Most birds choose not to fly in the dark. But bats can negotiate the dark enclosed passage of time, echo-locating moments of our life history that lie hidden there.

This memoir opens up my childhood in Belfast between the years 1950 and 1965. The last two chapters take a giant leap forward to the last few months of my mother's life. She died on my birthday in 2004. Her dying on the day of my birth connected us in a powerful way. During that time I began to discover my mother's

1

childhood and how it curiously intersected with and illuminated my own.

Ironically, there will be many birds flying through this memoir. I had to become blind as a bat to find them.

PAINS AND PLANES

My history begins in the dark.

I think I was about six or seven years old, and for some weeks, or maybe months, over a protracted period I dreaded night-time, bedtime and the dark. For me the approach of bedtime was synonymous with pain. It came out of the blue one evening as I lay in bed awaiting sleep. Sudden pain in my knees and thighs. The shock of it numbed me but as it grew chronic and intense I became afraid. I pushed back the heavy woollen blanket and tried bending my knees in the air as I lay on my back. I thought of an imaginary bicycle and believed that if I could pump the air furiously, I could cycle myself away from the pain. As I think of it now, it was a ludicrous notion, as I didn't own a bicycle and so had never learned to ride one. But the harder I pedalled, the harder the pain pursued me. I pummelled my thighs and knees but it was all to no avail. The next night, and for many nights, the pain returned, and with it my ritual bike ride. After several hours I fell asleep. This ritual went on for several nights. I suffered in silence. I was afraid of the pain but I think I was even more afraid of finding out what might have caused it.

Whatever my degree of physical discomfort, it was multiplied

3

by my fantastic imaginings. Were my legs dying? Did I have polio? Would I have to wear callipers and sit in the doorway watching other kids play, like the crippled boy in the next street? Like most frightened children, I reasoned things to extremes. But neither reason nor sleep relieved me from the pain that seemed to be waiting for me each night. I went sheepishly to bed telling no one of my anxiety. Pain even invaded my dreams.

There was a piece of stone in our house that someone had given my dad. He told me it was 'petrified wood' and tried to explain the process of petrification. He talked about how minerals and salts that are found in the ground dissolve and soak into the trunk of a fallen tree. These prevent it from rotting and preserve it so that over hundreds of years the substance of the tree changes, though its shape and form remain: it is fossilized and becomes a stone tree. My father was no academic, though he was interested in things and did his best to convey a sense of this magical piece of stone tree without letting the words 'petrification,' 'minerals' and 'fossilized' get in the way. But he didn't know what the dark held for me. In my dreams, my legs were petrified tree trunks. The idea of minerals and salts changing the composition of the wood had rooted itself in my mind and I dreamed that the bones of my legs were changing and when the fire in them went out, my legs would become like the petrified tree: dead logs of stone encased in flesh.

One night my mother found me sobbing and pacing the bedroom when I should have been asleep. 'What's the matter?' she asked. I resolutely intended telling her that it was nothing and that I simply couldn't sleep. But as I opened my mouth all the nights of pain and dreaming fell out of me and I complained between sobs of terrible pains in my legs. I never once mentioned the nightmares of petrification. She comforted me as we sat side by side on the bed, and explained that I should not worry. 'It was only growing

pains,' she told me. For a moment I was overwhelmed by the word
'only'. It seemed to diminish nights of torture much more than the
explanation did. Growing pain was also 'good pain', she insisted. It
told us we were growing up and 'that was good, wasn't it?' she
asked. I nodded, much relieved, and for the next few nights was
blissfully free of pain or nightmares. The efficacy of giving the
unknown a name is a wonderful thing, and if petrification was a
process of change in a substance, my mother's simple explanation
that growing pains were 'good' had erased the pain and dreams out
of me . . . but not completely. They went away for a while and then
came charging back.

Now I was armed with the knowledge that I was growing, and
that these pains were good. Besides, Mother always ensured that I
had access to a plethora of hot water bottles if I needed them. There
was a great big stone one that supposedly held the heat longest, a
floppy rubber one and a variety of lemonade bottles with stone
screw caps which had a thick red rubber band around them that
made a pressurized seal as you screwed it down. Armed with
Mother's simple logic and my regiments of hot water bottles, pain
became very familiar and I almost welcomed it. After all, it was my
guarantee that I was getting bigger.

It wasn't long before I began to question this idea as the growing
pains continued. How much pain equalled how many inches? I
would speculate. Did it move invisible and mysteriously through
the body to ensure that other limbs grew equally? If so, where would
it go next? My arms, my chest – and what would happen to my
head and feet? These questions created their own panic. Why did
only my legs hurt? I put this question to my mother. Again her
simple logic seemed to resolve everything. 'It was good pain but it
was also lazy pain and liked to stay where it was.' I shouldn't worry,
everything would be fine. I accepted this without confessing the

rising anxiety that I would become some weird daddy-long-legs human creature who wobbled about top heavy in every breeze. Though I never told her this, Mother obviously had some sense of it when she said, 'Be assured, your hands will always be able to tie your shoelaces!' If she was a mind reader, that was fine, but she was never able to dispel my fears completely: for months daddy-long-legged insects mocked me whenever I saw them. When I discovered one of these creatures in the living room, I would freeze in paroxysms of superstitious panic. One day when my dad attempted to catch the creature gently in his cupped hand to release it into the outside world, I remember telling him nervously, 'Don't break its legs, Daddy!'

However well my mother had sought to dispel my fears and answer my questions, I still resorted to marking the wall in my bedroom at head height. No one knew about the green crayon mark on the floral wallpaper. I put it there not to question my mother's explanation but to see how speedily this pain worked. When nothing happened, I remembered her explanation that it was a lazy pain. So I decided to suffer on and wait it out for a while. After a few months, the simple green height mark remained alone. I had thought that even after a few weeks I would have a ladder of green lines climbing upwards from the original. But the single green line stared back at me like a closed eye that refused to acknowledge my presence. It was then that I rebelled. This pain was no friendly bedfellow; no 'good guy' in disguise who had come to help me. Pain was a betrayer. It fooled me into believing that I was growing but secretly it was stunting my growth. Everything else in the world had grown in the last lot of weeks without all the pain, except me! Confused and angry, I refused to believe its lies.

Mother noticed the change in my demeanour. She knew the pains had not gone away but I was relating to it in a different way.

How was I feeling? she asked one day. Before I could answer, she continued with the question 'Still got the pains?' I wanted to be nonchalant but answered 'Yes, but they're doing nothing for me.' At the age of six frustration and resentment are deeply felt and hard to deal with but they are frequently openly expressed. Mother understood and answered, unforgettably, 'Well, son, it's a bit like baking bread, it's a long time in the oven before the dough rises!' So I forgot about the pains and after a while they forgot about me. I did grow though I never added any more marks on the wall. Other things were beginning to interest me.

Whatever the difficulties of my own growing pains, the adult world was undergoing its own. General Nasser in Egypt was nationalizing the Suez Canal, and Britain, France and Israel were all too ready to teach Arab upstarts that they were in charge and that the new world order was not about liberation but control. The Civil Rights Movement in America was in no mood to accept such notions of control. Liberation meant just that, and riots erupted as Alabama University was forced to admit its first black student. But monumental declarations of liberty and justice were quickly undermined, and the student was later expelled.

I remember the dissociated look on the face of the student as he was ushered by a retinue of black supporters through a mass of howling white faces: it reminded me of the boy in my primary school who arrived in class one day wearing spectacles with thick lenses set in simple round black frames. They highlighted his eyes and made him look gawkish. He was obviously self-conscious about his appearance, and a small group of his classmates soon homed in on this. In less than an afternoon they had invented the chorus that greeted him each day: 'Blind as a bat, face like a rat.' They would repeat this demeaning refrain, spitting out the consonants with great relish. A few of them would gather round him and place their hands over their eyes as they chanted, 'Owly eyes, you can't see, owly eyes, who are we?' To my credit, I don't recall joining in with this ritual. I only remember that his body seemed to get smaller while his eyes got larger behind the black circles of his glasses. After a few days the gang of bullies added to their torment by running up close to him with their arms outstretched, suddenly wheeling away from him like bats, avoiding an imminent collision. The boy stood silent or tried to turn from this onslaught, his eyes bright with held-back tears. While I was dealing with my growing pains and my hapless school friend was daily steeling himself against his bullies, the Hungarians were revolting against their Soviet over-lords. That's when I first understood the word 'refugee'. The cackle of our art deco Bakelite radio would spit out events, the number of people homeless and destitute, and the rising number of dead. The creamy-voiced presenter urgently spoke of 'the death count of those who simply chose to be free'. Death and freedom became big issues early in my life.

Meanwhile Elvis Presley was only twenty-one years old and already a millionaire. Arthur Miller, a bony playwright of distinction, married Marilyn Monroe, a buxom actress, also of distinction. Mr Miller looked like a neighbour I often saw cycling to work with his trousers tucked into his socks and his body enclosed in a great flapping gabardine overcoat. But none of our neighbours looked like Mrs Miller, though many of them tried. In this confusing world my mother stopped attempting to explain things with her simple comforting logic. Instead, if any question was put to her about our future by me or my sister, or if we innocently asked her about what was happening in the world we were hearing about through our radio, she would answer with a reassuring look that suggested she knew everything. 'Que sera sera! What ever will be, will be,' was her response to questions that were impossible for her to answer. My mother was not blonde and looked more like Eva Gabor or Hedy Lamarr but she was a million times more convincing than Doris Day.

Within the year Suez was forgotten and the 'Common Market' was set up to control the new order in a post-war world. Harold Macmillan became Prime Minister. He looked like one of the attendants supplied by funeral parlours to escort the hearse. My dad laughed at my observation and made his own, something along the lines, 'You might be right there, son. With him in charge we could all be following a coffin soon!'

I didn't understand what he meant, but in a world where in less than a year the Soviets – whoever they were – were ruthlessly oppressing a place called Hungary, had launched Sputnik 1 to orbit the earth and later sent a Russian dog called Laika into space. Mr Macmillan, with his pallid face and undertaker's top hat, was becoming insignificant. In school, we took to drawing pictures of space rockets and planets and Laika the dog. Meanwhile, black America was still on the move as a handful of black children were shepherded by a thousand armed troopers into previously all-white schools. Nobody drew pictures of that or even tried to explain the strange things that were going on in cowboy land. The radio, sitting above the gas meter cabinet, crooned 'Love letters in the sand' while Bill Haley and the Comets rocked around the clock and Elvis crooned 'All Shook Up', and I suppose that's how it really was in the complex, constantly shifting jigsaw of the mid-fifties. All shook up!

I remember watching my father listen intently to news broadcasts, especially about Hungary. I remember it only because Hungary to me was simply a place where, as its name suggests, everyone was hungry and homeless. Naïvely I asked my father about this and he answered quietly that I was very smart and that's exactly how it was in that place, then he mumbled something to my mother about how it could start all over again. Whatever 'it' was, my mother seemed unfussed and continued with the click-clacking of her knitting. She could knit like greased lightning for hours on end without ever looking at the wool or needles she held. She could hold long conversations and even read the newspaper while balls of wool passed through the quick magic of her hands and produced hats, gloves, socks, jumpers, cardigans and Aran sweaters in a matter of days. But she never responded to my father's remark or even acknowledged him. She kept on knitting blissfully oblivious to the world's woes or my father's concerns.

It was a dozen years since the end of the war. My father had been in the RAF and served in a ground crew team in many parts of the globe – in 'theatres of war' as Field Marshal Montgomery used to call them when the BBC broadcast a long-running series about the war. I remember his squeaky voice and skinny, pinched face, his beret and his swagger stick. I once asked my dad why I never saw *him* in the programme, but his oblique answer told me little: 'Maybe I didn't fight in his war, son!'

Trying to get my father to talk about the war was pointless. He would buy me toy soldiers, tanks, and all sorts of military trucks. He sometimes told me about the different places he was stationed: India, Egypt, Ethiopia and, curiously enough, Lebanon. I still have a photo of him wearing skis somewhere in the snow-covered mountains of that country with a local girl. They looked happy and playful and, wherever the war was, it was a long way from them.

Among the other war toys he bought me were several dozen Airfix model kits. They were not bought as presents to celebrate a birthday or Christmas; he just brought them home unexpectedly. I didn't recognize it then as I do now but there were moments when my father forgot all the personae that we expected from him:

father, husband, provider, workman and the other layers of roles
that hide a person, even from his family. When my dad was building
his aeroplanes he shed these accumulated guises and entered into
another world. Sometimes I think of it as akin to my mother's
hypnotic knitting. But it wasn't like that; her knitting was more
soporific and she could move in and out of these moments
instantaneously. Dad entered another world. It was one I could
share even if I couldn't fully be a part of it. Those weekend evenings,
he and I would sit studying the build plan for one of his models.
Dad's absorption was total. I sometimes felt myself older than him
and at other times in this aviation otherworld he was ageless. In
the opiate aroma of glue and Humbrol oil paint, we became unaware
of the world around us and beyond us. We disappeared into the
clouds of Spitfires, Stukas, Hurricanes and many more whose names
have flown away from me.

Dad spread out the plastic frames of moulded parts. He could
read their two-dimensional blueprints in minutes. He rarely needed
to refer to the manufacturer's plan kit. In his mind's eye he could
see the finished product in all its three-dimensional elegance.
Sometimes he would stare at the pieces and remark, 'Ah, she'll be
a beautiful job', or sigh and declare that the scale was too small and
'they should have enlarged it so that you could really see it'. I stared
down at the flat rectangle of pieces ready to be separated and
reassembled. They looked like a tableau of alien hieroglyphics
waiting to be decoded.

Dad had his own specialist tools for the job. Some of them must
have been liberated from my mother's dressing table: several silver
nail files, a tiny pair of surgical scissors, tweezers, small strips of
sandpaper, clear nail varnish, an assortment of darning needles and
several artists' brushes with stumpy stems and varying thickness of
bristle. All these tools were kept in an old tea caddy with a black,

red and gold oriental design. It had its own special spot on a shelf under the stairs. Dad knew how to pour precise amounts of glue on the smallest surface. Also, he could work in the tiniest of spaces created by the growing toy fuselage. I suspect that soldering thousands of fine wires as a telephone engineer had something to do with it.

He excelled at painting. He was an expert in camouflage but his 'birds', as he sometimes referred to them, did not sit all bright and shiny. Along the rivet lines on the fuselage he painted small spots of rust, and oil stains on the engine housing. Sometimes he toned down the colour along the wing ridges, explaining that that was where the aircraft took the greatest punishment from wind and rain. On other areas he would paint blotches of what I called 'dirty silver'. These were where weather or maybe gunfire had stripped away the paintwork. My dad's aircraft were real dogfighters, dirty and smelly and more authentic than the image on the box. As a painter he should have been a miniaturist. He painted every detail of the pilot's uniform. He painted skin tones and moustaches even though you could hardly see the figure when it was placed in the cockpit. He named most of the pilots, even the German ones, and made up stories about them. He took some of my infantry soldiers and cannibalized them for ground crew. One kneeling soldier whose arms were outstretched in the action of firing a pistol was modified and positioned to look as if he was carrying out a repair to a bomber's front wheel strut. Another soldier in the act of thrusting his rifle and bayonet was also transferred from the infantry corps to RAF ground crew. The rifle and its bayonet were carefully removed, leaving the soldier standing with his forward-thrust hands empty. Ground crew overalls were painted over his combat fatigues. If necessary, the item of army equipment moulded on the body of the soldier was painstakingly sanded off or removed by the diligent application of hot sewing needles. Ingeniously, my father threaded a 'hose' of wire encased in a black plastic sleeve through the man's hands and fitted a nozzle shaped from the waste of the plastic parts frame. The hose then ran to a discarded sewing thread spool painted to look like a fuel drum. The rifleman was now pumping petrol. Just to ensure that his handiwork was not too easily discovered, Dad even went to the extent of sanding off their helmets and painting thick crops of black hair on the rounded heads.

Few of Father's aircraft ever stood on mounted platforms like stuffed birds. Instead he suspended the models in different angles of flight by very fine lengths of fishing tackle. At night I shone the searchlight of my torch and watched these dogfights in the dark above me.

My real love then, and I suppose now, was the biplanes. At first glance they were rickety contraptions, but when you really looked at the finished model or flew it slowly above your head it was imbued with elegant, bird-like grace. Some of these early machines even took the names of birds: the Sopwith Snipe and the German Albatross DV with its centrally mounted wings, and long nose cone housing the engine. Hanging above my bed, its silhouette resembled a great gliding seabird. And there were other fanciful names like the Sopworth Camel and Pup, the Bristol Scout, and the Fairy Flycatcher, which I remember being described as one of the biggest fighters ever built. None of my biplanes ever seemed ugly. Quite the reverse. My plastic imitations of miracles of plywood, balsa and canvas had their own distinct personalities, which could not be summed up in a breakdown of technical data. They had human qualities of obstinacy, determination, pride and grace combined with a *risqué* sense of fun. Floating above me in the dark, they were more than mere models, they were gods that roared out of the heavens. With speeds in excess of 200 m.p.h., affording mankind the capacity to travel further than it ever had before, these cocky little contraptions had effectively jumped human evolution out of its skin. They had given man his wings.

But human beings do not make such evolutionary leaps easily. There is the story that is always associated in my mind with these fabulous machines which flew through my childhood memories. It happened in the countryside of northern Spain in the early 1900s. A biplane was being assembled from crates prior to a much-advertised flying demonstration. The huge crowd of country folk were not convinced about the miracle of flight. To their mind, anything that lifted men's feet off the ground was the work of the devil and they set about dismantling the infernal contraption, eventually burning it to a chorus of 'Down with science, long live religion!' The pilot and engineers barely escaped with their lives. The story might well have been forgotten but for an ironic twist of history some years later not far from where the peasants had their sacrificial bonfire. General Franco employed fleets of one of the most beautiful biplanes ever built, the Fiat CR32 which massa-cred the Republican forces wherever it found them and, with the help of the Luftwaffe, led to one of the greatest masterpieces of twentieth-century painting. But then maybe the evolution from aeroplane to warplane could be likened in artistic terms to the move from pastoral realism to Picasso's heart-stopping homage to the slaughter in *Guernica*.

The later names and descriptions of the fantastic aircraft say much about where that great leap forward had taken the human species. Gone were the bird names and comparisons of perform-ance with birdlike qualities. Now it was the the Hawker Fury, the Gloster Gauntlet and Gladiator; even the quaintly named British Bulldog, which marked the apogee of these adventurous machines.

It had a snarl about its appearance as much as its quirky name. I see it now in its smart livery: a chequered band of blue and white ending in Royal Air Corps roundels. It was the end of the road for flamboyant names and paintwork: the flying machines were now war machines. Plane-making was now in the grip of the Gauntlet and the Gladiator. I missed the sporting appearance and the dazzling colour schemes of the Boeing P-26 'Peashooters'. And I missed, above all, my flying boats, with their wings mounted above the fuselage and the propeller directly behind these wings. Maybe I liked them most because they had no real capacity to be warplanes. Their gift was to go where other planes could not. Maybe because of that real flying boats survived the wars even though my model copies would have no chance of floating on the calmest pool!

I remember Dad showing me how much better our model biplanes looked without their machine-gun. Though he painted the weapons and mounted them in position, he never glued them. As a child I always flew them around my room without their Parabellum or Lewis guns. These additions changed the whole drama of the aircraft. The sense of joy and exhilaration went out of them. But sometimes I turned traitor, and out of earshot of everyone I enjoyed the rat-a-tat-tat exploding out of my mouth as the Bristol F2b fired astern into the outlandish Fokker DR1 with its triple wing arrangement and a further tiny wing strung between its wheels. No aircraft could ever manoeuvre the way my birds could fly. But then, my models were gods.

Sadly, the day of stick and string dogfights were numbered as increasingly Dad and I assembled the single-winged warplanes. If there was something elegantly birdlike about the biplane, these new aircraft were distinctly shark-like. Menace and manslaughter were located in their design. I remember how Dad painted rows of white triangles forming a gaping jaw line above and below the exhaust fumes of the Messerschmitt. The information notes with these monoplane kits said little about speed or rates of climb: now the emphasis was on armament and how many machine-guns and cannons the plane had. Dad explained 'unguided ordnance' and 'dispenser systems'. I learned about freefall bombs, aerial launch torpedoes and unguided rockets. This was a different world and I had to learn different sounds to fly these craft.

Designed by engineers and physicists, who probably never flew, these aircraft had cantilevered wings and trailing edge flaps for greater speed and better take-off and landing. What struck me most was that the pilots were enclosed in cockpits and that the landing gear folded up into the undercarriage. Somehow they had lost their bond with humanity and the earth. They were characterless killing machines, ominous and joyless. Just like their names: Hawker Hurricane and Typhoon, Curtis Warhawk, the German Focke-Wulf. There were other German aircraft called the Wild Cat and the Hell Cat. Obviously, the bird planes of the First World War had evolved into these Frankenstein machines with a new, darker, demonology. They were never my favourites, perhaps because the pilots disappeared in their cockpits and became a function of the machine. Dad painted them but he rarely gave them names. Only the plastic pilots of the Spitfire and Mosquito had names. The names of men he knew from his service days. Those tiny painted pilots were a very real part of a shared mystique, between them, my father and myself. It didn't matter what national symbol was floated off the transfer paper to embellish the models; these imaginary aviators had transcended national animosity. They flew for sheer love of flying, relishing adventure, risking themselves and their aircraft to the limit.

It was during one of these building sessions that I asked Dad if he had ever flown. He casually told of how he had been in many of the real planes, except of course the German ones, some of which, he admitted, were much superior to the British. He had been on short service flights or simply gone on a joyride or two, never more than ten or fifteen miles from the airbase. 'Did you ever crash?' I asked determinedly. I knew there was a story in the family about my dad being 'lost in action' during the war. I had been told about it by Mum, how he went missing 'believed killed in action' and how my grandmother had received a letter 'from Her Majesty's Forces' confirming this. Dad looked at me for a moment and smiled, knowing I had been put up to asking him. There was no way he could evade the question. In any case, Mother would sometimes invade our shared secret world by suddenly remarking, 'Be careful you boys don't crash!'

Then he told me a story I have never thought to tell anyone else. He had been stationed in Addis Ababa when he and a few other 'mates' were invited by an American pilot 'to go for a spin'. All the friends happily agreed. During the flight, the aircraft developed problems, which got progressively worse until the plane was forced to crash-land in a remote mountain range. I can still hear my father quoting the radio operator's final Mayday flash with the words 'We're going down, we're going down.' 'Were you frightened? Did you think you were going to die, Daddy?' I asked, more spellbound than I have been at any time in my life. 'Yes,' he confessed, he was frightened. Obviously he didn't die; nor did anyone else.

The plane was broken into smithereens, and all the glue in the world couldn't fix it. I had a head full of questions, but Dad spared me. Some four hours after they landed, a tribe of about thirty or forty men appeared as if from nowhere. For a long time, both parties stood looking at one another, curious and afraid. Then the tribe disappeared. The American pilot said they looked like Ali Baba and his forty thieves. Dad and his friends spent a few sleepless nights in the body of the plane, awaiting the worst. Eventually the tribe returned with machetes, spears and several First World War rifles. This time the tribesmen were more demonstrative: if my dad and his colleagues were 'Deutsche' then their throats would immediately be cut and their heads removed.

A tense standoff followed with my dad and his friends pointing to the aircraft markings! The natives seemed to understand the bulls'-eye red, white and blue roundels, much to everyone's relief. Soon a sign language was established and the downed companions traded coins, watches, clothes and pieces of the aircraft for food. One evening, Dad explained, some of the tribe brought them a live goat and signalled that it was food for the airmen. My dad and his friends explained with their rudimentary hand signals that they did not want it as they had no way of killing and cooking the unfortunate animal. The natives understood immediately and, with equal swiftness, dispatched and skinned the goat before their eyes. Dad told me he felt more afraid of death at that moment than he did in the crashing plane. The liver and heart were left, as these were good things to eat without cooking, and the tribesmen departed. The next day they returned with a huge pot containing a foul-smelling stew, the legs of the goat protruding from the stinking gruel. The aircrew could neither refuse the gift nor refuse to eat it! For six weeks they lived like this, too frightened to leave the hulk of the plane. Luckily, it was spotted and at last a rescue team arrived and brought the crew down the mountains on donkeys. I still have a photo of that momentous day.

When he concluded the story he went off and came back with three knives that had been given to him by the tribe. Two were crescent shaped with crudely forged blades and bone handles. The other was a decorative and ornate stiletto. The first two were for skinning and carving the goat and the stiletto was reserved for the ritual of puncturing the jugular of the beast. Dad had told me this story as though it was only that, a story, and I marvelled at his words but when he produced the native knives, I was breathless with absolute awe.

In some strange way the revelation of the knives silenced me. It was as if I had stood before a holy relic and sworn a vow of silence. My dad was like that. He kept many things inside himself for his own reasons. It is something he has passed on to me.

Perhaps it was the silence the years had drawn over this story and the obligation the knives had placed on me, without my fully understanding why. But, when I read Yeats's 'An Irish Airman Foresees His Death', I hear my father's voice. I see his face, and know intuitively why he kept things to himself.

> Nor law, nor duty bade me fight,
> Nor public men, nor cheering crowds,
> A lonely impulse of delight
> Drove to this tumult in the clouds;
> I balanced all, brought all to mind,
> The years to come seemed waste of breath,
> A waste of breath the years behind
> In balance with this life, this death.

I have been told that my father's name is listed on a stone memorial of war dead in the Church of Ireland church near where he grew up in East Belfast. I have never been to see it but I love the idea of some stonemason carving the name on the epitaph while my dad was barebacking down the mountains on a donkey.

But he wasn't always the retiring type. On many occasions he could be the most outgoing of men. Mostly, I remember him painting. Not only his model aircraft; he used to adorn the mirrors and windows at home during Christmas with frescos of holly and robins, snow and candles or he would sit me on his knee and draw picture after picture of animals. But, although they were beautifully executed, his mouse was the same size as a horse, as were the alligator and the snake, the rabbit and the leopard. In the Noah's Ark of my father's imagination, all creatures were truly equal. He always insisted he couldn't really draw people. And when he tried, he proved himself right.

Which curiously brings me to this point. The surname Keenan is taken from the Gaelic O'Cainain, a family that as far back as history can record them, was established in County Fermanagh and County Louth before those places had such names. They were noted among the pre-Christian druids and also were scribes and illustrators in the early Christian Church. Principally they were historians to the McGuire sept. I like to think that my father – and perhaps, through him, I too – drew upon that ancient inheritance. I can see him even now as a medieval illustrator filling the marginalia of some ancient manuscript with his bestiary. And maybe, hidden under his scribe's bench, like the fragments of a dream, are drawings of weird fantastical flying machines! However, Dad's animals were not restricted to pencil sketches and painted mirrors. His love was as much for the living creature as it may have been for the art with which he re-created them.

In 1946, after he was demobbed, he married my mother in the same church where he had been previously named among the war dead. Marital domesticity required a steady job and regular income. So he became a bus conductor for a few years before joining GPO Telephones. What he had learned servicing warplanes must have equipped him in some way for this new technology.

I remember him singing in the morning as he stood in his vest and trousers at the kitchen sink sloshing handfuls of soapy water into his face and snorting loudly to prevent it sluicing up his nostrils. Among the refrains that drifted upstairs from these noisy early morning ablutions were 'Slow Boat to China', 'Somewhere Over the Rainbow', 'Mona Lisa', 'The Folk Who Live on the Hill' and 'We'll Gather Lilacs'. He only knew bits and pieces of these popular songs, but as he had no audience in our tiny two-up, two-down house, he sang with great gusto. Then he would don his navy overalls, a donkey jacket with great patches of leather across the upper back and shoulders, and he never left the house without his cap.

He was permanently on 24-hour call-out, so his van was often parked outside, from working late the night before. I could hear the consumptive clatter of the old diesel engine that seemed to take for ever to fire up, and then he was gone. Many nights, he didn't get home until the early hours. Or he would frequently be knocked up by his fellow workers in the early hours to go out on an emergency. Sometimes, it seemed, we didn't see him for days. He was always gone somewhere or in the process of going somewhere. His departures and arrivals were all too often in the dark; it gave him a kind of invisibility. He was a creature of the dark hours.

There were lots of other occasions when he did arrive home before we went to bed. Maybe my mother knew he would be late and allowed my sister and me to stay up for him. But sometimes his late arrival caused chaos in the house. Dad had a habit of bringing things home. I call them 'things' because my mother's reaction was invariably the outburst: 'Get that thing out of this house!'

The thing was always an injured animal or bird that he had picked up while repairing fallen telephone lines. There were rabbits and baby hares and hedgehogs. Once there was a polecat that my mother insisted was a ferret which had not run into the van (as my father had told us) but had been given to him by one of his mates. There were all kinds of stray dogs which resided with us for as long as they chose, or for as long as Mother agreed. There was even a baby fox, in such a state of malnutrition that we could not have kept it. And there were birds of all kinds. My father could never pass an injured or distressed bird.

However much Mother chastised my dad for playing St Francis to every injured and orphaned animal in Ireland, he was never put off his rescue work. She could just about put up with a shoebox of baby ducks until he got rid of them the next day. She even agreed to 'mind' a couple of geese overnight. But, if ever a wild bird was brought into the house, she put her foot firmly down; and if it was a big bird like a crow, a raven or, particularly, a seagull, her refusal could be almost hysterical. My mothers' rejected these birds not because she didn't want to be scraping bird droppings off the linoleum, or because she disliked birds. We had several budgies and canaries during my childhood, and often she helped choose them. But there was something pre-rational about her fear of having wild birds in the house. If they were brought near her she became distracted and began to tremble as if she was possessed. Her panic was childlike. Even after the creature was removed it took her some minutes to regain her composure, as she sat drawing deep breaths. Mother's reactions were extreme and sometimes frightened me. When I asked her why she refused to have wild birds in the house she spoke of bad luck, omens of illness and death. Once she said that the creatures were diseased and she didn't want their disease in her house. Even the thought of a wild bird in her house made her edgy.

Pragmatically, Father chose not to understand her superstitious reactions. When he rescued a bird that was any bigger than a sparrow he would bundle us kids in a blanket or one of his coats and we would sit in the back of his van, under a portable gas lamp that hissed out its light. Carefully he would open an old cardboard box to reveal a startled or sickly bird. He would tell us where he found it and what he thought might be wrong. Then he would carefully close the box and explain that he would take the bird to the vet or release it out in the countryside the next day if that seemed the appropriate thing to do.

Holding some of these birds, I was amazed at their weightlessness as I felt their trembling bodies in my own trembling hands. The quick blinking of the black pea of their eye almost hypnotized me. Around me was the incense of tallow, diesel, grease, oil and paraffin. There in the smelly compartment of my father's van, I was introduced to another of his worlds. The world of nature and the creatures who inhabit it. But it was especially my father's world and I knew he was happy to be lost in it. It transformed him in an entirely different way than it did my mother.

I have thought about this as I assembled the jigsaw of memory. In their relationship to nature, my parents seemed like elementally different creatures. But now I have revisited long-forgotten incidents of my childhood, the difference between my parents does not seem so acute. I think that, perhaps unconsciously, my dad was drawn to the 'wounded creature' inside my mother.

THE DONKEY

THE NEIGHBOURHOOD I GREW UP IN DURING THE DECADE OF THE 1950S is located in North Belfast and is known as Duncairn Gardens. A map of the area in 1888 explains why the name was appropriate. In that year the area is illustrated as a huge parkland estate with four gatelodge entrances. In the centre is Duncairn House, home of Lord Duncairn, replete with large formal gardens and a tree-lined avenue. Around it spread meadows and parkland. It marked a kind of boundary with the city. But the industrial surge of Belfast could not be stopped: it was no respecter of the property of landed gentry. Thirty-five years later the bacillus of backstreet housing had engulfed the estate. Row upon row of streets with the herringbone pattern of individual terrace houses outlining the DNA of urban development.

It was into these streets that I was born. I have been told that I was born at home by choice rather than chance. Such home births were common and it was mainly a matter of practical necessity. Women couldn't just go off to hospital leaving a house full of kids. If the husband and father was lucky enough to have a job, then he went off to work, labour pains or no labour pains. If he was, like many others, out of work then he 'cleared off' to the pub or to anywhere else where he would not be in the way. There was a great sense of community. An imminent birth in any one of them was rapidly communicated through the adjacent streets. Although a woman might have given birth in the privacy of her own bedroom it was a very communal event, and for weeks after the birth there was much coming and going by the local women, to greet the new arrival. Sometimes they brought clothes that their own babies had grown out of or they offered to 'mind the kids' for the new mother. Sometimes they would sit for hours drinking tea, suggesting names and discussing other recent events. Close neighbours 'ran for the messages' and cooked for the father of the new infant. It was on one of these occasions that it was decided which of the young girls in our street should help my sister take me for walks and generally look after me. Had I not had any sisters, the mothers of the street would have selected two of their own daughters for the job. In a very real sense the street was your family

In our enclosed neighbourhood no one locked their front door, even at night, and few people knocked when they were visiting. Or there would be a single knock, then a voice would call up the hall as the neighbour entered: 'Minnie, it's Bertha!' But mostly these women just blustered into our back room as if it was another in their own home. Only the men ever knocked and waited on the doorstep. If they were neighbours, they always called my mother Mrs Keenan. Occasionally strangers such as door to door salesmen, or what my mother called 'hungry people', knocked on our door: they would simply address her as 'Mrs'. If I heard the term 'Mrs' being used, I would shuffle to the door and peer half afraid and half curious down the hallway at the stranger. My mother kept a glass jar full of coppers in a cupboard in the parlour to pay into the gas meter. Any hungry people who called were always given a few coppers. Years later I used to sneak into the parlour and pinch a penny or two and when I had four of these I would buy a bar of Highland Cream toffee at the weekend. My cache of coins and toffee made me pretty popular with my mates Herbie Scott and Raymond Heald. I didn't know where the Highlands were, but it sounded like the 'Badlands' or even the 'Indian Lands', and the wonderful shaggy beast on the wrapper with its huge long horns looked like no cow I had ever seen in picture books or even on Sunday school outings to the country. But it did look like a cowboy cow! The horns were for scaring off wolves and to make it easy for the cowboys to lasso the cow. I told my pals my dad had met some American cowboys during the war and every week they sent me cowboy toffee. I even told them I had a cowboy lasso and silver spurs but could never bring them out as my dad had told me I had to learn how to use them on a horse and when I was big enough I would get a horse too. I suggested that we might go to America to buy it and the cowboys would teach me how to use the lasso and spurs while I was there. I don't know where this invention came from, but I do remember that my mates were better at physical things and were much tougher than me. Maybe the stories and the toffee were ways of buying my way into the gang, compensating for my own sheepishness in the rough and tumble of childhood. I was not a fragile child, but I was not a tough one.

One of my first toys was an old threadbare rocking-horse which for some reason I decided to name Moby. I am not quite sure why, nor has anyone been able to tell me. But apparently I would sit for hours pumping up and down furiously as I galloped through some imaginary landscape pursued by Indians or bad guys. Sometimes I chose to sit placidly on Moby's back scanning distant horizons. Or I would sit at his feet, usually hidden behind the family settee and talk to the horse, whispering secrets or planning great adventures. Moby was my invincible companion in whom I could confide everything, and however daring or impossible my journeys with him might seem to be, Moby would not fail me. One day my father complimented me on what a special stallion my equine companion was and then asked me if he was 'magic'. I informed him that Moby wasn't magic and that there were no magic horses but that he did come from a faraway land where the horses were super-strong and super-intelligent and that they could see and hear things other creatures couldn't.

Despite my denial, my father's suggestion had sent my mind spinning off, investing my stallion with all manner of wondrous qualities and abilities. Then Dad mentioned a flying horse called Pegasus and magical horned horses called unicorns. He wondered if these animals might even be brothers of Moby? I was adamant. Yes, they came from the same faraway land but they were not related. 'Moby comes from different bloodlines!' I knowingly declared. I noticed my mother look up from her knitting and stare question-ingly at my father. 'Bloodlines?' he asked pointedly. 'Where did you learn that big word?' 'Well that's how I know Moby is different,' I answered and continued to explain. 'Moby's bloodlines are special marks on his head and on his back leg. All the horses in Moby's tribe have them. That's how they know each other. Flying horses and horses with horns have different marks. They are like the tattoos that Mr McIlwaine has on his arms but little lines of blood run through the marks. Moby's tribe of horses have their own special bloodlines. No other horse has them.' Father smiled as mother returned to her knitting. 'You mean herds, son. Horses run in herds, not tribes,' he said kindly. 'Ordinary horses come from herds,' I corrected him. 'They can be caught and trained but special horses like Moby can never be caught or trained. They are too smart and they will only be friends with people that they choose.' 'I see,' said

Dad accepting my authority on the special characteristics of tribal horses. He turned on the chair and took up his newspaper leaving me to my fantasy world behind our settee.

For me, that clumpy old settee marked a boundary between my parents' world and my imaginary one. That ancient piece of furniture was variously the doorway into a hidden cave, or a waterfall behind which Moby and I would hide. Occasionally it was a huge boulder which hid us from the world around us, where I would light imaginary campfires and sketch sand maps to places like the Eagle mountains or the Great Lake of the Winds. I played alone here and although my parents sat only a few feet from me they might as well have been on the other side of the planet, or in a different world entirely.

Sometimes I chose to leave Moby to his silent world and instead of mounting him to be carried off into the vastness I would climb over the back of the settee, which had now become a small boat under full sail and I was away to some remote island. At other times I would excitedly plunge my hands and forearms into the back of the cushions to see what treasure I could discover. Often there were small coins, thimbles, buttons, keys, and all manner of household trivia. Sometimes I found swords and daggers, sometimes I found fabulous rings and necklaces of pearls. Sometimes I found secret coded messages which I had to take to my cave with Moby to discover who had left them there, and why. Over several days I would concoct elaborate stories around these imaginary finds. Moby always listened patiently. But I would never admit to the one truth: I had been the burier of this treasure. Mine had been the hand that had scripted the secret messages and drawn the maps, and if no one else could see them but me, then that, too, was exactly as it should be, for only I could sail the settee down white water rivers and out into beautiful remote lakes. Only I and Moby knew the wild places and the mountains.

Whatever adventures I elaborated in my head, their inspirational source lay in the world at the other side of our street. Every Saturday afternoon I took off with the rest of the kids to what we simply called 'The Donkey'. The Duncairn Picture Theatre was the biggest commercial enterprise on the Duncairn Gardens. Commended at the time of its opening for the quality of its structure and the originality of its design, it had a tea lounge at the head of the main staircase where one could take tea and watch the film. There was also a refreshment buffet. With twelve hundred seats, it was a large cinema with a selection of shops incorporated into the complex. Such scale and design suggest much about the kind of clientele of the cinema in its heyday. I imagined middle-aged women bedecked in fox fur with shoulder-length hair and rouged faces. Their husbands would wear smart suits with baggy trousers pressed to a razor sharp crease and would be wrapped in heavy worsted wool overcoats. All of them would have white shirts with well-starched collars and cuffs. The shiny blue and red ties would be always neatly knotted. The men would visit the refreshment buffet while their wives chatted over tea and discussed the fashion of the leading lady.

But by the time the hundreds of children from the streets that I grew up in started to arrive every Saturday afternoon, these genteel patrons had long since gone. The Donkey had lost its former grandeur. We were the scruffy, unwashed sons and daughters of artisans, shipyard workers, builders' labourers, carters and bakers. Some of us had holes in our shoes, patches on the arse of our trousers, and the clothes we were wearing today, our brothers and sisters probably wore a few days previously.

We descended on The Donkey like a plague of locusts and devoured whatever flickered in front of our eyes for the next hour and a half. There were the Three Stooges, Laurel and Hardy and Charlie Chaplin, but the inane comic antics were lost on me. Even the long-running sagas of Zorro, or of the Lone Ranger and Tonto, with their abrupt endings and an edgy baritone voice announcing: 'Will the masked avenger be in time to save the town? Will the faithful Tonto reach Kemo Sabe in time? Watch out next week when the Lone Ranger rides again', didn't excite me greatly. As the music swelled up in the overture to *William Tell*, hundreds of us were screaming and yelling our heads off so much you could hardly hear it. Zorro held my interest for a while and the Keystone Cops had the whole place screaming and booing. But, truly I don't think anyone cared what the continuing saga of the Lone Ranger would reveal. By next week we would have forgotten about the heroine tied to the railway lines or that the Indian was about to be blown up. We would be back next week roaring and firing cardboard pellets from elastic bands laced between our index finger and thumb. The sting of one of these cardboard 'bullets' if they hit you at close range on the back of the ear or in your eye really made you howl. If you were smart you sat with your collar pulled up round your ears and your neck squeezed down into your shoulders. Or you wore your da's cloth cap. The problem with that was that it would only be on your head two minutes before it went sailing across the auditorium, never to be seen again. Then you would go home wondering whether you should mention the cap, hoping your dad would think he had left it somewhere. Some people's da's could get very touchy about caps and were likely to give their sons a very thick ear for losing one. But if you didn't get blinded or have your ears pelted off you, then you could go scampering home with one arm stretched out in front of you as your clenched hand held imaginary reins. The other arm held out behind, you furiously slapped your buttocks as you lustily called out 'High ho Silver, away!'

The Donkey

Though I must have watched dozens of very badly made black and white westerns, I was oblivious to the poor story lines and their absurd characters. I loved the way they spoke and how the hero stared the bad guy straight in the eye. All the good guys had great relationships with their horses and more often than not the horse was the real hero, forever coming to the rescue; charging down the bad guy or galloping home alone to tell the ranch hands that its owner lay trapped or wounded in the hills. The idea of jumping on a horse and riding off into the wilds fascinated me. No wonder I didn't take to my father's story of flying horses and magical unicorns: they were altogether too otherworldly, and in any case I wanted my adventures to be my own. My secret world really had to be my secret. I couldn't cope with such complicated intrusions as my dad suggested.

Once, when someone bought me a matching pair of guns and holsters I chose to wear them the wrong way round with the pistol butts pointing forwards instead of backward. This meant that I had to cross my arms over my body to retrieve them in the ready to fire position. I also insisted my mum sew me a rifle sheath that I could wear across my back so that my hands would be free when I went hunting. Crossing the rifle in the opposite direction was my bow and another sheath, of arrows. I never liked Zorro or the Lone Ranger's love of masks but I did love the moments when the Indians painted their bodies, faces and even their horses with war-paint. One evening my parents found me with a black mask painted across my eyes and temples. The lower half of my face was covered in white from a tube of gym shoe whitener and I was wearing one of my mum's coloured scarves across my forehead. My dad asked, 'Well, what are you tonight? A cowboy or an Indian or can you not make your mind up?' I don't know what I said, but the final part of his question really was the answer. Even at an early age I was drawn to the underdog and the outsider. In some part of my naïve innocence I had mixed my blood with the wild man and was at war with civilization.

The street I lived in now was called Evolina Street and next to it was Syringa Street. The names stood out exotically from the other street names. Like Ilchester, Kilronan, Mervue, Mackey and Collyer Street. I never did get to know the meaning of Evolina. Somewhere in the back of my mind is an idea about a flute-like instrument from ancient Greece or a plant with flute-like flowers. Syringa, I later learned, is a lilac. Because the words Syringa and Evolina end with that pronounced 'a' sound, I assumed they were somehow related. Perhaps the syringa plant had been cultivated in the formal garden of the original Lord Duncairn's home, and possibly Evolina was another such plant with its roots back to the ancient world. However exotic the name of the street I grew up in, there was little exotic about its inhabitants. Most of the men had jobs in the ship-yard. William McNabb was a boilermaker. Freddie Hyland was a caulker. Harold Heald, my friend's father was a riveter, and all the streets around us were awash with fitters and shipwrights, riggers, platers and welders. In the bigger houses that fronted the tree-lined avenue from which the whole area took its name, there was a master mariner, a master boatman and several ranks of engineer from first to fifth. The men of Evolina Street who had not acquired a trade were either unemployed or picked up work where they could. Herbie Scott my other pal's father was a plumber's helper. Robert Gorman was a labourer, Tommie McIlwaine was a seaman, Johnnie Corbery a slater. William Black was a clerk in a shipping office and his neighbour James Radcliff worked in a grocery business. None of them by name or profession could be said to live up to the ancient Greek origin of the street they lived in. Yet as I grew older and thought of my neighbours, the fathers of my friends, and of the

seamen, shipwrights and shipbuilders who forged raw iron, and
bent and riveted it into titanic creations, I felt that each of them
could be an Argonaut on Jason's ship in search of the Golden Fleece
and that Homer would not have found any want of material or
inspiration had he been born in Belfast.

But one man did stand out from the others. I only knew him as
Mr Thompson. He was a projectionist who worked in the local
cinemas. We knew him simply as the 'pictures man'. Perhaps it was
the fact that he wasn't involved in the robust physical labour of the
other men in the street, and that he worked nights and weekends
unlike his peers, that set him apart. I remember him setting off on
his bicycle with his trousers gathered at his ankles and held there
with thick rubber bands. His black bicycle had a carrying frame
fixed over the rear wheel and a basket attached to the handlebars.
Some of my friends thought this made it a sissy bike, and dismissed
Mr Thompson outright. As a younger man Mr Thompson and his
bike had couriered Pathé and Movietone newsreels between cinemas;
his diligence in ensuring the news was delivered in all weather helped
to get him a job as an assistant projectionist and eventually projectionist. When he cycled off in the mornings he either had a leather
satchel-like bag slung across his back or an ex-army canvas kitbag.
When he returned, his basket or his bag was full of books.

Sometimes my friends and I would find him engrossed in a book
on a bench in Alexandra Park. For my friends this was simply
another reason to dismiss him. Few of our fathers had the time or
the inclination for reading, and even if they had they would hardly
go to the park to do it. Parks were for pushing prams or playing
imaginary games. But whatever Mr Thompson's difference from
the other men, he was a source of curiosity to me. My father used
to say that he had one of the best jobs in the world: 'There aren't
many men whose job allow them to eat, read and work all at the

same time without getting soaked to the skin or blown away altogether.' But I thought of his work differently. I thought of that moment in the cinema when the house lights lowered and the searchlight beam of the projector suddenly materialized. As it lit up the great heavy curtains that fronted the screen, they slowly opened as if the beam had its own invisible power. And indeed it had, for in this moment every eye was hypnotically glued to the screen until it came alive with the various studio logos, MGM's roaring lion, RKO Radio Pictures' radio mast radiating its Morse signals, the eagle of Republic Productions hoisting its vast wings against the skyline or Universal's little aeroplane circling the earth. I was drawn to the logos of Universal and RKO. Because of my own interest in model planes I knew that no plane could circle the earth. It was completely out of perspective, like the radio mast on top of the planet in RKO's logo. But then that was the magic of these movie houses. They recreated perspective. Time and culture shifts were effortlessly effected. History was distorted and reinvented in an instant and we were transported beyond reason or caring. And Mr Thompson was the magician in his magic box who made it all work. High above us, up beyond the gods, suspended in his own secret enclosure, he carried us screaming yahoos out of the Donkey and dropped us in wonderland. We became heroes, immortal avengers, saviours of mankind. Bathed in the projector's searchlight, we lost ourselves in Mr Thompson's magical worlds.

The 'pictures man' intrigued me. His mystery was enhanced by the knowledge that he not only controlled this world but he had access to films we never got to see, either because we hadn't the money, or we were too young, or because they were only screened at night. Sometimes we got tantalizing hints of these forbidden movies when the 'coming attractions' preceded the Saturday matinée. That's when I really envied the pictures man. He had secret knowledge. He knew everything before the rest of us.

But no matter how the lesser beings in the auditorium of The Donkey roared and screamed at the antics of their celluloid heroes, a different kind of awe silenced the place when *The Ghoul, The Walking Dead* or *The Mummy's Curse* was the cinematic feast on offer. They may have been classed A category and forbidden to under-sixteens, but it was a regulation that was never put into practice. The fact that they were forbidden and that they were guaranteed to scare the living hell out of you, made them irresistible. They were also a challenge to our childish male egos. None of my mates dared admit just how frightened they were. None of us admitted to sleepless nights inhabited by Boris Karloff, Bela Lugosi or Lon Chaney. But all of us acted out a lumbering Frankenstein with outstretched arms or Kharis the mummy as we chased girls across the playground. Oh yes, we were fearless heroes until the night when you lay alone wondering if by drinking a brew of tana leaves the dead could really walk the earth again. I remember the Mummy's hand: the image of that disembodied piece of flesh haunted my sleep for weeks! If it wasn't a disinterred Egyptian prince then it was the terrifying white face and lascivious mouth of a Transylvanian prince that lurked behind my bedroom curtains in zombie silence waiting for me.

The pictures man awed me precisely because he sat in his cosy little box and watched this parade of horror and heroism. It was as if these conquerors and creatures of the damned had come to him first to seek his approval, for he could destroy them utterly with the flick of a switch. Mr Thompson of number 3 looked nothing like a hero but I was drawn to him. He was the omniscient god who feared nothing and knew everything in his light box in the sky. The lanky bespectacled man I saw coming and going from the house at the top end of our street was no ordinary mortal!

On occasion I tried to follow him, hoping he would recognize me and talk to me. Maybe I might find out some secret about him that, like a password, would gain me access to his hidden world. But there were no secrets. More often than not he simply went to the corner shop on Halliday's Road for potatoes or bread, maybe tins of peas or beans and a packet of Senior Service cigarettes. Sometimes, if I saw him sitting on his bench in the park, I would disengage myself from my mates who were intent on catching small fish we called 'spricks' as if that was the greatest thing in the world. While they fought over who should fish from where or who had the sole right to catch a particular 'sprick' which was smaller than their little finger and thinner than a pencil stub, I paced up and down past the pictures man hoping he would notice me. I tried to see what he was reading. It might be a tattered paperback, or there were books with diagrams and drawings which were incomprehensible to me. One was a novel called *The Cruel Sea*. The title was mysterious; it made the pictures man even more elusive.

One evening I asked my dad if he thought Mr Thompson might know everything? 'Well,' he answered, 'he certainly sees more news reports than most other people and he does read a lot of books . . .' He paused and studied me for a moment. He knew the nightmares that had frequently brought me into my parents' bed had their origins in Mr Thompson's cinema but he never mentioned this. He continued: 'Anyway, nobody knows everything and you shouldn't believe everything you see!' This was not the answer I needed. I was already having difficulty believing that the pictures man I saw most days was just Mr Thompson. Even as I look back on those times, and when I consider how the men of Evolina Street could well have sailed the Argonaut, I am forced to ask: what of the resident of number 3? That quiet, skinny bespectacled man who looked nothing like a shipwright, a rigger or a master mariner. Now, I can see him better than I did then, high in the ancient crow's nest with his searchlight scanning over the dark waters as his voice calls out, borrowing the words of Cecil Day-Lewis:

> Enter the Dream House brothers and sisters,
> leaving your debts asleep, your history
> at the door: This is the house for heroes,
> and this loving darkness as far as you
> can afford.*

* Cecil Day-Lewis, quoted in *Standing Room Only* by James Doherty (Lagan Historical Society, 1997).

GRAVEYARD GHOSTS

I AM NOT SURE HOW THE IMAGES THAT FUEL OUR NIGHTMARES TAKE UP residence in our unconscious, or even why, but I am sure that the horror stories that unfolded each Saturday afternoon in the Donkey were only one source of my all too frequently disturbed nights. I suppose my mother's constant assurance that my monsters were not real, that they were merely a silly old story, eased the tension of my sleepless nights. If they were not real then they could never really hurt me. Anyway I convinced myself of the elaborate theory that the Wolfman, Frankenstein, Dracula and all the other undead were really trapped inside the searchlight beam of Mr Thompson's cine projector. They could not escape from it and he could freeze them like a statue or make them disappear. And if they could only inhabit the projector's cone of light, then they could never enter into the darkness of my bedroom. After a few months, I learned how to deal with these demons by limiting their power to affect me or by simply refusing to believe in them. They were only stories, after all. To be doubly sure, I never shone a torch in my bed at night just in case ghosts could move magic-ally from one source of light to another. But there were other stories that seemed to have a firmer hold on reality. They seeped out of the stones and mortar of the place I was growing up in. And because they had this relationship to reality, they were harder to deal with.

One such place near where we lived was Clifton House. A great imposing rectangle of a structure, it had been built in the late 1700s and stood completely surrounded by its own grounds on an elevated site. A tall wall topped by heavy wrought-iron fencing enclosed it. It was originally built as a poorhouse and hospital combined for the indigenous poor and ill of the rapidly growing city of Belfast. As the city prospered and grew, so did Clifton House. It added to its extensive buildings a wing for 'lunatics', a reformatory, and a House of Correction to clear the streets of beggars, thieves and prostitutes. A graveyard came later. This was the chosen resting place of doctors, surgeons, mill owners, importers, clergy and anyone who thought they were someone in this rapidly expanding industrial city. Ominously, the grounds also contained several mass graves. One for those who were too destitute to pay for their own interment and two more for the uncounted numbers who died from the many fever epidemics that took hold of a city that swarmed with more people than it could cope with. Typhus, dysentery, smallpox and cholera swept through the overcrowded and insanitary backstreets like a biblical plague. To this day no one knows how many corpses lie piled one on top of the other, or who these unfortunates were. We only know that they are there, stranger clinging carelessly to stranger in the impossible embrace that only discarded corpses can make.

The thing I remember most about Clifton House is not its grotesque Gothic history so much as the silence that surrounded it. The place was a stone's throw from the bustling city centre. It sat alongside bus routes out from the centre and seemed oblivious to the streets, shops, offices and other institutional buildings which had been built around it. It was as if this particular part of the city's history existed in a special timeless space of its own.

On occasional Fridays Mother would go shopping in town. Friday was 'divi' day and the Co-op headquarters was a short walk from the original poorhouse. The Co-op coalman shouldered a bag of slack and a bag of coal through our house and out into the yard once a week. Mother shopped when she could in the local Co-op and I licked stamps to put into her dividend book. Once a month or longer, depending on what was stored up in the divi, me and Mum descended on the 'Co.'. I have never forgotten our divi number: 70368. Likewise, my social security number many years later when I queued up in the unemployment offices round the corner from the Co. The queue in the Co. and the queue at the dole marked a large part of our lives. In one it was women and their children picking up a few shillings and in the other it was men, also picking up a few shillings. They too had their special number. Poverty still brooded over us like the poorhouse in Clifton Street. It was a living reminder. Clifton House was no well-preserved historic artefact: the old and the poor still lived there. They were like ghosts. I never saw them. Still, the solitariness of the place fascinated me.

Taking that walk to the Co., Clifton Street was a mystery to me. At the top was Carlisle Circus, a roundabout with a statue of a man called Roaring Hanna, a blood and thunder, old-style evangelist who was obviously more intoxicated by a vision of perdition than those who lived it day by day. To my young mind Roaring Hanna raised high on his plinth staring wide eyed and bull faced into the sky was an image of the giant from 'Jack and the Beanstalk' roaring at the sky as he scanned it for the missing giant stalk. There was something desperately lonely as he roared his 'fee fi fo fum' like a mantra, trying to make the ladder to heaven appear again. I never knew who the real Roaring Hanna was until many years later. For me he was the homicidal giant who had become earthbound and was raging to get back into the sky.

The descent from the Circus down Clifton Street to York Street where the Co-op stood was increasingly surreal. On the left stood a huge building with great muscular Corinthian pillars holding up a huge triangle of stone with an obscure frieze embossed on it. Above this, and seeming to be riding through the clouds was a statue of Prince William of Orange mounted on his white charger with his sword arm raised, calling his followers to attack. Standing as a child looking up at this figure, I could see no structural connection between it and the grandiose building it rode above. It hovered like a celestial angel or an apocalyptic horseman.

A few yards beyond Clifton House a Catholic church stood squashed between a small hospital known as The Ben, a collection of shops and small stores, a newspaper office and an assortment of solicitors' offices and other offices whose purpose I have long forgotten. Years later, when I began reading Charles Dickens and discovered the grubby, officious clerks and office functionaries who fill the background of his books, I thought of those soot-stained second-floor offices. I imagined wrinkle-faced little men with gold-rimmed glasses peering down at Mother and me as we walked past; their inky fingers would fumble in greasy waistcoats and the shoulders of their jackets would be smothered in a fine coating of dandruff.

It was the small chapel that interested me. Obviously, I never went into it. Being christened in St Barnabas, Church of Ireland in the leafy thoroughfare of Duncairn Gardens, it did not even cross my mind to do so. In any case, I had been warned enough times by my mates, their big brothers and their fathers – when alcohol had made them garrulous – that if I entered a Fenian church the most serious afflictions would befall me. I would suddenly acquire a hump on my back, or a club-foot. My speech would turn into a stammer and I would constantly dribble as I tried to speak. I would undoubtedly turn into the ugliest creature on two legs that no girl would want to kiss and that animals would flee in fear from. I would have a smell permanently about my person. I'm not sure I believed much of it but, just to be on the safe side, I never went through the chapel gates. However, I did always run ahead of my mother so that I would reach this building before her. I would stand at the cast-iron railings that enclosed a small yard to the side of the church. Set well back from the pavement towards the rear of this yard stood a statue of the crucified Christ surrounded by the Virgin Mary and Mary Magdalene. The figures were carved in white marble, yet surrounding them grew soot and rust stains and the accumulated weathering that had encrusted the stonework. The marble figures seemed to glow where they stood. There was nothing remarkable in the artistry of the tableau. Even Christ's cross seemed sunk too far into the ground. The two Marys had to be carved kneeling so that they could look up at the figure on the cross. I thought that if they stood up they would be bigger than the upright cross. Consequently I formed the impression that Jesus was really a very small man. Not quite a dwarf, but certainly nowhere near the size of the men I saw going off to work in the mornings or sometimes stumbling out of the pub on Friday. For a while I connected this impression of Jesus with the various curses that were attendant on entering a Fenian church. Maybe you would grow smaller like the small Christ hung up in the side yard of the church. Maybe the two Marys weren't kneeling either. Maybe their limbs had shrivelled too! I'm not sure I retained that consideration for very long, but I always stopped to stare fascinated at this group of stone figures. I am not really sure why. Maybe it had something to do with the fearsome prohibition and curses or maybe it was simply that this quiet marble vignette was right down at street level. To my childish imagination, other statues were surreal, partly because of their elevated status on great stone plinths or atop some Greek or Roman edifice. This group of figures was small, like me, and its echo was quiet.

But Clifton House seemed to be the anchor point that held all these colliding images together. Maybe it was because the house and grounds were hidden behind a wall and an iron fence. Maybe it was its curious history, or the stories that stole out of that history and took up residence in the side streets of Duncairn Gardens and with the people who lived there. Like the cinema, Clifton House was as full of stories as of graves. But the stories that emanated out of the grounds of it lingered longer in my imagination. They didn't peter out when the house lights went up. The graveyard of Clifton House was full of corpses stretching back hundreds of years – but not all the graves were occupied! You see, this graveyard was the preferred hunting ground of the body snatchers!

I first heard about these people from an old night-watchman who was employed to watch over a building site a few streets from where I lived. I am not sure how old he was but he looked ancient. He would sit up all night in a small wooden hut just big enough for himself and a sleepy old dog that lay at his feet. The interior of the 'watchie's' hut was lit by a low-burning hurricane lamp. The old man always had a parcel of egg and onion sandwiches and a tall brown medicine bottle with ribs moulded into the glass and its prescription label still intact. My mates and I knew it contained cheap fortified wine not just because of the blackening red stains at the corner of our watchie's mouth but also by the smell, and the frequency with which he took his medicine.

To keep him warm he burned a brazier full of hot glowing coal. As the winter neared and the evening closed in, we were drawn to the watchman's hut like hornets to a honey pot. The combined aroma of egg and onion, cheap wine, burnt timber and the musk of his old wet dog were irresistible. They added to the warmth of the glowing brazier. The old man seemed to enjoy our company and he had the same allure for me as the pictures man. 'There's coffins in that place, all laced up like a docker's boot with iron wires so's nobody can get the dead body out of them. But the body snatchers in Clifton graveyard were too smart for that. Them boys was not gonna be put off by a couple of yards of coiled iron or ten feet of bolted plate. Anybody that's up to no good has to be a bit more smarter than the rest of us, has to have a bit more upstairs in the brainbox. These men would sneak in the pitch black of night with a shovel, a few hooked poles and a bit of rope all wrapped up in a couple of baling sacks they probably got from the shipyard or one of the mills up the road.' My mates and I all knew about the shipyard as most of our fathers worked there. We also knew about the mills as we had mothers, aunts and even sisters employed there. These realities made his story all the more intriguing and we sat entranced as the watchie and his fire heated our bodies. Firing our imagination in the incense of egg and onion, he continued:

'You see, the thing is, the snatchers would be watching the grave-yard every day so's they would know when somebody was buried there. Then after a few days when everyone had finished visiting, they would sneak in with an old oil lamp same's that one of mine and they'd find the freshly dug grave faster than a pair of ferrets. They would dig up the head part of the grave and smash open the top of the coffin. Then they'd stick their hooked poles in the graves and hoist up the dead person by his shoulders. Just like lifting sardines out of a tin. Then they would swiftly wrap them up in their burlap bags and whisk them away on an old horse and cart that was waiting outside for them. They always dug the earth back so's nobody would know a thing. Swift and silent, that's the way them boys worked. In and out like a baker's bread paddle.' He paused for a moment. 'People say you can sometimes hear the awful moans of the dead being hoisted up out of their coffins if you pass the graveyard after midnight.' The watchie took another swig of his medicine, then as an aside he asked pleadingly if any of our parents smoked and suggested that we could all be body snatchers and steal him one or two cigarettes some time! 'But that wasn't the end of their cleverness cos they had to get the dead bodies out of the city altogether. Edinburgh in Scotland and London, that's where they went – and can you imagine how they done it?' He took another swallow, his lips shiny and red from the wine. Then he asked some of us to throw a lump or two of timber or a shovel of coke on the fire. 'You can't put a body in a postman's bag now, can you? So you have to be dead smart, and the boys in this business were all of that and a bit more. You know what they done?' The watchie's eyes looked into each of ours, burning the story into our imagination. 'Well,' he said, 'they simply dropped the bodies into barrels of salty water: sealed them up, painted the word bacon on the barrels and off they went to the surgery schools in England.' The speed with which he delivered his explanation had the words falling from his mouth like bodies dropped into brine barrels.

We all sat in silence. The watchie's gummy mouth chewed his sandwich and the flame in the paraffin lamp flickered, moving a momentary shadow across his face. As it flared up again it seemed to freeze his image. He stared into the brazier motionless. The overcoat he wore was several sizes too big and the scarf bunched up at his throat made it look as if his head had been set on his shoulders from some other body. Tufts of hair grew out of his ears and nostrils, his cap looked like it had been poured on to his head and the broken peak of it had a greasy sheen from the number of times he had handled it.

I never got to know his name, but someone gave him the name 'oul cough syrup' because of how he would take a sup of medicine every five minutes. He glowed in his confessional of a hut. I did pinch a couple of Woodbines for him, and when I gave them to him a few nights later, he said simply through his gummy lips, 'Ah nails for my coffin son, God bless you.' Then he winked at me.

How he knew I body-snatched the cigarettes was beyond me. After all, I could have asked for them, explaining who they were for, but I didn't. I did what he had suggested as if he had Svengalied me into it. There was no one else with him when I presented my offering of tobacco, and, being a bit awed by him, I walked off in silence. He called after me: 'Don't worry, son. You'll never be punished for doing someone a kind turn!'

Perhaps the night-watchman sowed the seed that the horror movies nurtured, for I know that the graveyards in Clifton House spat out more ghosts that took up residence in our neighbourhood and were called upon when our mothers wished to chastise us or warn us from doing something. We were threatened that the Wolf boys would get us and 'smit' us with scarlet fever if we had been particularly badly behaved. If we were uncooperative and sulky it was the ghosts of the spinster sisters who would visit us and make us talk. These ghosts grew out of the story of two sisters who had lived together all their lives. One of them, named Jane, died in bed beside her sleeping sister. When the other sister Mary woke she found she couldn't wake her sister, so she kept complaining 'Jane won't speak to me.' Mary died a few hours after her sister, still intoning the words 'Jane won't speak to me.' Those same words were still occasionally directed at a child who got into the sulks. If your mother teased you with the words 'Jane won't speak to me' she was reminding you that sulky silences would certainly mean a visitation from these two withered old women who would scare you into talking.

Another ghost who haunted me and was another parental threat was that of Antonio Da Silva, a Portuguese sailor who was hanged for the murder of a fellow sailor in Belfast. The story goes that Da Silva loudly insisted on his innocence up to the moment of his execution. As a protest and in a final act of proclaiming his innocence, the sailor insisted on being hanged wearing a white surplice. He was executed on a rocky foreshore of Belfast Lough on the curiously named Three Sisters, which was a construction of three tall upright posts joined by a crossbar. Da Silva was left hanging for several days looking out to sea with his dead eyes before being buried in Clifton House in unhallowed ground set aside for murderers.

The story of the Portuguese sailor was not just a piece of history: there was a local belief that the ghost of Da Silva was still haunting the streets looking for people whom he would transport to his native homeland to leave stranded there, pining and lonely for their home just as he had been left. 'Be careful or Da Silva will get you!' I heard that threat before I knew the story, but I don't remember it being addressed to me. Initially I thought of 'Da Silva' in familial terms, with da as in the familiar term for father. Thus Da Silva was to my mind a kind of malign father who would take you from your own family. Understanding the ghost in this way somehow brought it closer. But when I was told the real story of the Portuguese sailor, with a group of us roasting potatoes on a piece of spare ground near home, it did not diminish the fear of Da Silva; it only changed the nature of it.

One evening, when I had displeased my mates for some reason, they gathered round me repeatedly chanting 'Da Silva'll get you,

Da Silva'll get you.' For many nights I lay awake dreading the sleep that Da Silva, with his bloody knife and white surplice, could enter into and carry me off to leave me alone and tormented on that rocky shoreline.

I was not the only one in my family who suffered from the ghostly overspill of Clifton House. On our visits to town, Mother would often meet neighbours and stop to chat. I instantly took myself off to the gates of the big house, where the large entrance gates provided the only open view of the building. I never dared go inside the gates, even so much as to put a foot inside them. This was the repository of so many stories that I stood and wondered who would still live in such a place. The fact that I never saw anyone move about the house or the grounds made it all the more forbidding yet intriguing. And then there was that silence that the whole place seemed enclosed in. It was the silence of anticipation. To me, it was the kind of silence that seemed to be holding something back, like the calm before the storm.

Any time my mother caught me hanging about the entrance or climbing the wall to peer through the fence, she would chastise me: 'Come you away from those gates. You never know what will happen to you hanging about them.' Her scolding may have varied a little but the emphasis was always the same, that 'something' might happen to me. As with most kids, the warning went in one ear and out the other and the dreaded consequences of my curiosity burst like a bubble the moment the command was out of my mother's mouth. Many years later when I was too old to be chastised and when I understood more about the place, I thought I understood my mother's anxiety.

History records that many sick children were left at the entrance gates of this house by parents too ill or too poor to look after them. Numbers of babies and orphans were also deposited at the gates and left to the mercies of the poorhouse administrators. Though my mother would not have witnessed it, her mother and many other grandmothers in the area must have known of unwanted babies and children huddled at the gates, sometimes wrapped in newspapers and a blanket.

Just over a year before I was born my mother gave birth to a son who was anacephalic and consequently incapable of surviving outside the womb. The unfortunate child was taken from her at birth. She never saw or touched it. It was gone the moment it arrived into the world. Apparently it was given to my father and he and a midwife immediately removed the baby from the delivery room. The dead child lay in the mortuary for a few days and was then taken off and 'buried in a shoe box'. It was a day or two before my mother was told the sex of her child, and that he had been buried. For some months my mother was withdrawn. She never asked where the child was buried or even what he looked like. The passage from womb to tomb was too instantaneous. Even when she was sufficiently recovered from post-natal stress my father refused to tell her where the child's grave was, or to take her there. In his own way, he had wanted to spare her any more pain and for himself he did not want to relive the anguish of burying his first son all over again. Apparently the months that followed were very difficult for both of them. Even forty years later there was still an edge of resentment in my mother's voice when she recalled my father's actions. I suppose the profound emptiness she must have felt on the birth and death of this child was never really filled up by understanding. When you lose something so precious, the memory of it never goes away even if the object of such memory has. Even when you get over the anger, the cruelty, and the lacerations of grief, the emptiness remains. Sometimes you go on for a lifetime trying to fill the void.

I remember on many occasions Mother suddenly suggesting 'Maybe we'll go for a walk', and off we went. But the walk invariably ended up in a graveyard. To me it was another playground or a park and I loved these walks. The fact that often we went on our walks in the rain never seemed unusual to me. But my mother walked slowly, studying the headstones as if she was turning pages in a book looking for a part of the story she only half remembered. I suppose that in some confused way that first child was amongst the ghostly gathering at the graveyard gates of Clifton House. That dread warning that 'You never know what might happen to you if you hang about there!' was simply an instinctual outpouring from that point where her personal history intersected with the history of the place.

ST BARNABAS AND THE
BLITZ KIDS

MY MOTHER WAS NOT THE KIND OF WOMAN TO BE HAUNTED BY GHOSTS. At least not on the surface. She was a strong woman, determined to the point of defiance. She had spent most of her young life working in the linen mills. Over the years, she had acquired the status of a kind of shop steward for her fellow women workers, with a steely protective temper. She had little time for the male charge hands and overseers who strutted the factory floors roaring orders at the loom workers as if they were indentured slaves. When Minnie McClean was about they kept their distance and their mouths shut. Throughout her life my mother had little respect for male authority figures. She was tough and uncompromising with any man she considered abusive to women. She was, I suppose, a prototype feminist without understanding the concept. But her battle to improve working conditions and rates of pay for women in the factory where she worked was unremitting and knowing the ferocity of her temper, no man willingly entered into a dispute with Minnie McClean. No matter how little my mother might have gained in terms of working conditions, whoever was arguing with

51

her was bound to lose much more in terms of authority and male ego! If my mother had been born a man I'm quite sure she would have made a fearsome street fighter.

The area I grew up in was famous for its street fighters. At one time in its history it was known as 'Lions' Den' but as the area grew and took in more streets it became 'Tigers Bay' I suppose because, like its namesake in Cardiff, it was a rough locality. Street fights were legendary. They were a form of free social entertainment and always attracted a big crowd of onlookers, both men and women. Local history records that many of these contests originated in a pub called the Willing Mind! A curious title for a rough public house. The name of the place has a sense more of philosophic or religious enquiry than of the meeting place of fist fighters. In any case, philosophic or intellectual debate was a piece of foolish extravagance that resolved nothing for the inhabitants of Tigers Bay or the frequenters of The Willing Mind. There was only one decent way to resolve an argument and that was for two men to strip to the waist and attempt to beat the pulp out of one another outside the pub. Now if it was late in the day, and much drink had been taken and it was a case of the flesh being willing but the mind too inebriated, then the fight would be held over until a Sunday morning when half the locality would make its way to the brickyard on the Limestone Road where combat would ensue. The brickyard, or 'The Pit' as it was known, provided a kind of miniature amphitheatre for the assembled audience of men, women and children. However bloody and brutal these contests became, they were always conducted within the laws of an unwritten rule book and a code of honour. The winner of a dispute could not walk away from the battle with his head held high if he had broken any of the rules, and he would never be allowed to live down such disgrace.

These bloodbaths created local heroes but also served as a ritual which in a curious way cleansed and bound the community. If no rules had been broken and the code of honour was upheld, the victor and the vanquished were applauded and respected in equal measure. The spectacles had something that neither rituals of faith or the regimented learning of the schools could offer. Two bare-chested big men slugging it out on the 'altar' of the brickyard on a Sunday morning excited our spirits. We applauded the winner because he had overcome, and we loved the loser the way we all love the underdog.

However, these fights were the exception rather than the rule. Generally Sundays were a mixture of austerity, boredom, un-fulfilled expectation and anticlimax. On Sundays everybody dressed in their Sunday best. Housewives redeemed their husbands' suits from the pawnbroker's, fresh creases were wet-ironed into old trousers, shirt collars were starched and ties that had been handed on from my grandfather or dead uncles were steamed over a kettle. Mother always ironed my father's trousers with a sheet of brown paper, so as not to leave a sheen on them. When she had finished, the paper was carefully folded and returned to the cupboard.

On Sunday morning when I came downstairs I would find everyone's shoes lined up in front of the fireplace, all of them gleaming. It was a ritual with my dad to collect up all the shoes on Saturday evening. Then he would place a small stool in front of him, spread a newspaper on top with each pair of shoes lined up beside him. He had a wooden box full of brushes and assorted polishes, and an old screwdriver which he called 'the muck-raker' for scraping away caked mud from the instep and soles. I don't think he cared much about the necessity for dressing up on a Sunday; he simply enjoyed cleaning shoes. He said it was something he picked up from his days in the RAF and that a good cleaning and 'feed' of polish gave the footwear extra longevity. But whatever he said about it, I also know that he simply enjoyed the task. He enjoyed restoring our battered shoes and giving new life to them. Every morning I saw them I always thought that they looked newly alive.

For most people the dressing up was as automatic as it was unconscious. People did it because everyone did it. Of course, having done it they had to find some reason for it. So Sunday also became a 'day out', which meant a family walk in the park or a visit to the cemetery or maybe a visit to relatives, though I don't seem to remember too many of those.

Sunday was also about religion, of course. It was about going to church and, more particularly for us kids, it was about Sunday school. St Barnabas was the local church of Ireland, which was located about midway down the main thoroughfare of the Duncairn Gardens. It was small but had lots of bulk. Its Victorian mock-Gothic granite and limestone declared that though it wasn't big, it was boss. The meagre little redbrick mission halls of the lesser denominations seemed sad or pathetic and certainly second hand in relation to St Barnabas. The avenue of trees that lined the road added to its small but still stately appearance. To the side and set back from the church was the parochial hall where Sunday school was held. St Barnabas sat almost opposite the cinema. So between the Donkey and 'Barney-Baps', the kids of the Duncairn Gardens could expend their enthusiasm. On Saturdays we could cause murder and mayhem encouraged by the Lone Ranger, Zorro, tribes of bloodthirsty Indians, vampires and the ghouls of the undead that the cinema gave us. On Sundays, washed, scrubbed, polished and pressed like cardboard cut-outs of ourselves, we went off to Barney-Baps where we recited the Lord's Prayer, the Apostolic Creed and verses from the Book of Common Prayer. We mumbled our way through hymns which told the story of 'a green hill far away, without a city wall where the dear Lord was crucified, who died to save us all'. Most of us couldn't read the hymn-book but we knew the words and the tune from much repetition, and sang with giggling gusto. St Barnabas was less exciting than the cinema but somehow it was more edgy, more daring to have a laugh in the House of God!

I always went to church with Brenda, my elder sister. Mother shushed us out of the house with a couple of coppers for the collection. Because I was still young and curious at the time I sat with my sister's girl friends and took the whole thing very seriously. The children's sermon, which was delivered by the minister before the main sermon, seemed patronizing. There were stories about friendship and betrayal, about charity and greed. There were stories about dying and faith. But they were just stories. The minister often looked to the parents for their approval as he tried to explain the 'moral' of the story; and I watched as they all smiled back at him in unison. They looked as if they were dead or else like clockwork dolls. I remember the night before seeing some of them roaring and screaming abuse at one another, usually about money, or debt or drink!

But when the minister moved on to the main sermon, I was more inclined to listen, for his demeanour seemed to change. Sometimes his authority became grisly and threatening; or he spoke as if he was pleading, and on other occasions he'd address the congregation with gravity and understanding. I loved his stories about Isaac and Abraham, Cain and Abel and the one about the woman who enticed the general into her tent and cut off his head while he was sleeping. I was enraptured by the story of the Temptation of Christ and the plagues in Egypt. For me, where there was blood, there was life, and the Donkey across the road was reeking with the stuff every Saturday afternoon. At the end of each matinée, we all charged out of the cinema transformed in a way that we never were by church.

I never gave up going to the church on Sunday. I liked to hear stories rather than see them. My curiosity was more than aroused by the preacher's continued insistence that his stories were about real people with real consequence. I wanted more of the stories and less of the hymn singing and mindless reflection. So, I insisted on going to Sunday school after the service. My mother tried convincing me that I was too young. When my insistence turned into tears, she gave up and ordered Brenda to take me with her. Brenda duly did as she was commanded. Within a matter of weeks, something happened at Sunday school which caused a lifelong schism between my mother and the church. One which I have passively inherited.

I cannot recall at first hand the detail of the incident, but I do recall its aftermath. I remember how the parochial hall was divided into eight areas, each with its own circle of chairs with up to twenty or more children. In each circle the children were of a similar age and at the head of the circle a young man or woman in their twenties led the group. They were the teachers. After prayers they would relate some biblical story then ask the group about the story and what it meant.

For the first two weeks I sat on the floor in front of my sister and listened as everyone spoke about the story the teacher had related. But I wanted to hear more stories, and began to wander from group to group. The story of Jonah and the whale absolutely fascinated me. Moses and the burning bush and then the tablets of stone set me alight with all sorts of questions. Jesus taking a whip to the moneylenders was better than Zorro any day.

I wandered from one circle to the next swallowing all the stories and listening to the answers that the teachers provided to the groups' questions. My head was full of its own questions about the Flood, the snake devil . . . if Moses was a magician? And why didn't Jesus give Judas some money, because he could make wine from water and magic up thousands of fish for thousands of people? My head was spinning with all the stories and the confusion they were creating. Sometimes questions just popped out of me, much to the teacher's annoyance. They knew the stories but didn't seem sure of the answers. Lots of times I wasn't sure of the questions in my head and I wanted to sit on my own and play. But Sunday school was for praying, not playing. It was for learning, not looking out of the window. These sentiments were expressed to me and my sister a few times. They didn't mean anything to me because they weren't answers. Sometimes, Brenda would tell me that I mustn't keep wandering off, that I had to stay with her until I was old enough to go into a group of my own and then I should stay there until I was ready to be moved on to the next group. None of her advice worked for me. However, things were to resolve themselves by the ministry of God himself.

It was a Tuesday, I think. Mother always started to sort out the week's washing on Tuesdays. Someone was knocking at our door though it was wide open. A neighbour would have walked in, having called up the hall. Again there was a knock at the door, but no one was heard coming up the hall. Mum suggested I go and see who it was as she was busy. I didn't like going to strangers on the doorstep, so I sneaked into the parlour and squinted through the window. A figure in a large black overcoat stood with his back to me. He was looking about the street while he waited. As he turned to knock again I saw the white collar at his throat. He didn't see me and knocked again.

'Mummy,' I said, rushing into the scullery. 'It's the minister man from St Barneys.' My mother looked at me for a second then said

'I wonder what he wants?' She left the washing in its separate piles on the floor beside an old tin bath. There was a bottle of bleach, a big lump of carbolic soap and a glass-ribbed washboard standing at the ready while a huge pot of water was steaming on the stove.

Ministers were important people and one had never been to our house before. My curiosity was tempered by apprehension. I heard myself silently repeat my mother's question 'I wonder what he wants?' Strange men at my mother's door, whether they were clergymen or not, never got more than a dismissive 'he' when being referred to by Minnie. I waited some minutes before the sound of my mother's voice drew me to the doorway and into the hall. I stood out of sight and listened. The minister's voice had lost its clerical authority. 'Well, Mrs Keenan I was simply trying to explain—'

He never got to finish the sentence. My mother wouldn't allow him. 'There's no need to change your tone of voice to me. Disturbing your Sunday class, is he? Talking too much, is he? Running around the place, is he? Or do you mean he's not good enough?' 'Believe me, Mrs Keenan, I was not trying to imply anything . . . perhaps if I could come in for a moment and we could—' Again my mother cut him short. Whatever apprehension I had about him calling at our house, I was beginning to feel sorry for him. God love him, he was like the dumbstruck Moses before the burning bush as my mother flamed up at him. 'You can't come anywhere in my home. In fact you can take yourself away to Hell's Gates from about the place.' I could see the clergyman wither in the heat of her rage but Mother wasn't finished yet. 'And you can rest assured that neither me nor any of mine will darken the doors of your church again . . .' This time the minister tried to interject: 'I'm terribly sorry that you feel this way, I was—' 'Don't bother feeling sorry for me, save it for yourself, for you are more in need of it than I am.'

The minister stood in silence and my mother silently eyed him, daring him to speak again. He did. He spoke slowly and evenly, attempting to regain control of the situation and his own dignity. 'I think I should leave the matter and wish you a good afternoon.' He was in the act of turning to leave but did not want to be seen turning his back on a woman. He might have spared himself because my mother was not about to let him have the last word, however conciliatory. 'Wish what you like for I want none of your wishes. And the next time you're standing up in that pulpit of yours be careful that collar doesn't choke you.'

For a moment I was sure the man was indeed choking, but it was with anger rather than righteousness. He turned sharply and walked away. My mother watched for a minute then came back into the scullery. She was boiling more furiously than the water in the huge saucepan.

'You'll not be going back to that Sunday school or that church.'

And with that she grabbed the bleach and carbolic and tossed them into the bath before stirring the boiling water over them. 'A dose of this down his throat might do more for his soul than all the Sunday school in the world. Suffer the little children my backside!'

I never did darken the doors of St Barney-Baps ever again. The church is long since gone, as is the cinema, but the incident remained lodged in my memory for a long time. St Barnabas marked some turning or perhaps I should say some turning-away point in my life. The saint himself remains as a kind of obscure talisman for me even if the incident of the minister and Minnie has faded.

Barnabas is reputed to have said to the author of his epistle: 'No one has learned a more excellent lesson from me but I know you are worthy of it.' I like to think that those same words had some meaning for me too in relation to the Sunday school affair. I confess

I am deeply drawn to this man, with his quirky but elaborate notions of a numerical prophetic code hidden in the Bible. He was a real rebel who had no time for the obligations and prohibitions of Jewish orthodoxy. An ethical revolutionary and brilliantly imaginative apostle who I am sure would have loved my mother and blessed me.

So even if the doors of the church were closed against me, I choose to believe that old Barney-Baps stayed with me, and I am happy to confess that I was baptized in the house of this rascally old saint. As for what happened in the Sunday school that required me to leave, I don't know exactly. Maybe the old man's spirit came home to roost in me as I obviously got up the minister's nose, big time.

My early but enforced retirement from the congregation of St Barnabas was something of a godsend. Freed from the restrictions and regulations of a Christian upbringing I was able to make the world my own. The people and stories that inhabited the streets of the Duncairn Gardens and the New Lodge Road were more interesting than the biblical stories with their moral undercurrents and the dreaded consequences of not living a Christian life.

There was the story about a character named 'Buck Alex', a one-time street fighter turned semi-professional boxer. What made Buck Alex famous was not his fighting skills but the fact that he kept a fully grown tame lion in his tiny two-bedroom terraced house. The boxer and the king of the beasts could often be seen out for a walk. The lion was sometimes held by his master with an old piece of rope, or sometimes by a skinny dog lead fixed to one of Buck Alex's belts buckled around its neck. There were lots of stories about the lion and how it came into its owner's possession. One suggested he had won it in a circus prize fight, another that he had beaten up the ringmaster, the strongman and the lion tamer for whipping the animal then stole it from its owners, who were in no mood to protest. The lion in return became Buck Alex's faithful friend and bodyguard. No one said a bad word about Buck when the lion was with him for it was believed that the creature could smell a malicious thought or intention long before the supposed perpetrator could come within shouting distance of its owner.

A more exotic story was that Buck Alex had jumped ship as a young seaman in Africa and had ended up fighting some giant of a Zulu king. In recognition of defeating the Zulu warrior he was given the lion because the Zulu thought Buck was as fierce and courageous as a lion. There were more stories that I can't remember, but the stories and the lion made a great showpiece when Buck the boxer entered the ring. The lion would always let out a fierce roar as his masters' opponent entered and the spectators roared out twice as loudly. Sometimes Buck Alex sang a song either before or after a fight. I was told that there was one opponent, a huge black man with a strong Liverpool accent, who roared back at the lion as he entered the ring. But Buck was not to be outdone and began chanting a Zulu war song. The Liverpudlian was so astonished by the fearsome mumbo-jumbo that Buck was making up as he sang that he was seized by terror. Buck Alex 'the Lion of Africa' hardly had to lay a finger on the other boxer and the fight was over before it had begun.

Then there was Taty Metafsky the Russian Jew who ran an enterprising business replacing broken windows. Many houses had to call in Taty as many a window was 'put in' during the course of some domestic upheaval. Taty, it seemed, was something of a psychic. Apparently the greater the number of pieces of broken glass, the greater the problem at the heart of a particular marriage. Sometimes he would console the feuding couple using the medium of his trade, suggesting that, like a pane of glass, they should try and see beyond their differences. Alternatively he might explain the difference between a marriage and a piece of glass, suggesting that a pane of glass cannot be stuck back together but that a marriage can. Perhaps the quality of his counselling struck a chord with the women of the house. I suspect Taty got the business of replacing the window because of his sympathetic charm, and he knew it too. Taty was never short of work or money. Some women even believed that his windows brought good luck with them and would keep out the demons; for a while anyway.

My escape from church and Sunday school attendance did not bother me but I had not escaped the necessity of 'dressing up'. When I complained about this to my mother she would always answer, 'We may not be good enough to go to church, but we are the equal and better than many that does.' I was able to convince her that there was no point in getting all 'cleaned up' unless we were actually going somewhere and she agreed, with the proviso that 'we'll not shame ourselves on a Sunday'. I was never too sure what she meant by that but I never questioned her.

On Sundays, especially if it was raining, I was often given the task of cutting up some toilet roll. We had an outside toilet housed in a brick cubicle at the far corner of our yard. I was sat down with a pile of old newspapers and a pair of scissors and was left to slice them up into about six-inch squares. When I had a sufficient pile I would take the pointed end of the narrowest blade of the scissors and drive a hole through one corner of the sheets, then thread a cord through this end and tie it in a knot. The toilet paper was hung from a nail driven into the mortar of the brick wall of the outhouse toilet. Some neighbours kept at least one proper toilet roll in the cupboard for visitors. My mother used to laugh at the idea, suggesting 'there would be no lords or ladies eating at number

30', the number of our house. She laughed even louder as she told the story of her friends who had a whole box-load of these toilet rolls. 'She's always lived a bit above her station or maybe she's expecting the whole of the royal family over for dinner.'

Often, my father would carefully go through the news-sheets before I cut them, to catch up on items of news and this could lead to heated discussions between my parents or anyone else who was in the house. I remember angry talk about a woman called Ruth Ellis who was going to be hanged. My mother was incensed that a group of men that she called a 'jury of fools' should take only half an hour to hang a woman. My father, on the other hand, was angry about what he called the 'colour bar' on the buses in England. I wasn't sure what a colour bar was until he explained. My father's contention was that the English were 'plenty glad enough to have coloured people help fight the war for them.' And he was unhappy about the election of the Conservatives' new leader after Winston Churchill, for 'Churchill was an old warhorse who could never manage peaceful politics.' Dad saw strikes, economic problems and industrial unrest as the new war to be fought. 'Aneurin Bevan and a Labour government is the only party to see the future straight,' he pronounced. I thought that this man Bevan was like Moses and that maybe there would be another war. When I asked about this, Dad laughed and answered 'No, son, I think he's a Welshman and Wales is a long way from Egypt, though there is sure to be trouble there yet. Some people want to own and control more than their share of the world and that always causes wars.' He mentioned a big canal called Suez, and I got it mixed up with toilets and sewers! Over the years I learned a lot about the world from our newspaper toilet sheets, things that Sunday school could never teach me. Even as a young boy I quickly became aware that wars weren't over just because my dad was no longer fighting in one. He tried to explain about the island of Cyprus and how it was fighting for its freedom. That word freedom again: it seemed to be at the centre of lots of things our dad got exercised about. Suez, he explained, was a bit like the parting of the Red Sea, only this time it was the parting of the land by a sea canal but this had happened in Egypt and the people should be left to manage it themselves.

Dad had been stationed in Egypt and some other Middle Eastern and North African countries during the war. He had shown me a photo of himself taken near the Pyramids and the Sphinx. I saw him drinking tea with Egyptians whose flowing clothes made them look like refugees from an Ali Baba story. To my thinking, these photos confirmed that my dad knew what he was talking about even if I didn't. Although I did know it was somehow important.

If the weather was really good the lot of us would go to the local park, which was all that remained of the original estate of Lord Duncairn. It was named after Princess Alexandra but local people dropped the title and called it Alexandra Park. All my mates insisted on using the masculine form as they would not be seen dead in a 'sissy park'. My sister always brought her doll and pram. She had two favourite dolls which she sat in the toy pram facing each other. Of course I took no interest in dolls and prams but I know that my sister had the only black doll in all the streets that surrounded ours. If there was a 'colour bar' problem on the buses in England it certainly wasn't allowed to happen in our house. I cannot remember the names of these dolls except that the black one had an exotic and foreign-sounding name that my father had suggested. In the park Mother would sit knitting while Brenda and the twin dolls entered their own make-believe world. Dad and I would remove our shoes and socks, roll our shirt sleeves up to our shoulders and go in search of spricks and tiny elvers in the stream which flowed into the park from the hills surrounding the city. In no time our jam jars were full of fish and baby eels, but Dad never allowed me to bring them home and I never complained.

Sometimes we might go to the waterworks, which was across the road from the park. This had been constructed in the middle of the nineteenth century to provide water for the growing number of industrial mills that were opening up in the expanding city. It consisted of two large, square reservoirs, fed by streams from the hills. In its heyday, the waterworks hosted spectacular firework displays, aquatic dramas and fêtes of monsters and mermaids. Military and local bands played music regularly to everyone who came to listen.

The waterworks of the late 1950s had lost its gay charm. Men still fished for brown trout in the upper lake. Kids still splashed and shivered in the lower lake as the mountain streams brought their coolness with them. Many years ago a miniature railway had run round the reservoirs but it had fallen into a state of disrepair. Men still poled model yachts. We would sit and watch the mass of small white sails lean against the wind and glide across the water. Several swans overwintered in the reservoirs and the great white galleons of their bodies moved through the armada of tiny yachts with imperious dismissal. Maybe it was the dreamy lethargy of this place on a sunny Sunday that relaxed my father, for that's where I learned about the Blitz and how lucky we all were to be alive.

Every time we went to the waterworks we came upon a group of old men who sat together in one of the sun huts that were sprinkled around the grounds. Most of the men had a dog with them. They wore old gabardine overcoats and well-polished lace-up boots. Some had scarves tied at their throats like cravats, others trilbys that had obviously been thrown away by some of the wealthy families who lived in big detached houses along the Antrim Road. All of them wore poorly fitting suits that had probably been purchased cheaply as an unredeemed item from the pawnshop or had been handed on from a family member who was either twice or half the size of the suit's present owner. One or two had double-breasted blazers with grey flannel trousers. On the breast pocket an elaborate badge had been embroidered with gold and silver threads that glowed against the more sombre shades of red, blue, green and black.

I was fascinated by this collection of old men. They were at the waterworks any time we visited. Everyone seemed to know them and always said hello as they passed. Mother was aware of my interest and quietly whispered to me with a bright smile that they were 'The War Office', further dazzling me by explaining that the men with the badges on their coats were the 'Major-Generals' – then laughed at my amazement.

I couldn't see through her humour and often went over to the men on the pretence of wanting to stroke their dogs. Their conversation was always about the Blitz and the bombing of streets that I knew were only a short walk from my own. When I heard the names – Mileriver, Lawther, Hillman, Hogarth and Edlingham Street, Cliftonville Road, Halliday's Road as well as York Street Mill – and the devastation that occurred there, I could hardly believe it. My streets were a real war zone: the limpid scratched images of the black and white Movietone news that was shown before our Saturday matinée were no longer pictures of a faraway place and time. The talk in the War Office gave them an added immediacy and reality. When I overheard mention of the Luftwaffe and the names of German bombers and fighter aircraft, I was in territory I knew. The War Office descriptions of throbbing aircraft engines in the night sky, the sound of the air raid sirens and the whistle of descending bombs, all excited my imagination. All my model aeroplanes came flying out of the mouths of these old men and I could hear the street collapsing under the weight of the bombs.

Over several months I picked up fragments of stories about the carnage caused by the bombings. There was the story of the mad flautist who lived alone and rarely left his house. He could be heard at all hours of the day and night, blowing his compositions out into the streets. Such was his obsession that on the night of the worst bombing his mad music played louder and harder and sweeter than ever. No one could identify the body found in the rubble of his house, partly because it was so long since anyone had seen him. They found broken flutes, the burnt remnants of hand-scripted sheets of music and a collection of books about music and the great composers. I wondered about this incident for a long time. The mad musician's bravado inspired me. Many years later, I came to the conclusion that the man must have had little fear of death. For in his own reclusive way, he had been living with the dead.

Then there were stories of the families who fled from their homes to take refuge in some empty house in a safer area. One such family was buried alive when their safe house collapsed. Rescue workers were forced back from their efforts when the severed gas mains ignited. The story has it that the people attempting to remove the rubble broke into tears and covered their ears at the sound of the burnt children crying, 'Mammy, Mammy, my feet are burning!' Many neighbours could not bear to disinter the bodies when the gas fires had been extinguished. The charred bodies of the children were deposited in soapboxes to be buried. Even though there were enough coffins, no one could have afforded one.

And it wasn't only humans who lost their lives. Everyone knew the milkman who delivered by horse and cart. His stables were near the top of the Duncairn Gardens. The man had a great love of horses and kept more than he required for his milk business. He also kept three or four dogs in the stables to ensure that anyone who fancied his horses couldn't make off with them in the night. The night of the 'Big Blitz' made that precaution horribly irrelevant. No bombs landed on the stable, but the buildings collapsing around it made it impossible to get in or out. Everything was destroyed in the inferno and the howl of frightened dogs combined with the high-pitched whinnying of terrified horses must have turned the night into an explosion of utter evil. The smell of cremated flesh in the morning underlined the horrors of the night.

Of course, the men in the War Office didn't only talk about the Blitz. They talked about their dogs, the events of the previous week and the likelihood of catching any fish in the top reservoir. They argued about whether Woodbine was a better smoke than Park Drive or Senior Service. Inevitably, they retreated to the war years. Gathered in their small sun hut they were leftovers from another time, plucking memories out of the air, arguing and laughing behind clouds of cigarette smoke. Like the badges on their blazers, the past was a badge of honour. It conferred on them the obligation to be a witness. In the wisps of smoke and sunlight shafting through open latticework of the walls they recited the names of the dead and sometimes cursed their passing in their coarse accents. The sun hut was no silent mausoleum: it was full of arguments, swearing and funny stories as the old men talked about their dead friends. I didn't know the people they spoke of, and could hardly understand their humour. My mind was caught up in things like the parachute bombs that exploded before they touched the ground killing everyone near them by draining the air from their lungs.

My father often disputed the old men's ideas and suggested that I shouldn't believe all that I heard. 'Some of them fellas would tell a lie that would hang the whole neighbourhood,' my mother said. Like most children, I was inclined to believe my parents. But on other days, Dad would stop at the end of a street and point out how one side had more houses than the other. The shorter side ended with derelict ground full of weeds and young sycamore trees and was often littered with bits of old cars or prams. 'They came down in the Blitz,' he said, pointing out where three or four houses were missing. Like all the other kids I knew lots of spare grounds. We played football or marbles on them. We lit fires and roasted spuds in the ashes on them. We had our own wars over the owner-ship of them and we got a rap across the ear for coming home in a filthy state from them. Now, my father's information made them different. Sometimes he knew the names of the families who had had homes on these spare grounds. When I asked if they had died there, he answered that he didn't know or that 'some people died and some people didn't'.

I couldn't cope with such ambiguity, yet I made good use of it. On days when Raymond Heald and the Scott brothers and I went playing on one of these derelict sites, I made up horrifying stories about how the people had died there and said it might still be possible to find some of their bones buried in the ground. I even tried to suggest that there were ghosts, but my pals ridiculed the idea, and my more fanciful stories too.

Whatever stories I was making up, there were plenty more that roamed round the street, echoing the ever-present past. One was the belief that the Luftwaffe had a special unit of airmen who had all been personally converted by the Pope and whose job it was to destroy every Protestant church in Belfast. The idea went over my head. I gave it little thought. After all, I had been excommunicated, in a way. Some time later, I listened as my father read something in the newspaper about how the Protestants of Belfast objected when the City Hall flew a flag at half mast on the death of Pope Pius XII. Could the story of special units of the Luftwaffe be true? For years afterwards, I had my suspicions about the real significance of the German Iron Cross emblazoned across my model aircraft.

THE SWIMMER

DAD LOVED THE OUTDOORS. ON SUMMER MORNINGS, HE WOULD BOIL the kettle until it steamed, then pour the hot water into a basin which he would carry with him into the yard. While he sat on a stool or chair, Dad would go about his daily ablutions with great enthusiasm, splashing water everywhere. Occasionally he used a cut-throat blade to shave with. He loved to sing as the blade scraped across his face. I thought he simply needed a good scrub because his work was often dirty and smelly, but it was probably that Mum wanted to use the sink to wash dishes or clothes. Dad was happy to be relegated to the yard. He wasn't obsessed with dirt or cleanliness. It was more than that: Dad was like a child around water. Water cast a spell on him and transformed him.

I had my first encounter with this in Alexandra Park. After a sleepless night when my growing pains had subsided into a series of disturbing dreams I awoke to the sound of my father's singing and sluicing. The noises he made blew away the dreams at once. I came down the stairs more asleep than awake and stood in the doorway of our scullery and watched him. He was unaware of me for some minutes and I was content to stay and watch, attracted by the animal abandon with which he washed. After some minutes he turned to me, vigorously drying his ears by pushing the towel into them. 'Bad dreams again, son?' he said without making any fuss about the fact. I nodded, half afraid that the acknowledgement might bring the dreams flocking back. 'Well it's very early, but it's going to be a big bright day. So why don't me and you go off to the park and maybe the waterworks, just the two of us?' I was swept away by the suggestion. Most of the street was still asleep. The milkman hadn't even arrived, rattling us all awake with his empty bottles and aluminium crates. And I had never been outside the front door or beyond the yard at this hour of the morning. In no time we were gone. The empty streets were new to me, though I had made this walk hundreds of times. Dad was quiet too. He never did talk much unless I asked him something. So we stole through the streets like a couple of conspirators. It seemed like no one else in the world was awake.

When we arrived at the main gates of the park, they were locked. But there were plenty of bars missing in the wrought-iron railing that enclosed it so we squeezed ourselves through. Dad first, then I handed him the small army canvas bag he had brought with him and finally I stepped rather than squeezed myself into the forbidden parkland. I was afraid of the park keeper catching us but didn't say anything. Dad walked briskly across the grass and on to the pathway. His casual demeanour made me forget the keeper, but not my sense of being afraid. The park, like the streets we had walked through, had lost its familiarity. The lack of distant traffic noise and the absence of voices of other children shouting and playing made the place seem twice as big. The trees I had tried to climb seemed larger and the bushes and shrubs that I had played hide-and-seek in did not invite me at this unearthly hour.

Instinctively we headed to a natural embankment that was crested by several well-formed trees. One had great muscular branches that grew out over the sloping landfall. Years ago someone had climbed the tree and crawled out along one of these branches to attach a rope, which drooped down and dangled over the embankment. It provided hours of fun for local children who would swing out from the edge and then drop to the ground. It was a constant challenge to see who could swing out the furthest and drop from the greatest height. When I went to the park with my parents and sister, I would watch the other lads screaming in panic and delight as they flew out from the hilltop and then plunged like a shot bird to the ground. I watched from a safe distance, never daring to join them. But this day, Dad hoisted me on to the 'Tarzan swing' as it was called and pushed me out. I clung on like grim death as the ground beneath me receded further and further. I was dreading that Dad would push me out even more when the swinging rope turned back on its arc. I said nothing as his hands received me then launched me back even further and higher into the empty air. I clenched the rope but felt only the numbness of my hands. I was glad we were alone and desperately hoped my dad could not see me white with fear. Suddenly I thought of his plane crash into the mountains and simultaneously heard him call 'Drop.' The noise of the command blasted into me and I released my grip and fell to the earth.

I landed easily and rolled a few feet to where Dad stood waiting. I was dumbfounded by what I had done and the fact that I was still in one piece. 'You see, son, I knew you could do it,' Dad said. He was genuinely thrilled and it spilt over into me. I was amazed at my feat and was annoyed now that no one except Dad saw me fly. Something new bubbled up inside me. I felt tingly and unafraid. The park seemed less big and foreboding. 'Want to try again?' he asked. 'Yes,' I answered, surprised by my sudden confidence. For twenty minutes he pushed me then encouraged me to run with the rope in my hand, launch myself off the precipice and drop at the highest point of the swing's incline. 'You'd make a great para-chuter,' he commented encouragingly as I completed another flight and fall. The remark brought me closer to him and our model aero-planes and to his unspoken adventures during the war. Now I was glad no one else was here. I didn't mind that the rest of the screaming jumpers hadn't seen me. When he suggested that we go swimming my new-found confidence fell from me faster than my fall from the swing. I didn't want to say no, but my fear of water was so great that I couldn't speak. Part of me also felt that to say no or to make some other feeble excuse would erase the magic of the past hour. 'Come on,' he said, picking up his haversack.

Instead of walking in the direction of the waterworks, we walked quietly towards the lake in the centre of the park. Swimming here was forbidden. The lake was surrounded by a low iron fence which was only three feet high. So it was not meant to keep people away from the deep water, only to emphasize the prohibition. I had never seen anyone swim here, except a family of swans. I had heard that the lake was maybe forty feet deep. The banks down to the water's edge were steep and overgrown with tall weeds. One reason I think Dad liked this park was its informality. It was more like the countryside than the term 'park' suggested.

'You wait here and mind this stuff. I won't be long,' he said without looking at me. I was immediately relieved and immedi-ately apprehensive. The edges of the lake had swathes of water reed growing and beyond that a film of algae that looked like green confetti. Only at the centre could you see the still black sheen of unmoving water. It looked pretty at first glance, especially when the swans moved across it. But the thought of it was ominous, and the swans scared me. They were not like the birds in the reservoir lakes who were used to the proximity of people with their toy boats and the fishermen and families who often fed them bait or breadcrumbs. The lake swans never got close to human beings because of the fence, the bank and the reeds. The lake was their home and they patrolled it with austere assurance.

Dad stepped over the fence with the rolled-up towel and swimming trunks he had brought in the small haversack. Within minutes, he had changed and was descending the bank. 'Daddy, Daddy, what about the swans?' I asked, becoming more fearful by the second. I had seen the waterworks swans hissing and charging at dogs they thought were too near their nests. I had watched them stand up and spread their wings, flapping furiously. 'The swans won't come near me,' Dad assured me calmly as he slid down through the waist-high weeds and entered the water like a sea snake. He breasted the reeds and the water without a sound. A few water hens scurried out and skimmed to the far side of the lake. Other birds called out their warning at his alien presence in the water. Everywhere else around us was complete silence.

But Dad was no alien here. He swam on through the algae into the middle of the lake. I saw his head and face crusted with the green scum and his black shiny hair sitting on top of the water. He looked like a seal that had suddenly emerged out of the black depths. Then he disappeared again, only to reappear a few seconds later. I watched him intensely and felt lonely and afraid. He moved across the water as if his head was fixed to a submerged stick and an invisible hand was moving it under the surface. He wasn't himself. There were no signs of movement of a body beneath the dull water. For a moment I hardly recognized the thing in the water. All I knew was an overwhelming sense of distance between him and me. His hand came up out of the water and made a slight wave. And then he was swallowed up by the lake again. I knew the wave was an encouragement for me to be unafraid; but it was a passing gesture, as if he was only half conscious of me or anything else. There in the middle of the lake he hardly made a splash or a ripple. He seemed so content. Water was his element and he melted into it. I didn't know him. I only knew the man who made aeroplanes and who brought home animals. This aquatic beast who looked back at me like a ponderous seal, rolled languorously as a beaver, shook his wet hair and snorted like a water buffalo, was from another world.

If anyone was the intruder there, it was me. I wasn't part of this man who an hour ago had encouraged me to fly and be unafraid. I recalled that he had only brought a towel and trunks for himself. Obviously his decision to come here was premeditated around this swim. Something more than wanting to bring me this early in the morning had called him here.

Then I saw the swans emerge and move across the lake like two patrolling gunboats. I wanted to shout a warning but was afraid. I watched as they bore down on him silently and swiftly. I knew that at any moment there would be an eruption of water and wings blasting around my dad. 'Daddy, come on, hurry up,' I urged. He didn't seem to hear me or notice the birds. Then he calmly swam away and ceded the centre of the lake to the swans. They accepted and their bodies sank a little in the water as they ceased their pursuit.

Dad remained a few feet away, watching the birds while they began preening each other. Then he swam to the bank and emerged slowly from the water. His face, shoulders and chest were clotted with algae. It was as if he had grown green scales on his skin. He dried and dressed himself quickly and I knew we would go home now. Something had been appeased. The elemental gods of air and water had touched us separately and it was time to leave.

BALLOO

IT WASN'T ONLY THE LAKE IN THE PARK THAT REVEALED MY FATHER'S affinity with water. Many years later he purchased our first car. Every Sunday saw us drive to somewhere along the coast with a blanket and flask of tea and sandwiches. We went to so many places that I hardly remember their names. There, he used to sit at the wheel of the parked vehicle for what seemed ages staring out at the ocean. Sometimes Mum would doze in the sun while we played or paddled on the beach. When we returned, Dad would be quietly watching the waves.

He took me swimming on his back. 'Just think I'm a great big turtle,' he said and I clung on tightly to the island of his back as he sculled us both out beyond the breaking waves. At one place there was a raft moored a couple of hundred yards from the shoreline. Dad would roll me off his back and hoist me on to the bobbing raft as easily as lifting a pillow. Then he would swim off a few yards and roll and dive like a porpoise. I was never afraid on the raft, I sat, content to watch as he swam underneath the raft and popped up blowing the sea from his nostrils. It was his way of letting me be in the middle of the sea with him even though I couldn't swim and was too afraid to learn. Dad never tried to coax me. In fact, he never pushed me in any direction. He was never anxious about me: I think he believed I should be left to my own devices and should choose my own way into things. I suppose most children are in awe of their dad, and I was too, but it was more than that. He wasn't just the great giant who could do things that I couldn't. He was more a presence around me than a real person. Even if over the years of my growing up we talked little, I always felt him looking on, watching over me.

Most years we rented a bungalow for our summer holidays in an area of coastal countryside, some seventeen miles south-east of Belfast, known locally as Balloo. To most people, this is the name of Kipling's and Walt Disney's lovingly tender but heroic bear in *The Jungle Book*. My Balloo, the place, was an equally fantastical part of my childhood.

To the outsider, Balloo was no more than a conglomeration of fields, rutted lanes and outlying small farms. In the midst of this unmapped landscape sat half a dozen rickety bungalows, built on stilts with long, overhanging verandas; a perfect setting for any Disney fairy tale. Uncle Hartley, Aunt Audrey and my cousin Michael frequently joined us, and sometimes my other uncle, Maurice and his girlfriend Jean came for the weekend. Uncle Maurice drove a big black motorcycle with a sidecar. It had a badge with a pair of wings springing from the centre of a huge wheel on the fuel tank. The letters BSA were embossed on the design, which my uncle said meant 'bloody sore arse'! Jean agreed with this, as she was the one who had to ride in the sidecar up the rocky road that led to our bungalow. You always knew when Maurice was coming as you could hear the choking roar and crashing gears of the BSA as it bumped its way towards us. Uncle Maurice always wore a brown leather skullcap and goggles. As soon as he laid them down, I was off with them and into the cockpit of the sidecar from where I screamed through the skies. I was tail gunner or navigator to the imaginary pilot, riding above me on the big BSA.

Our bungalow was built on stilts so that rats couldn't get in, and snakes and lizards too, or so my father used to whisper, tantalizingly, in the gas-lit evenings. That forbidden place underneath our floorboards excited and challenged me. But only in daylight did I venture there. In the evenings, my chosen sleeping quarters was the veranda. I snuggled up on an old moth-eaten sofa, wrapped in a few ex-army blankets, and gave myself up to the fantasies of the night. I loved the sense of freedom of those evenings on the porch: they conferred on me a feeling of ownership and of adulthood. I was allowed to sleep on my own outside the security of the bungalow. I liked it when Auntie Jean made some remark about how safe everyone would be with me keeping guard outside.

I loved listening to the bungalow shut down for the night. The gaslights were silently extinguished. The adult conversation ended as everyone retired. I am sure my parents and relations sometimes forgot I was listening to them beyond the clapboard walls. I overheard things I could never admit to overhearing the next day, and there were references to people that confused me. Some woman was 'too much of a Jezebel for her own good!' I thought Jezebel was a great name and wondered who the woman was. And there was another woman who fed her husband dog meat in a stew every Friday night when he was too drunk to notice. 'If he spent less time with his greyhounds and whippets he might get a proper meal on Fridays.' Unusually, my mother's voice was sympathetic towards the unfortunate husband. 'If you listened long enough to that woman's stories and looked at the two of them stood together, you'd think twice about who wears the trousers and who's hard done by!'

There was talk about who was in debt, who was taking what to the pawnshop, and there was talk that confused me about the outside world, a long way from my secret sleeping place. There were heated conversations between my dad and Uncle Hartley, about the nuclear bomb. Uncle Hartley, a Welshman, had been in the army during the war. 'There isn't a bomb big enough, boyo!' he would declare. If he thought he was losing an argument he would say things like 'Victory to the valiant' and 'To the victor the spoils!' Or else he would get really excited and slap the table, saying, 'Look you Jack, boyo, there are no referees in war, and principles don't stop bloody bullets. It's kill or be killed and I don't care how it's being done as long as it's not me or mine that's being killed!'

Sometimes Dad got as frustrated as my uncle. 'It's not war any more, it's slaughter and you can't talk about principles if you can count the dead in millions overnight!' There was talk of another war, which they called the 'cod war', with a country called Iceland, and they debated about the riots in England between the blacks and the whites. Mother, Aunt Audrey and Aunt Jean talked long into the night about babies that were born with no arms and legs because the mothers had been given drugs when they were pregnant. A strange-sounding word entered my world: Thalidomide. I had never heard it before. It sounded like it had come from another world or another language. To my mind, it was the name of a monster.

I only half understood the adult talk, for I was usually half asleep. These conversations filtered into my dreams. My sleep was haunted by horrible limbless monsters, soldiers made of ice, and fighting fish. But always in the morning, I awoke to the soft cooing of wood pigeons that had come to roost on the corrugated roof. My father cooked breakfast in his vest and braces. His singing woke everyone and they tumbled into the kitchen cranky and hungry. Breakfast was a generous free-for-all, and the home-made soda farls and tattie bread fried crisp in hot lard hardly reached the table before they were scoffed down. The country air made famine victims of us all.

The walks around this unmapped countryside created a hunger for rural things that still gnaws at me. We had to walk two miles and back to purchase our eggs. A couple of dozen cost a 'tanner' (sixpence) and you took what you could get, chicken, duck, or on occasion 'duck all'! You walked everywhere for everything. We collected water in white enamel buckets from a spring well at the bottom of the garden. In a farm a few fields away, we could buy fresh farmhouse butter and potatoes and fresh vegetables. On many occasions I would sit on my veranda with my sister shelling peas and broad beans into a pot. In the scullery, Mum boiled beetroot, which we all had to eat. She swore it had more medicinal qualities than all the pills in the world. Dad loved his mushrooms: break-fast was not really breakfast without lashings of fried mushrooms and he knew all the best spots in the fields around us to find them. If I was awake early enough, he would take me foraging with him. Sometimes, it seemed we were gone for hours. On these high, bright dew wet mornings, it was as if only he and I were alive in the world. We found more than mushrooms. We found fields full of rabbits, saw hares boxing, or caught the white flush of a disappearing fox's tail. We found nests full of speckled eggs and hungry fledglings. But it wasn't always a pastoral idyll.

There were also some frightening moments. Once I walked into a farmyard with my cousin and Dad to purchase eggs. For no reason that I can remember, a cockerel attacked my cousin. It flew up on his chest and neck, clawing and crowing, with Michael screaming in apoplectic fear. Everything happened in a moment, and my father's urgent, volatile attack on the crazed bird imprinted Michael's terror on my innocent imagination. I can still see the blood and red welts on my cousin's neck and chest, and the farmer stomping towards us growling, 'What the Hell's Gates . . . !' And grabbing Michael as if he was the accursed creature himself.

I experienced a new kind of fear that day. It wasn't the fearfulness of the moment, though the image of the mad blood-crazed cockerel remained with me for many years. It was the unpremeditated nature of the attack. Something unknowable and evil had entered my world. It was without cause or reason. My cousin's unearthly screams and his uncontrollable trembling announced its arrival. I was not the victim, but something in me was also scarred. The image of my father grabbing the psychotic bird off Michael's chest, the way he threw it to the ground and the force with which he kicked it, launching it into the air, was something I could hardly believe of him. The bird lay silent a few feet from us and shook. Dad walked towards it and I was convinced he was about to tramp it into the ground. He stopped and stared at the dazed creature then removed his coat, wrapped my convulsed cousin in it and walked off cradling him like a newborn. 'There, son, don't be afraid, that old bird is dead. He won't hurt anybody again!' Watching him as he walked away, I felt dreadfully lonely and more afraid than my cousin. I looked at the farmer. We had got to know him well over the years. He looked back at me vacantly, then lifted the limp bird and walked off in the opposite direction. 'Come on, son,' my father called out to me. I ran after him clutching at the hoard of mushrooms I had secreted in the front of my jumper. It seemed to take for ever to reach home, and every footstep ached with the noise of Michael's exhausted sobbing.

Later the farmer's wife called to enquire after Michael, and to inform us that the cockerel had been slain by the farmer and if Michael or his family wanted to see for themselves, they would be welcome. There was much discussion as to whether it would be good for my cousin to see that the creature was well and truly dead.

Michael's father thought that he should have witnessed the creature's execution. But the women chastised him. In the end my uncle
went alone to view the corpse. That evening, the men drank bottles
of Guinness which had been opened and left to 'cook' in the hearth
in front of an especially big fire. When the froth climbed up the
neck and formed little white caps on the top of the bottle, they
were ready for drinking. No one mentioned the events of the day.
Conversation was muted. The radio played and the women talked
about going into the nearest seaside town to buy a present for
Michael. He sat in the corner, wrapped in an eiderdown, sipping
at a home-made milkshake. No one mentioned what had happened;
but no one forgot it.

Balloo wasn't far from the sea. A few miles from our bungalow
was the tiny harbour at Groomsport. Early each morning a collection of small boats, packed to the gills with fathers and sons, set
out to catch the evening's supper. With Dad's addiction to the sea,
it was inevitable that we should be regulars. There was a great sense
of camaraderie on these boats. Most people were holidaymakers
who, like ourselves, had been coming to this part of the countryside for years. There was ribald good humour between the men. If
it was a Sunday, most of them had come along, not just to catch
fish but also to nurse a hangover. Soon there was an exchange of
banter about who was going to catch what, and who was incapable
of catching anything!

It took maybe an hour and a half to get out to where the fish
were expected to be. Dad never bothered much with the banter but
sat watching the ocean or made bets with me about who would
catch the first fish. There was an unspoken rule governing the boat
we always went out in. It was that it never returned empty: we
stayed at sea until there was enough fish for everyone to take something home. I once heard the skipper say, 'This might not be the

Sea of Galilee and I can't make miracles, but no one goes home without a few fish for the pan!'

When our craft reached its destination my father squeezed lead weights on to my line and fixed white feathers on the black gleaming hooks. Everyone on board had their own tackle box and their own favourite bait and lures. But Dad didn't go in for any of this fancy stuff. He swore by his white feathers and they always seemed to work. The idea of using bird feathers to catch fish was its own kind of miracle, and how the boatmen knew just where to stop in a heaving grey ocean told me that even if the skipper couldn't make miracles he still possessed a special kind of power. As the boat shuddered to a stop, we plopped our lines into the sea. Each time I hoisted my flimsy line it was alive with flapping fish. And flapping is precisely what my heart was doing. Mostly they were mackerel. Occasionally, there were some flat-fish, maybe a cod or two. Often there were dogfish which were immediately returned, or perhaps if the bait bucket was empty they would be swiftly dissected. Sometimes the anglers would catch ugly writhing conger eels that scared me as they wriggled furiously along the bottom of the boat. Often it rained, and then the fishing was poor. No one dared suggest that we return. Dad and I sat shrouded in a great black waterproof, sipping hot tea and munching biscuits. Everyone told jokes or stories to dispel the gloom. But most times the two tin basins stowed in the centre of the craft were filled to the brim within hours and we headed home, shivering but conquering heroes. Often Dad and I had enough mackerel for every bungalow in Balloo.

The bungalows are long since gone and the rutted laneways are no longer there. Balloo is still not on the map. But it's there in my memory. Sometimes I watch *The Jungle Book* with my son Jack. He has my father's name. He loves Balloo the bear with the same wonder that I loved Balloo the place. But it's all gone now. The wooden bungalows fell apart from long disuse. People had knocked some of them down, intending to replace them. They never had. The rutted lane is now a proper road. A smart redbrick house looks across the fields where I picked mushrooms. The small farmstead has gone. The fleet of fishing boats is gone. Maybe it's best that the boats are gone. The vacant space they leave behind has the effect of embalming history. Years later, when we ceased going to Balloo, I asked my dad what the farmer had done with the cockerel he had to kill. 'Plucked him and made soup,' he answered nonchalantly. I swallowed hard at his words. I remembered that only a day after the attack on my cousin the farmer had left the pink pimpled carcasses of two chickens with my mum. His departing words were, 'One of them for roasting and the other only fit for making soup!'

CONGREGATION
OF WOMEN

IT HAS ALWAYS BEEN DIFFICULT FOR ME TO GET A PROPER FIX ON THE man my father was. From the long reach of history, I see him in flashes. He was untypical of the men I witnessed growing up. In him the Planter and the Gael, the Covenanter and the Cavalier, lost themselves in comfortable contradiction. There was astuteness hidden behind long patience, a quiet but determined dislike of class attitudes or humbug. He had the ability to see beyond the ordinary and mundane but either hadn't the capacity or hadn't the desire to communicate to others what he saw. Behind that silence there was a touch of the 'shorter catechism'. He had a sense of responsibility and a vigilant if complex conscience. But I always felt that he was influenced by imagination and generosity of heart. He had a countryman's capacity for honest sentiment. Whatever his reserve, something mysterious yet gay and exciting lay undiscovered there. Throughout my childhood this compelling, undisclosed man stood as an isolated figure in the landscape. His presence was an assurance and a guarantee, yet always at a distance. And this was both comforting and confusing. Sometimes I wanted to get closer not for affection – for I never felt the lack of that – but to know him more, to be taken into his world. For years I studied his face. I still have a photo of my parents on my desk. Whatever else I may read in his face it is still the handsomest I have ever seen.

My mother's world was so different. It was jam packed with things happening and people coming and going. There was a frenetic energy about her, and her life seemed supercharged by it most of the time. I cannot remember my mother ever sitting still; she was always on the go, a proper study in perpetual motion. I can still see her in the scullery standing at the sink with the tin bath beside her, her arms moving like pistons up and down the glass washboard, suds seeping out of the clothes and through her hand as if she is bleeding soap. Then she would rinse the items at the sink, plunging her hands in both hot and cold water without the slightest hesitation. I hated the sight of the red fleshy lumps they became. If she wasn't washing clothes then she was on her hands and knees with cotton rags polishing the linoleum in our hall. The heavy odour of paraffin and silicone wax hung about the hallway for days. Afterwards, it was upstairs to make the beds. Mother could toss and shake blankets like a matador. Then down to the kitchen to chop up soup vegetables which were left to slowly simmer, their soupy aroma mixing with the silicone wax. I was often sent to the shops to get the messages. Off I would go, with the list of provisions written on a scrap of paper and wrapped tightly round a brown ten shilling note. If it was only a few items, I had to repeat them once in front of her, then over and over again to myself all the way to the shop on the corner of Halliday's Road. When I returned I would find her at the ironing board. She would stand there for ages, her arm flashing dextrously backwards and forwards creating neat piles of pressed clothes from several pillowcases full of wrinkled jumble. This hurricane of energy that was my mother powered through her chores in silence.

Unlike my father, my mother seldom sang, and the transistor was rarely on. When it was, she was oblivious to it. It was as if music or melody was somehow in the way. Mother had her own rhythms and needed no accompaniment. In the evening when there was nothing left to do, she sat snugly in the corner of the sofa beside the fire knitting furiously, the needles click-clacking with such continuous intensity that they became a low-sounding rhythmic hum. I accepted this outrageous energy of my mother's as the normal way of things and I never complained about it, because her energetic preoccupations left me entirely to my own devices. Our separate worlds coexisted, mutually content.

But there were times when the regimented order of my mother's routine was broken. It was a rare occurrence and lodges itself in my memory because of its rarity. Mother would often stay up when everyone had gone to bed. Perhaps she couldn't sleep until those banks of energy that drove her were entirely used up. When my dreaming sleep woke me and I lay anxious in the dark, I could sometimes hear her moving about in the house below me and I would sneak down the stairs wanting the comfort of the big fire. Before I reached the last stair I would hear her humming some tune and then breaking into a chorus, her voice pitched high and airy yet soft. It was an old song from long before my mother's time but she had picked it up in snatches from her young days working in the mills.

> You might easy know a doffer
> When she comes into town,
> With her long yellow hair
> And her pickers hanging down,
> With her rubber tied before her
> And her scraper in her hand,

You might easy know a doffer
For she'll always get a man
Oh she'll always get a man
You might easy know a doffer
For she'll always get a man

You might easy know a weaver
When she come into town,
With her oul greasy hair
And her scissors hanging down,
With a shawl around her shoulders
And a shuttle in her hand,
You will easy know a weaver
For she'll never get a man
No, she'll never get a man
No, she'll never get a man
You will easy know a weaver
For she'll never get a man.

The clipped speech and consonantal dead weight of my mother's accent was rounded off in the melody. The song was about working women but it was also about animosity and rivalry and pride; the man who may or may not be got was a secondary thing. Mother half sang, half hummed the way people do who remember a song through accidental hearing or repeated association. When I entered the room, she would be sitting with sheets of newspaper spread on her knee, her fingers black from Brasso cotton as she rubbed and polished the brassware that decorated our hearth. She stopped her work and showed me how to apply the polish. I watched the brass dull as the polish settled on it, then saw it come up gleaming as she rubbed a rag of cotton over it. She didn't mind me being there, nor did she ask me why, beyond the rhetorical question, 'Them old growing pains again, is it?'

I only ever heard her sing and hum in the curious way she had of running one thing into another before the first was complete. It was always done *sotto voce* as if she didn't want to be heard, or perhaps the memories that the inarticulate song recalled were too special. Whatever the reason, these almost inaudible harmonies were part of the way she worked. I remember her standing on a chair so that she could reach our front windows. Her fists were full of newspaper soaked with paraffin, her arm curved across the glass in great sweeping movements. Her lips were moving more like a whisper than a song. She looked right through the window and through me as I sat in our parlour watching her. She was like a giant marionette. When she came in I told her she smelt of paraffin. 'It makes them shine better and the rain runs off them faster,' she said. That was my mother: if she couldn't sing, she could make the rain run fast!

However, Mother's energy was not centred on our house. If there was a neighbour who needed something done, Mother would be there to do it. She would paint doors, climb ladders to paint window frames, scrub floors, cook other people's dinners or tend to sick neighbours. Her energy was boundless, but sometimes it was fuelled by anger: anger at the husbands who refused to do the work themselves, anger at doctors who fobbed off her sick neighbours as if their illness was somehow their own fault. My mother's concern was driven neither by morality nor social altruism. If there was a kind of Mother Courage complex about her, it was driven by something less easily definable: something relentless and enduring.

Our house fairly buzzed with the presence of women. Usually they came alone; only very rarely do I recall women coming together. I don't remember many of them by name. They addressed my mother as Mrs Keenan, but she hardly ever used this form when talking back to them. Only if her visitors were very old did she call them Mrs followed by their surname. Mostly she gave them their first names, Annie, Margaret, Agnes, Patsy and Irene. There seemed to be lots of them and lots of names and faces I have forgotten. But some remain, partly because of the frequency of their visits and partly because of the smells that I associated with them.

There was 'Dizzy Lizzie' who walked up our hall followed by invisible traces of lavender-scented talc and sharply sweet perfume. Lizzie was a dreamer and the moment she sat down, Mother took up her knitting. Lizzie was always going somewhere. One week it was to London, another week she would be full of talk about how much she had saved for her long-awaited trip to America. She had a sister in Devon who had married a farmer and she was planning to visit her in the summer. Though she had never been there, she could describe the farmhouse and the country round it at length. Everything there was either 'beautiful' or 'wonderful' or 'unforgettable'. Sometimes she brought a bag with her own knitting in it, or else she would crochet. If she was knitting, it was always baby clothes or if she chose to crochet it was a baptismal blanket or a coverlet for a pram or cot. While Lizzie's hands worked, her mind wandered. She had been to Blackpool and some-where in Scotland before she married. But she and her husband had grand travel plans. Lizzie talked and crocheted and Mother sat knitting silently and hardly listening to a word. Dizzy Lizzie always stayed for an exact amount of time. She drank a cup of tea and at the end of it she would stare into the bottom of the cup and ask, 'I wonder what's in my tea leaves?' Mother's answer was always the same: 'Now I wouldn't know that Lizzie, why don't you go and find out!' But Lizzie never did. Often if she had finished the garment she was working on she would leave it with my mother, telling her that she probably knew someone who would need it.

When I once asked why the woman was always leaving her baby clothes, Mother explained that she had no children of her own. After she finished her tea and left, I might ask when she would go to London or America or wherever she happened to be talking about, and Mother would simply answer that her husband was not the travelling type and that it cost a lot of money to go to the places she spoke of – perhaps more than Lizzie would ever have! There was such a sense of finality and inevitability about my mother's explanation that Lizzie's stories of her proposed travels ceased to excite me. While my mother sat knitting I played with my toys as Lizzie delivered her monologue of faraway places.

There was another woman who called only occasionally. She was always well dressed and wore high heels. Unlike the other women, she knocked and waited in the hallway until she was invited in. Mother ushered me into the back kitchen as she directed this woman into our parlour and I was always curious: 'Why does that woman talk funny and what's that smell?' My mother's answer was curt and she informed me that it would be the only answer and I was not to bring up the subject again. 'She talks like that because she's from the Antrim Road and she smells like that because she drinks gin that's from the Antrim Road too.' The woman only called two or three times. She wore a fur collar and a hat. I was fascinated by her collar; it looked like a fox lying across her shoulders. I could see its face and its dark, staring eyes. No woman in our street wore such clothes. After a while I forgot the woman, but the image of the fox draped across her shoulders remained with me. In my dreaming imagination I got it all mixed up with those images of Jesus the good Shepherd with a lamb strung across his shoulders. I knew that foxes killed lambs, but the woman did not appear to be bad: she was too clean and polite. Maybe there were lots of foxes in the Antrim Road, or maybe she just liked them. When I asked Mother about this she agreed with my suppositions and left the matter at that.

Then there was the woman from the next street who was always sobbing into a handkerchief and apologizing for it. Mother tried to reassure her the way she did with my sister and me, telling her not to worry. The neighbour was concerned for her child who had polio and wore callipers. She was constantly anxious about what would happen to her daughter if anything happened to her. The husband had died a few years ago and she had two other children. How could her daughter with polio learn at school? Would she never marry? As the woman spoke she smoked and coughed into her handkerchief. Mother let her talk; she had heard this story so many times. But sometimes she could bear it no longer and she would round on the neighbour. 'In the name of God, stop whingeing and fretting over nothing. You're worse than the child itself. There's many who have less and they have got by and managed better than most. What about young McAllister in Syringa Street? That child would put a smile on anybody's face. To listen to you, you'd think you wished that child of yours dead.' The last sentence fell like a hammer blow. The woman ceased sobbing and coughing. She was silent but her face was awash with tears. Mother sat watching and waiting, then her voice would turn soft. 'Ah Agnes, there are many women around here who have lost children. There are some I know who cannot have them, and they spend their days doing things that mean nothing because they are afraid of the emptiness . . . The days have neither shift nor shape on them . . .' Sometimes my mother would say more, encouraging the distressed neighbour, but more often she rose from where she was sitting and went off to make tea. It always seemed to work. The crying mother wiped her face and drank the tea gratefully. When she left, the smell of tobacco and polish remained.

The young crippled boy in the next street was probably the most popular kid in the neighbourhood. The rest of us used to go and play outside his house while he sat in the doorway. His deformed legs never allowed him to join us as we played a game called 'Fall the best'. One boy positioned himself flat on his stomach a few feet from the cripple and pretended to have a machine-gun in front of him. The rest of us lined up several yards from him and then, one by one, charge at him firing our Tommy guns. The prostrate sniper would rat-a-tat-tat each of his assailants to death. We fell down in the most dramatic fashion. Young McAllister would then choose who fell the best, and that person then took over the imaginary machine-gun and the murderous process would begin all over again. The Saturday matinées had taught us all to 'fall' with an amazing bloody grace.

The girls had no interest in war games. Instead, they would sit around McAllister telling stories, ignoring us completely. It was obvious that the young boy had little interest in our heroics and he would listen and laugh at the stories and jokes that were presented to him like a garland. Sometimes the girls held skipping marathons. Two of them would stand some ten feet apart with a rope in each hand running between them. They wheeled their two hands in turning circles, one clockwise, the other anticlockwise, the ropes running between them, laced into one another without ever touching. This created a fluid oval at the centre of the alternately turning ropes. At a given moment one or two of the girls would enter this oval and jump lightly when the ropes made a slapping sound as they touched the ground under their feet. Sometimes two groups of girls would gather at each end of the turning ropes. Two girls, one from each end, would enter the skipping ropes simultaneously and skip to the chorus of a song being sung by their friends. Then they would pass out from the rope, running to the end opposite to where they entered. The next two girls would repeat the action and so it would go on, with an endless figure of eight being made by the girls' entrance and exit from the ropes. The songs changed from one chorus to another. The subjects of these street rhythms were completely unrelated yet the girls knew instinctively which chorus would come next without any prompting. These songs were usually about childish flirtations. They were stories of romantic pursuit and stolen kisses. Some had riddles built into them in an attempt to divine the name of a future husband.

She is handsome, she is pretty,
She is the belle of Belfast city
She is courting, one, two, three,
Please can you tell me who is she

Albert Mooney says he loves her,
All the boys are fighting for her
They rap at the door, they ring at the bell,
Saying O my true love are you well

Out she comes as white as snow,
Rings on her fingers, bells on her toes.
Ould Jenny Murray says she'll die
If she doesn't get the fella with the roving eye!

I loved to watch them. The whole dizzying ballet of the spinning ropes, the skippers entering and exiting with effortless assurance and the background of their songs was much more intricate and challenging than our thespian death throes at McAllister's feet. The skipping was irresistible and before long, I joined in with the girls. But before I was allowed to skip, I had to serve my time learning the ropes. As I swung the ropes, the girls sang while my comrades-in-arms lined the footpath jeering me with taunts of 'skipping sissy' or 'sissy knickers'. But soon I was running in and out of the ropes like a swallow. With some songs the ropes had to be turned at tremendous speed and the skipper had to do 180-degree turns and then hop-skip on alternate feet. It all seemed so easy: it required no understanding or timing or technical expertise. You only needed to fall into the rhythm of the songs and the spinning ropes. Then you didn't really skip, you hovered inches above the ground. McAllister clapped and laughed loudly at my act of treachery in going over to the other side. He cheered jubilantly as I performed inside the madly turning ropes. His enthusiasm flowed into me and I skipped with stubborn joy and smiled triumphantly at my mocking friends. I was never sure why McAllister took such delight in my defection. A part of me likes to think that just for a day or two my antics gave him the legs that he would never have. Whenever I did play 'Fall the best' after that he always made sure that he picked me 'the best' above anyone else!

One time my mother explained that McAllister had been to see several faith healers and some had even come to his house, but all to no avail. 'There are some people whose mind refuses to meet up with things,' she said obliquely. The words puzzled me. The tone of her voice was sympathetic and she continued, 'No one can pull miracles out of the air, you have to make your own.' When Mother spoke like this I was never sure if she was talking to me or to herself. Much later, I came to think that a part of my mother secretly wanted to believe in miracles. Another part of her detested the falsehood of such things because in her eyes, they led people astray and only reinforced the neediness of those who believed in them.

There were days when there weren't enough kids to play our street games. However, the girls were never at a loss, and usually impromptu concerts were performed for McAllister. I was either too shy or too conscious of the sissy label to join in: I took a position beside the crippled boy and watched the show. I always wanted to ask him what the faith healers were like, what they did to him, and why nothing had happened. Though I never went to church, the word 'faith' troubled me. I thought it was so easy to believe in things!

Some women who called at our house were less welcome than others, especially the woman who smelt of cats and ashes and who slunk up the hallway like a cat. As soon as she announced herself, Mother would declare that she was about to go out herself. But invariably, she made her a cup of tea and a sandwich of butter and sugar. This woman talked about nothing in particular; mostly about her cats. She had a houseful of these creatures. Mother never really listened and would busy herself with washing at the scullery sink. As soon as she had finished her tea and sandwich, Mum would gently hurry her out the door pretending that she was in a hurry herself. The woman's parting words were that she was off to buy herself a pastie supper. 'Doesn't she ever eat anything else?' I asked one day. 'I don't think she knows how to,' my mother replied, then volunteered that the 'poor woman' had stopped cooking when her husband died many years ago and had lived on sweet tea, sugar sandwiches and pastie suppers ever since. Later my sister Brenda told me, half smiling, 'Everybody calls her "Tate and Lyle".' I smiled back knowing that anyone who went to the shop for sugar always asked for it by its brand name, Tate and Lyle.

And then there was Lily who fascinated me and scared me at the same time. As my mother explained it, 'poor Lily had grown up before her mind had'. Her clothes were old fashioned. When she wore make-up, her cheeks would be rouged up as if she had a rash and her lipstick smudged well beyond the outline of her lips. Lily loved flowers or, rather, weeds that flowered and she would scour the waste grounds and derelict sites in the streets around us to find them. Often neighbours took Lily with them when they were taking their own children to the park. Lily thought she was in heaven. She was rarely seen without a handful of wild daisies, buttercups, purple scabious, red clover and other flowering weeds. She never knew their proper names and invented her own simple names like 'Auntie Emily' and 'Tickles'. All of us children were expressly forbidden from making fun of Lily. 'Lily is a special person,' my mother told us.

When Lily called at our house she walked in and sat down like she lived in the place. She always had her handful of flowers and weedy leaves. She liked to give them as a present with the simple expression, 'For you now, Mrs'. She never added the surname, as she never remembered it: she called everyone Mrs. My mother made a great fuss of the present and fetched a jug of water to place the flowers in. Then she would talk to Lily with simple childlike questions. Sometimes her answers shocked us and Mother would look at me with a stern warning in her eyes and her finger raised, threatening that I was not to laugh or repeat what I might have heard.

Often Mother would help remove some of Lily's indulgent make-up and on occasion would give her a small medicine bottle with some of her own perfume, slightly watered down. At other times she asked Lily to help with her knitting wool. Lily would nod in agreement and ask if she could have two biscuits for helping. Mum bought her wool in long skeins which had to be unwound and rolled into a ball for ease of knitting. When Lily thrust her hands out in front of her in one urgent movement I couldn't help laughing nervously, for it looked as if she had suddenly produced two imaginary six-shooters and was about to blast my mother full of holes. Mum smiled, allowing me my laugh, then placed the long loop of wool over each of Lily's hands. 'Do you like this colour, Lily?' she would ask as she pulled a strand of wool backwards and forwards across Lily's hand while creating a compact ball of wool in her own hands. Lily seemed fascinated by the action of the wool. 'What are you going to make?' she asked. And when Mum answered her, she always asked if she would knit her some gloves. Mum hated knitting gloves but politely asked what colour Lily would like. Her answer rarely changed. Gently she would set down the wool, walk to where the 'flowers' had been placed and then, pointing to each colour in turn, say: 'Like this and like this and like this.' Mother's reply rarely changed either. 'OK, Lily, I'll just have to look and see if I have anything like that.' Lily was satisfied. When the wool had all been unwound into balls Lily, Mum and I would sit down with cups of tea and biscuits. Lily hated to be given a plate of biscuits that were all the same shape. To her, there were less biscuits if they were all the same. But if they were assorted shapes and colours, she clapped her hands in delight.

Mother never worried about the rainbow-fingered gloves. She knew that Lily would never remember asking for them. But there was something Lily never forgot: her flowers. Ten minutes after she had left the house, she would return, walk calmly to the jug, lift the flowers gently and walk unconcernedly out again with an affectionate 'Bye, bye Mrs. Bye bye, Brian.' We both returned the cheerio as if nothing had happened. Mother would smile at me and shrug her shoulders. 'Maybe she has somewhere else to go?' I knew that Lily forgot many things. Perhaps that was why everyone loved her. But it worried me slightly that she never forgot my name. Even if I hadn't seen her for weeks, Lily always knew my name!

Looking back on those times I think it was that constant frenetic energy which surrounded my mother that drew all these women to her. The Mother Courage persona wasn't something studiously learned or consciously acquired. My mother was tough and uncompromising about many things and that toughness spilled over into compassion. But great displays of tenderness were not part of her character: perhaps she saw it as a weakness, or even an injustice. Mother was always poised for action. Tenderness and outpouring of sympathy only sidelined you from action; from doing and saying what needed to be done and said.

I suppose my mother and father were two sides of the same coin. They were collectors. Just as my dad insisted on bringing home orphaned and injured animals from his many nights on the country roads, so too, my mother gathered to herself women who were in some way wounded or troubled or simply despairing. Father had a gentleness about him combined with a sense of reserve or even mystery. I was in awe of my father. I didn't worship or fear him. I respected his presence and his comforting reserve.

My mother was everything my father was not. When it was first explained to me that the figure on a penny coin was Boadicea the warrior queen, I thought of Mother. I even tried to imagine her standing on her chariot behind two horses as they reared in the air, their nostrils flaring and the muscles of their flesh hard as congealed lava. I liked this wild image of her. It frightened me a little. Once I caught a glimpse of her washing herself at the sink. The whiteness of her breast was nothing like the triumphant image on the coin. Boadicea would have charged fearlessly into battle leaving a wake of bloody corpses behind her. The warrior queen would have bathed herself in the blood of her victims. Watching my mother at the sink that morning with her blouse ruffled about her waist as she washed her upper body, I could not imagine her as the blood-drenched queen. Yes, she was stubborn, defiant, even fearless. She had a temper that withered hard men. Certainly she could eviscerate enemies with her tongue and was afraid of no one, but I could not see her leaving a trail of corpses in her wake. All the women who came to see her were victims in different ways and she took them on to whatever chariot it was she rode and carried them away or went to fix whatever needed fixing. But it wasn't just her resilience and reckless willingness to take on the world that drew all these women to our house. They came to her because she knew the anguish of victimhood. Somewhere in her experience she had drunk from that cup.

HERCULES AND THE PIGS

ROBERT MCCARTNEY WAS A SMALL BOY AND I HAVE NO IDEA WHY WE
befriended each other. He lived about a dozen streets from my own.
That was out of my neighbourhood so we only shared school time
together. Robert's height and slight build meant that he had no
interest in the boisterous games and girl-baiting that seemed to be
a major pastime in school. But Robert was fascinating. His dad had
been a seaman and now worked at the docks. Mr McCartney must
have been something of a storyteller, as his son could tell fantastic
stories about the places his dad had been. As we sat in school sewing
long strands of coloured raffia through a wheel of cardboard and
string, we talked of Africa and America. He spoke about storms at
sea and how a sailor had lost his hand because of rope burns. One
time his dad had even brought a small monkey home, but had to
sell it to the pet shop in Smithfield. I knew the shop and had seen
monkeys there so I believed him. Maybe his father's stories about
his travels to foreign lands compensated for my own father's silence
about the war. The fact that his dad was a seaman and mine an
airman made us brothers in some kind of way. Robert and I always
sat together to drink the free milk that was rationed out to every
schoolchild at the time. Often his milk was stolen. Robert would

sit saying nothing as the boy who stole it gulped it down in front of him. Furiously, I would storm up to the front of the class and take another bottle for him. My act of sympathy and rage at injustice confirmed our friendship. Most days we walked home together, except on the days he was absent. I think he was sick of school more than he was sick. One day as we were about to part company at the gates of St Barnabas he asked me why I never went to church. I didn't really know the answer and simply told him that I got sick every Sunday. After many months of this playground friendship Robert asked me if I would like to go the docks with him: he went there most Saturday mornings so he could help his dad. On this particular Saturday there was a large shipment of cattle and pigs coming in and they needed people to help with the unloading. The words 'help with the unloading' seemed so grown up. I was more than keen, even when he told me I had to be outside the church where he would meet me by 7 a.m. 'No later,' he ordered. The confidence with which he snapped out the words encouraged me though I hardly needed any encouragement. 'You'll need a big heavy stick,' Robert called out to me as we parted.

Most Saturday mornings were spent scouring the local shops for wooden boxes and fruit trays. Myself, the Scott brothers and Raymond Heald chopped these up to make bundles of sticks which we sold door to door as firewood. We made enough money to pay for the afternoon matinée, with some spare coppers for sweets. The toss-up between going to watch the Lone Ranger and herding my own real life cattle was an easy one to make. 'Mum, I'm going to Robert McCartney's house tomorrow morning, we're going to watch the cattle boats with his dad. I have to be there at seven o'clock.' Mum seemed content. She knew Robert and also knew that he and I 'could have come out of the same yolk', as she put it. I didn't mention about the stick or the fact that we would be 'offloading' the animals. 'You can get up and have breakfast with your dad but if it's raining you can forget it,' she said. It didn't rain on Saturday morning and Robert McCartney and I hurried towards the docks. I hadn't brought a stick but my companion suggested that I shouldn't worry too much as we could steal someone else's. 'There's always something lying around,' he added when he saw my look of anxiety.

I am not sure what I expected when we reached the dock. I had an idea of a harbour lined with ships, people toing and froing along gangplanks, but instead I found myself in a great timber and tin shed, taller than any hayshed and big enough to swallow up half a dozen of the houses from the street I lived in. The place was full of men and only a few kids like ourselves, and all of them sat together on a pile of boxes smoking and watching McCartney and myself. There was an air of viciousness about them like dogs waiting to attack. I was dreading having to walk past them but my school chum strode past like he owned the place. Sheepishly I followed, weaving my way past men sitting in small groups or others who were moving about with urgency. They were like the men who clear the circus ring after every act. Everyone seemed to be shouting or laughing in a loud, bantering way. Some men were giving orders and some were telling their gang boss exactly what they could do with their orders. The language was without restraint, as was the way it was delivered. Boxes were banged about, handcarts collided as their owners cursed and threatened one another. Some of it was obviously good-natured: 'You shouldn't have had that last pint, Charlie, you're still half-cut!' But other exchanges were withering. One carter in a hurry to pass us called out, 'Are you two wee shits fucking frozen or what? Move, for Christsakes, come on.' The violence of the command petrified me but McCartney was having none of it. 'Move yourself, you blind bollocks.' I was stunned. I had never heard such language or seen such brazen bravado in my friend before. At school he was quiet and shy: here he was altogether another creature. The little boy who sat beside me at school was suddenly ten feet tall, growling and snarling back at anyone who gave us offence.

Winding our way through the deafening pandemonium was terrifying but I soon learned that everyone shouted because they had to and as no one seemed to listen, they roared all the more. Whatever insults were slung from one man to another they just filled up the chaotic babble of the place. We were walking to an area that was being fenced off with sections of wooden stockading. It marked out a clearway from a wide gangplank that had been let down from the side of a ship. I looked up to see the top half of our boat but it was obscured by the corrugated iron roof of the shed. All that was visible of the ship's hull was a long wall of iron. The clearway ran from the boat into a section of yard outside the sheds. The yard was subdivided into lots of animal pens of different sizes. Men were loitering about everywhere.

My eyes were drawn to a movement near these pens. Several huge Clydesdales were being moved around or put into harnesses. A few were slowly being backed into their carts, and Robert and I walked over to watch. He explained that his dad was a tallyman and had to check the number of animals and which carter collected them. We found his father without too much trouble. He wore a soft, tweed hat rather than the cloth cap everyone else seemed to be wearing. Pencils jutted out from the hat at each ear. His coat had lost any shape and hung from him like a cloak. Rolls of paper and tails of string busted out of his pockets. The beautifully patterned scarf he wore looked so out of place that I whispered to ask my friend if his dad had a sore throat. 'No,' he informed me, it was so that people would know him if they were looking for him. 'The tallyman is the man with the cravat,' he explained. I looked around me: sure enough, no one else was wearing such a flamboyant scarf. He also had a very wide belt that was adorned with brass carvings. I really admired it and thought how my mother would enjoy polishing the brass until it gleamed. I couldn't resist remarking on the fabulous belt. 'That was my grandad's; he was a carter and them's miniature horse brasses he got specially made. See that big brown horse there – that was my granda's when it was a foal.' The brown horse looked nothing like a horse to me. More like a statue of a horse. It was immense. We both walked over to the great beast. 'You stay here while I go off and get you a stick,' my pal ordered.

I didn't need to be told again for the massive beast held me hypnotized. It was everything a horse shouldn't be. It was bulky and inanimate. The big black collar around its neck must have weighed more than I did. I could not imagine this preposterous animal charging at breakneck speed across the cinema screen. As I stood trying to convince myself of the equine credentials of this giant, it stared back at me in somnambulant oblivion. Its eye was as big as a cricket ball and its coarse eyelashes looked like the bristles on a yard brush. The beast's head was sunk into a huge filthy nosebag. The size of its head stunned me. I thought it was three times the size of any horse I had ever seen. I could only imagine the weight of it and gasp. Both McCartney and myself could have stood inside the nosebag.

The animal's big black eyeball never moved. The whole demeanour of the creature suggested that it had long tired of the world and had philosophically concluded that mankind was a species of confused consequence which spent all its time and energy making as much noise and fuss as was possible for no reason other than to fill up the empty space around itself. The animal munched abstractedly at the contents of its feed bag. I approached, full of nervous awe. It shifted its weight from one huge foot to another; amidst all the competing bustle and noise trapped inside the shed the movement appeared elegant and graceful for a creature of such tonnage.

At first, I was too enraptured by the horse to notice its handler approach and fiddle at the bridle. 'What's its name, Mr?' I eventually asked. 'Hercules,' he said, then, looking at me for only a second or two continued, 'He's the biggest, strongest workhorse in the whole of Belfast, but blind as a bat. He can't see more than a few feet in front of him. I doubt if he can see too much of you.' He paused for a moment then looked directly at me and winked. 'He likes you to talk to him . . . and after a while, when he gets to know you, and like you – he's very choosy, you know – he even talks back to you!'

I was momentarily caught up in a whirlpool of fascination about this gigantic horse and what I was supposed to say to it when Robert suddenly appeared from under its belly and handed me a heavy, gnarled walking stick. 'My da says if you lose that he'll throw us both in the drink!' I was too amazed by my pal's ease in walking right under the mighty Hercules to take in the warning about the walking stick. 'Come on,' he urged. 'They'll be offloading soon.' I followed after my diminutive friend, amazed at his careless courage.

Already men were lined out along the makeshift clearway that led from the gangplank. At my pal's bidding we took up position opposite each other at a gap in the clearway. Robert's instructions were direct: 'Make sure nothing gets past you. Anything that looks like it's going to try to escape, give it a good poke or whack it as hard as you can.' I was so overwhelmed by how he became a different person in this noisy aggressive world that I accepted everything he said. I felt myself becoming tougher and stronger as if I too was part of this strange new world.

At the head of the gangplank I heard an explosion of noise unlike the raucous background sound that constantly rattled around the shed. It was an inarticulate mix of roaring and grunting, and squeaking and swearing. Suddenly the gangplank was alive with dozens of pigs skidding and stumbling over one another. It was as if a giant broom had swept them there. As they struggled down the incline of the gangway, another wave of stinking pink flesh and muscle followed, and then another. The confused movements of the pigs attested to just how frightened and angry they were. The smell they brought with them confirmed how sickening the sea journey must have been. I gagged, and felt sick and nervous myself.

When the animals reached the dockside the men lining the clearway started shouting and striking at them with their sticks. However confused the boat trip had made the pigs, this sudden violence terrified them. They began to squeal and charge at the sides of the clearway to escape. This encouraged the men about me and they kicked and slashed and swore at the frightened pigs. The men's eyes bulged with violence and contempt.

Apoplexic with fear, I watched as the squealing, foul mass of pig flesh hurtled towards me. I wanted to run away but I was trapped in the appalling din of the animals and the fanatical excess of the men around me. Out of this miasma I heard Robert shouting urgently, 'Don't let it out, don't let it out!' I looked in front of me and was confronted by a pig that had all the dimensions of a baby rhinoceros. It tossed its head and waved it from side to side and bellowed out the most terrifying and unearthly sound I had ever heard. The brute was enraged and determined to break out of the cordon of men. I was the weakest point in the wall of violence and abuse that enclosed it. The deranged rhinoceros had chosen to savage me to escape. I stood motionless, hearing the bedlam about me diminish. Suddenly, I felt myself being scooped into the air. Below me, I heard the irate pig howl and snuffle at the same time.

The man who had hoisted me out of harm's way with one arm had simultaneously cudgelled the big pig several times on its snout. I watched it charge off with its mouth and nose bleeding. 'That big bastard would have ate you whole,' he said still flushed from his victory. Then his face softened. He must have felt me tremble as I gasped for breath and choked with sobs. 'Never mind, young fella,' he said. 'You leave the big ones to us big boys. You and your chum there drive them as hard and as fast as you can and we'll keep them in.' Obviously he knew my pal, for he called out, 'Hey young Bob, you and your mate get in there behind them and keep them moving.' McCartney dashed across the clearway, kicking and prodding pigs as he went. 'Come on,' he said, grabbing me by the sleeve and hauling me into the pink mêlée. In the midst of all this grunting and groaning, I had little opportunity to think about what felt like a close call with a hospital visit. Robert was swatting and flushing the pigs around him and encouraged me to do the same. I did it automatically, listening as he cursed and whacked the stubborn beasts. Then suddenly, I was laughing hysterically, cursing and whacking and driving the beasts like I had been born to it. When we had successfully manoeuvred the animals to the pens we ran back to the end of the gangplank and jumped into the thick of it again shouting and slapping pigs as if we were in a marching band. I couldn't get enough of it.

THE LONG WALK

OUR MOVE TO THE EAST OF THE CITY WAS A SUDDEN THING. IT WASN'T
unusual for people to change houses where I grew up. Most people
rented their houses. When there was little work for long periods
and the tenants could not keep up with the rent payments, they
packed up and did a moonlight flit to another house, leaving their
debts behind them. If there was no empty house to shift to, people
loaded up handcarts with their furniture and belongings and stored
them with relatives and friends. In the meantime, they stocked the
house with old pieces of broken furniture which neighbours had
intended throwing out. Orange boxes and tea chests served as
cupboards and there wasn't a matching plate nor un-cracked cup
to be found in the newly furnished house. It was a ploy for the
bailiffs who might have sought to obtain rent debt by confiscating
household goods. Even clothes went to the pawnshop for safe-
keeping. One of the women who called at our house remarked how
half the Duncairn Gardens turned into Jerusalem on the first
Monday of every month. The idea confused and intrigued me. At
first I thought it had something to do with the church; like Easter
and Christmas when special services were held. But I had never
seen anyone dressed up like Jerusalemites or whatever you called

them. I remembered the word Pharisee and thought that that's what you called people from those times in Jerusalem. After the woman had gone, I thought about this odd transformation she had spoken of. Later that evening as she was preparing the dinner, I asked Mother about this, saying that I had never seen anyone dressed up as a Pharisee coming or going from St Barnabas. She laughed, telling me that I could see more than enough of them every Sunday. Then she explained that at the beginning of every month, the streets were full of rent collectors and moneylenders knocking on people's doors trying to collect payments on debts, loans and long-overdue rent. The 'tick-men', as she called them, were like the moneylenders and the 'short change merchants' that Christ chased out of the temple. Though I hadn't gone to church or Sunday school since my mother chased the clergyman from the front door, I still had my quota of biblical stories from school. Also my sister had a bible with lots of illustrations and sure enough, there was one of Jesus upturning the tables, and wrecking the stalls set up in and around the synagogue. He obviously had a temper just like my mother's. I thought he would have made a great Red Indian chief, with his long hair, swarthy skin and raging deep brown eyes. I even gave him a name: 'Raging Bear.' I bet old Saint Barnabas would laugh at that apostasy!

With all this talk of Jerusalem days, Pharisees, tick-men, money-lenders, moonlight flits, bailiffs and even a Red Indian Jesus, my mother's proclamation that we were moving to a new house seemed to betoken dire circumstances. I couldn't believe we were so poor we had to move. I knew my mother sometimes bought cracked eggs because they were cheaper. And for the same reason, bought a bag of beef cuttings and a shin bone to make a big stew which would last a weekend. But I always had my own clothes to wear instead of someone else's hand-me-downs. My sister, who was about sixteen, had gone to work in Gallagher's tobacco factory and I watched her hand over her wage packet every week. No Jerusalem men ever knocked at our door, as far as I knew. When Mother informed us that we were going back to where we came from, I was doubly confused. How could I have come from anywhere else? I was living where I grew up and didn't know anywhere else. When she explained that we were moving to East Belfast where she and Dad grew up, it meant nothing to me. She could have been talking about Timbuktu or Upper Silesia. Some days later I asked her if all the really poor people moved to East Belfast. She knew exactly what I was thinking, and reassured me, telling me how my dad had a good job with 'the telephones' and we could buy a house instead of paying rent: 'Especially to Harold McLean.' She said the name with complete distaste. It was some time later that I learned that the Harold McLean to whom we paid the rent was the same Harold McLean who was my grandfather!

The whole problem of our impending poverty – the only way I could understand this flight to the East – was resolved one evening, as my sister and I, along with my mother and father, stood in the back room of a small butcher shop on the Beersbridge Road in the east of the city. The butcher owned the house we intended buying, though he did not live in it. He was preparing carcasses for the next day. He wore a white coat with a navy and white striped apron over it. In areas the white stripes had all but disappeared under the brownish stain of blood. The room was heavy with the odour of raw meat. I had never seen so much meat before. Three enamel basins were piled high with what I knew as beef cuttings. 'Sausage meat,' said the butcher. 'I'll be here for a few hours before I get this lot finished.' He pointed to several carcasses hanging from a rail by great S-shaped silver hooks. Some were covered in a skin of muslin. The butcher noticed my interest and said, 'See them two big fellows, well, they're cows, the other two are sheep and them three will be pork chops, sausages and bacon before I go home.' Then he turned again to my parents and said something about finishing a few quick jobs before they settled business. I looked around me and saw silver-coloured trays and huge plates waiting to be dressed with all manner of cut meats. Another two large bowls were filled with big chunks of brown liver which I later told my mother looked like dried-out jellyfish.

The butcher seemed to be arm-wrestling with one of the animal corpses. But it wasn't wrestling. Instead he was systematically reducing the animal into different cuts and joints which he would place on a specific tray or plate. Beside him were a saw, a heavy cleaver and several knives of different lengths. He handled each implement like an extension of himself. His saw ate through bone as if it was melting it and the cleaver broke open the breastbones in supreme single blows. Each time he took up a knife, he flashed it back and forth on the sharpening rod almost oblivious to the action he was making. Then he cut sections of beef as if it was a watermelon. At times half his body disappeared as he crawled inside a large carcass. It looked as if the dead animal was devouring him: butcher and beast had become one hideous abstraction. Dad decided to leave him to his work. He said we would go and see the house on our own and call back in an hour. The butcher nodded his approval and we left.

Number 37 looked like all the other houses in the street. But it was very different from the house we were leaving. It was a small redbrick two-up, two-down house. It didn't have the long hallway or parlour of our old house. It didn't have the bay window or the tall fireplaces. The yard was smaller and the scullery was tiny. It did have a small garden which, my father jokingly suggested, 'you could just about fit a coffin into!'

We didn't stay long in the house; there was little to see in its small, empty shell. I remember the faded wallpaper and the nails where pictures had once hung. When we emerged from it the redbrick street seemed smaller than I first thought. I missed the long row of bay windows. I missed the colour. Every house in our old street had been painted. Most of them were different shades of shipyard grey, or British army green or air force blue. They were all rendered in war surplus paint and every year or two every house was painted over in some admixture of these colours.

The street we were coming to live in was called Mayflower and the two parallel streets were Heatherbell and Foxglove. At right angles to them all was Flora Street. Behind it and running the whole length of it were row upon row of allotments sealed off by sections of tar-stained and corroded corrugated iron. Running past the allotments at the furthest end from the fence, there was a river.

Dad was enthusiastic about the allotments and said we might get one. He also pointed out that the streets were all named after wild flowers. He showed us a small knot of pinky-purple weeds which he said were foxglove but most people called them 'lupins'. Heatherbells were a smaller plant, with more flowers that were a different colour of red but he was sure that there would be none growing here. 'Whoever named these streets must have come from the country,' he said.

Mother and Father seemed content to be coming home. Part of me was charged with some small curiosity about this home-coming. If these streets were close to my parents' childhood, then what could they mean to me? Maybe I would get closer to them both. Maybe the tug of memory would play itself out and somehow pull me into their childhood and I could know them as they were. Not just as they are: Mother and Father, the twin pillars that held open the creaking doorway into life. But as we walked back through the densely packed houses, I began to have my doubts. The place seemed too closed in. The serried ranks of tiny houses plus the pattern-work of the red brick pressed in on me like an accordion closing. The discordant wheeze that the instrument made seemed to be mortared into the street.

Dad airily proclaimed that he grew up only fifteen minutes away and that Mother had lived just across the railway line from him. This volunteering about childhood romance relieved me. For a moment, I imagined a young man emerging out of the pall of locomotive smoke as he crossed the tracks to his girlfriend who was waiting anxiously at the other side. Some cliché from the matinées had unearthed itself, with my mother and father playing the lead roles. 'Are there any picture houses?' I asked. 'Lots, son. There's the Castle and the Willowfield and the Ambassador and the Picturedrome, and you can walk to them all,' Dad confirmed. 'Did you go to them when you were young?' I continued. Dad smiled at Mum and explained that he had taken her to them, but when he was a boy he went to a place that he called the Picture Palace. 'It was no place for courtin',' he commented. Then he proceeded to tell me how the cinema divided the front and back stalls by barbed wire! He laughed at my amazed expression. It obviously encouraged him. 'There was half a dozen hard men who kept everyone in check. One of them had a long whip that he cracked around your ears if you were too noisy. The sound was always breaking down, and everybody started jeering and throwing things. Sometimes they had talent shows.' He talked about an Indian strongman who could lift an iron mangle with his teeth. There was also another cinema, where you could see a fiddle player with flowing locks down over his shoulders, who played wild music as he jumped and sprang around the stage. 'Everyone knew him as Morelli the "Mad Fiddler". More people went to see him than the picture. Anyway, most people couldn't read the words on the screen.' He paused for a moment, obviously remembering the scene then he laughed again. 'You know, there were some places that doused you with disinfectant just to make sure that your fleas didn't transport themselves to the "bigwigs" from the fancy houses at the top of the road!' This time both Mother and I laughed and she added, jesting with him, 'So that's why you wear the bay rum and Brylcreem!' He looked at her and smiled. 'Do you remember the night someone smuggled in a box of pigeons and released them during the film?' Both of them laughed, and I was drawn into their laughter. They seemed to be enjoying memories of the courtship and their intimacy made me feel that perhaps our new house might not be so bad. It was much smaller, but that would bring us closer together. My sister was not so optimistic. She was older, had long-established girl friends and a few secret boyfriends that she kept quiet about. She had just started her first job. Now her own adult world had been suddenly closed on her. I could sense her disappointment and anxiety. I had my own, but there was little we could do about it. We were moving and we would have to get used to it.

When we returned it was obvious the butcher had not been idle. Several of the carcasses had been reduced to trays and plates full of meat. A few animals remained hanging in their white muslin shrouds. The butcher stood knotting his tie and adjusting the tension in his braces. 'Away into the front shop,' he commanded. 'I've just switched on the cooler in here.' We waited in the shop as the man followed after us. 'Was everything all right for you?' he asked. In a kind of nervous subservience both my parents agreed that everything was fine. The man was too busy buttoning his coat to listen. It was obvious he wanted to be out of his shop as soon as possible.

Dad approached the counter and withdrew a large manila envelope from his inside breast pocket. Mother stood between my sister and me with a hand resting on each of our shoulders. We knew without her telling us that it was a warning to say nothing and stand still. I watched as Dad started to count the banknotes he had withdrawn from the envelope. 'No need of that,' said the butcher. 'I never mistrust a man until I have reason to.' He took the wad of money, pushed it back into the envelope and slid it into the back pocket of his trousers. The sheaf of banknotes astounded me. I was still under the impression that our move had something to do with being poor but the exchange between my dad and the butcher changed all that. In fact, the butcher now looked nothing like the man I had first encountered. In his grey flannel suit and neatly knotted tie with maroon and green diagonal stripes, he could have been a 'collector' for the Mafia. When he placed a neat trilby hat with a shiny black band gingerly on his head I was half convinced that he had stepped out of one of my gangster movies. I walked out of the shop in a trance and stood as my father and mother engaged in some more conversation with the man. When they had finished, he locked the shop door and shook my father's hand. Then he remembered something. He quickly opened the door, ran into the shop and re-emerged with two large brown paper parcels tied with string. 'There you go,' he said. 'That will seal the deal good and proper. I may have lost a house but I'm sure I have gained a customer!' Mother thanked him, insisting that he should not have been so generous. With final goodbyes, the butcher gangster strolled off in one direction and we took the opposite.

'How much did the house cost?' I asked sheepishly as we waited for the first of our two buses home. 'A lot more than your dad just gave him,' Mother answered, knowing immediately that I thought Dad had paid for the house then and there. 'That was only key money. It will be a long time before we own it.' She paused for a moment before saying forthrightly, 'But it will be ours and we will have only ourselves to thank for it. Harold McLean can have his house for we'll have ours, and there'll not be a stick of what we put into it left in 13 Evolina Street!' Obviously my grandfather had done something that mother was not about to forgive in a hurry. Only occasionally did he call into our house. To me he was a stranger who didn't know me any more than I knew him. 'Leave it now, Minnie,' my father said consolingly. 'We've enough to be worrying about over the next few weeks.' On the number 30 bus back into town I surveyed my new 'homeland'. Green gas lamps lit up streets that were not my own. There was no tree-lined avenue here like the Duncairn Gardens. From the top deck of the bus I watched as we passed by little shops closing for the night. Newspaper vendors were already taking up positions outside the pubs and calling out 'Tele, six't Tele' in high-pitched voices that sounded like a yodel. The sixth edition of the *Belfast Telegraph* seemed to have street sellers everywhere. The bus trundled on. Our new house was no longer a stone's throw from the city centre and I knew we would never go walking into town again. I leaned towards my sister and whispered, 'Do you like it here?' 'No,' she hissed. 'I think I hate it!' Then she turned to look out on the streets below. I saw her face reflected in the window. She was biting her nails and studying the nightscape as we passed through. Two bus rides right across the city was too much for visiting friends.

All our family connections, my many aunts, uncles and cousins, lived somewhere in those streets. We very rarely saw them at our house in Evolina Street. Now it seemed that might change, now that we were moving to 'our own side of town', as my parents put it. I felt no enthusiastic sense of belonging. As the bus moved through the protectorate of East Belfast and I listened as my parents called out familiar landmarks I knew they were trying to encourage us. Brenda sulked defiantly while I pondered the big issues like what kind of games they played over here. The bus reached the city centre and stopped opposite the front of the City Hall. Beside the bus stop was a big fancy shop called Robinson and Cleaver. It was the kind of shop that you only looked in the windows of. 'The likes of us might be stared at if we went in there,' Mother said to my sister, who was gazing distractedly into the fabulous display windows.

My attention was elsewhere. Casually I slipped my hand out of my father's and walked to a spot near the main entrance to the store. A small man with tufts of grey hair jutting from below his cloth cap sat on a small stool. His old jacket was buttoned right up to his neck, which was well wrapped in a heavy woollen scarf. His trousers were baggy and shiny and so voluminous you could hardly see his feet. At first I thought he might be a beggar but shops such as Robinson and Cleaver would not tolerate such a person camped on their doorstep. Instead, the man was a musician – but such a musician as I had never seen before.

The little man's knees were pressed together holding the grip end of a long saw. The saw pointed directly up into the night sky while the musician bent down to lift something up from his feet. He wore fingerless gloves, which I had only ever seen on men who drove cart-horses. Then he took up what Dad explained was his fiddle bow, holding it in one hand while he 'waxed' it with a stub of something in the other. His waxing arm ran lavishly up and down the length of the bow several times. When he stopped he laid the bow across his knee, then reached up to take hold of the top of the saw blade. Slowly he pulled his arm down and away from him, forcing the saw to make an arc. He held it for a moment, long enough to attract the attention of some passers-by. He took up his bow and pulled it slowly, backwards and forwards across the straight top edge of the saw.

It sounded like nothing like I had ever heard. It was music. It had melody in it but no perceptible tune. I could hardly believe my eyes or my ears. Dad encouraged me to move on but I was in no hurry and my pleading look permitted me to stay. Few of the passers-by did stop to watch though many seemed to know him, calling out his name in a greeting or bidding him 'good-night Charlie' as they dropped a copper or two into a box at his feet. The musician always returned the greeting and never missed a thank-you as money fell into his collection.

His left arm tightened and loosened the tension in the saw's arc while his bowing arm moved in long or short strokes against the blade. Sometimes it moved position, altering the pitch. It was obvious that he was making up the melody as he went along. The music had a strange, unsettling intensity. Then it squeaked and skipped and jumped like a cat chasing mice across a polished floor. I loved it all and extracted a few pennies from my father to pay for my pleasure.

As we walked off, the little musician made a long sad note on the saw. Abruptly I turned to look at him. His face was ruby red. He made a grimace, feigning sadness at our departure. Then he smiled widely; some teeth were missing and some were barely stumps. The sound of the saw turned soft and happy. 'Good-night young fella, God bless you wherever you are going,' he croaked. I was spellbound and walked away in a trance. How could that little old man have known about our impending move? I wondered in silence about the musician's magical insight. It was all too curious and strange.

Our second bus journey, this time up the Duncairn Gardens, seemed shorter than the previous one. Mum was busy discussing with Dad who she would share the parcels of meat with. 'There's far too much for us, and it won't keep in the meat safe. The Scotts will be glad of some and maybe Peggy Linton too, and I'll cook some of it for old Bobby. He won't remember the last time he had a bit of beef!'

The Long Walk

I had a lot to think about that night. If we were avoiding poverty by moving east, why was my mother handing out sides of meat as if the holy golden calf was tied up in our back yard? And if we weren't poor why were we moving? I wasn't sure whether I wanted to exchange my friends to be near my relations. I hardly knew them, and it didn't bother me in any way. As for the little wizened man with the musical saw, how did he know everything?

I am not sure how long it was from our visit to the butcher's shop to our eventual move but it seemed like several weeks; perhaps more. Meanwhile, Dad moved bits and pieces of furniture to our new house in the Post Office Telephones van that he brought home every night. All my pals were aware that I was leaving and asked me lots of questions, none of which I could really answer. I do recall having a recurrence of my sleepless nights. Some of the dreams were distorted echoes of that visit to the butcher's. They included images of the muslin-wrapped carcasses, only this time the creatures retained their heads. The cow, the sheep and the pigs were there, a cross between a glove puppet and a carcass. The butcher was there too, in his white coat and striped apron. He kept sticking his head and shoulders into the body cavity of the carcass saying, 'Where's my head? I've lost my head!' The dreams were not frightening: they were more like a macabre mixed-up Punch and Judy show. There was also something about bunches of red flowers and funerals and rows of houses with no front doors. It was all very interesting. But although not in the least scary it betokened some kind of concern, and I wondered if this was the reason for my long walk. But in truth, the long walk simply happened. I hadn't planned it, nor had I spoken to anyone about it. If I had, I would most certainly have been prevented from leaving the house. I place it as the significant first of many long journeys I have made in my life.

*   *   *

It was a Saturday morning, but this particular Saturday was different. I have no idea why. I didn't bother joining up with the rest of the gang, but instead took myself off to Alexandra Park. It must have been around ten o'clock and there were few enough people there. None of the local kids had as yet commandeered the 'Tarzan' swing. So I played on it alone for fifteen or twenty minutes. I wasn't feeling too energetic. In fact my sense of the whole day is that it was enclosed in some energy-sapping mist. I walked through the park aimlessly. I stopped to watch the swans briefly then paddled about in the stream watching the darting spricks without having any desire to catch them. I dried my feet on the grass and with clutches of dock leaves; they were great for pressing on your skin to relieve the sting from nettles. For maybe another twenty minutes I lay on the river bank and watched the people who had come into the park. They came and went and I registered little more than their passing. It was time to move on.

Across the road stretched several acres of playing fields which by now would be buzzing with junior football teams from all over the city, togging out for their matches. I hadn't the slightest interest in football and I had only ever ventured into the Grove, as it was called, on one other occasion with my dad. We stood watching a game not far from the gate and left quickly due to a sudden down-pour of rain. The Grove, I thought, stretched on for what seemed miles. So I went there, not knowing why, and not having enough curiosity to ask myself why.

I walked through the green acres only half aware of the people around me. There were lots of kids, huddled in groups changing into their football gear, balls were being kicked about excitedly and coaches were shouting encouragement and advice. For a moment the clashing colours of team jerseys, seen from a distance, appeared like mad butterflies. But the thought was gone as soon as it appeared.

That was the way it was that day. People passed in and out of my sightline like apparitions. A pack of mongrels excitedly hunting down an exhausted bitch on heat distracted me. Momentarily I felt sorry for the poor animal and thought how I might try and rescue her. In the end I left the dogs to themselves. Old men with their pets on a lead passed by me. Old women in pairs chittering away to themselves held my attention for no longer than their passing conversation lingered in my ears. I walked on and on enveloped in my own thought. It was as if I was invisible.

I came to the end of the playing fields. I knew I should turn back as I had never been this far before. Something nudged me on and I had neither the energy nor the desire to resist. I exited the Grove and walked through street after street after street, always following a straight line as best the street geography would allow me. I had no idea where I was and even less of an idea where I might be going. The streets were different. There were fewer houses in them than in my own. Each had a small garden to the front and back. These streets were quiet as if the people who lived in them didn't know the world existed outside of them. I walked through them like a ghost until I came to a major road. It was heavy with traffic and lorries. It should have been the natural end to my wanderings. I stood on the wide footpath listening to the numbing noise of the moving traffic. I walked alongside the roadway as if caught up in the backdraught of its movement. Across the road was a wall of hoardings, advertising Bovril, Inglis Biscuits and Camp Coffee. Beyond the hoardings were a few small commercial enterprises all very run-down, and beyond them was a wide patch of overgrown waste ground with a railway line running through it. I couldn't see what was beyond the raised ground of the railway embankment but I knew there must be something.

The road I was walking alongside seemed to be a barrier: it was deflecting me from the straight line that I felt myself to be following. I was following something, though I had no idea what that might be or why it was nudging me on. The arrow which had fired itself inside me was arcing its way across the road beyond the hoardings and small workshops. Its trajectory pointed straight across the jungle of wasteland, over and beyond the embankment on which a train was cannonballing along.

I crossed the road hardly aware of the moving traffic then found my way through broken fences and over walls on to the waste ground. It was full of old paint cans, bits and pieces of machinery, rusty bed ends and the remains of prams. I hesitated to examine them. Prams' wheels and axles made the best go-carts (or 'guiders' as we called them). I found some and smashed them off their pram bodies; I would have the fastest and tallest car in the street with these beauties. Before my thinking was waylaid, I set the wheels aside, hid them under an old rusty car door, and kept following my imaginary arrow.

It seemed to take ages to plough my way across the wasteland. I could hear the roar of the road behind me as the railway embankment loomed up. I was too far from any streets for a proper fence to be erected stopping people like me from gaining access to the line. Instead an old rusted barbed-wire fence stretched along the bottom of the embankment. I crawled through it without a cut or a tear and climbed up the hill of earth on my hands and knees, avoiding the swathes of nettle that were taller than me. As I got near the top, I became worried about what would happen if I were caught. I was a trespasser and I would be prosecuted just as the sign said. For a moment, I mixed up prosecuted and electrocuted and stared in terror at the glistening railway lines as I crested the embankment. The shiny steel radiated a warning but its hold over me was momentary for when I looked across the line I became

exhilarated and dashed over, sliding down the opposite side of the
embankment fearless of nettles, barbed wire, prosecutors, electro-
cutors or anything else. There in front of me, not more than twenty
or thirty yards from the railway bank, was the sea, and as far as I
was concerned the waves were clapping and applauding my final
arrival.

I charged across the remaining foreground heading directly for
a small section of sandy beach. It appeared to me that the sun was
shining directly on it and everything else around it was shaded by
the cloud cover. I ripped off my shoes and socks and could feel the
warm sand followed by the cold water. This was where my arrow
had landed and I felt a glow of real happiness to be here. My long
walk had brought me to this elemental meeting place where the
world ended and the ocean began.

I sat on a rock for some time, caught up in my mood of fastid-
ious idleness. There was no noise where I was. The road, the house,
the traffic had all sunk behind the embankment. I was alone and
more miles from my home than I cared to think, and I didn't think
about anything but being here. The city had all but disappeared,
and all I could see as I looked back in the direction I had come
was the horseshoe shape of the hills that surrounded my city.

I don't know how many hours I spent in this magical place. I
walked the tidal line of my little beach delighted with the debris
of driftwood, tin cans, old bottles, single shoes, fish boxes and shells.
A scruffy little dog came charging up the beach barking and doing
insane pirouettes in the air. He too had obviously crossed the line
and was caught up in the joyous invisible bubble that enclosed this
place. He remained my only companion for hours. We entered into
each other's enthusiasms as if we had known each other for years.
At one point in our sojourn at the world's end, a train came roaring
and belting along the track. It seemed colossal as it charged and

clattered past us. I waved animatedly at the people in the carriages. They stared back as if they couldn't see me. I watched as the train got smaller, then in an instant it disappeared round a bend in the track.

It was time to go. The world had come crashing past me and disappeared. I too had to leave my enchanted beach. The scruffy dog barked as I crested the embankment. Then he too scampered off and was gone. I retraced my steps as best I could remember them. Inevitably, I became lost. Whatever had nudged me here, it wasn't pushing me back. I had to depend on memory, but there were too many streets. I ended up in an area of gorgeous leafy avenues and big majestic houses. Birds flew about everywhere. I had never seen so many birds so close up – only pigeons ever landed in our street. We called them street pickers and sometimes tried to 'wing' them with our catapults. But here, there were robins, blackbirds, thrushes and God knows what else. If I was lost, I didn't mind. Until I became hungry.

I dared to enter the driveway of one of these palatial homes and knocked on the door. A well-dressed woman with short hair opened the door and looked at me with a puzzled smile. 'Yes, son?' she asked. 'Please, missus, could you giv'us a drink of water and a piece?' The woman smiled wider. 'You want a sandwich, you mean,' she said, correcting my vocabulary. I nodded, afraid to open my ignorant mouth again. 'You just wait there a minute,' the lady said as she turned and walked up the hall. I could see along the broad hall and up the stairs. At the landing was a lavish stained-glass window with a crest of arms above a name and words in some foreign language surrounding it. It was a bit overpowering and I was about to leave, when she returned. She handed me a long glass of water and a sandwich cut in a triangle! I drank greedily not because I was thirsty but because I wanted to go quickly. She insisted

I eat the sandwich and as I munched she asked, 'Wherever are you from, young man?' I noticed her eyes were darting round to see if I was alone. 'Duncairn Gardens, missus,' I answered. 'Holy mother of God! What are you doing away up here on your own?' she asked, genuinely anxious. I didn't know what to say and blurted out about returning someone's dog that I had found and could she tell me the way to the Grove. 'Oh dear, I wish I could take you there . . . but it's easy if you're a smart lad, which I'm sure you are.' She seemed even more concerned but gave me directions before running up the hall and returning with an apple, some custard creams and a big Paris bun. 'Now you be careful,' she smiled, delighted with my surprised face. I found my way back to the Grove playing fields without any bother. The footballers had all gone though there were small groups of kids everywhere, still kicking a ball. Men were still walking dogs and old women were still bustling their way home from somewhere. I passed through the Grove and across to Alexandra Park. It too was much the same as it had been in the morning. I even had a momentary feeling that I really hadn't been away anywhere . . . except for the big fat Paris bun in my hand and the two tiny silver and blue and cream and yellow shells in my pocket. They had the shape of tiny fantastic magical trumpets. So I had been somewhere!

We moved by instalments over several weeks. I never really noticed the house slowly becoming emptied of all its familiar bric-à-brac, but when everything was finally packed and gone to our new home in the east, I too was glad to be gone. The house in Evolina Street grew more and more like a waiting room. It was cold and unfamiliar. I spent most of my time in my friends' houses, uncomfortable with the sterility of my own.

Eventually it was time to leave. Mother and Father had said their goodbyes over the previous weeks. On our last day, my mother suggested that Brenda and I should go and say goodbye to our friends. My sister skipped off, happy to be gone from the vacant house but less happy about the move. I was unable to see my friends: I just wanted to sneak away without anyone knowing I was gone. I felt as if I had done something wrong. Moving had somehow become an act of betrayal and I could not face my friends. Mum suggested that I write a letter to them but when I asked her sheepishly if they could come and visit she explained that that might not be a good idea. I was saddened by this. Mother's excuse that it was too far or too many bus journeys away neither convinced nor consoled me. There was something in the way she said it that made me think she was glad to be leaving and that there were some things she did not care to remember – and maybe some people that she did not want to see again. I knew there was little point in asking her. Mother was not good at sharing her feelings. She never spoke about them and it was impossible to discern any emotion in her face, ever. I think she later tried to explain our moving as a new phase in our lives though she never elaborated much on what that meant. She talked to me about a new school just at the bottom of our new street. Brenda would get a new job; maybe working in a shop instead of a factory. But they were vague notions that revealed little. How she understood this new phase, or indeed what it meant to her, she never explained.

The network of streets I was going to live in were not constructed on a lord's estate but were developed on pasture and farmland that had once been the countryside nearest to the old town of Belfast. In a way it was like changing time zones and eras. I was leaving behind a world shaped by relative poverty, sporadic employment fed by the shrinking linen and textile industries with their weaving and spinning mills. Away from the tobacco factory and small businesses such as bakeries, hardware and furniture merchants, carters and haulage merchants, upholsterers and bacon curers. I was moving to the east, to the industrial heartland of not only Belfast but the whole of Ireland.

THE MAN WITH THE
WALRUS MOUSTACHE

EAST BELFAST WAS AN INSULAR BUT BRILLIANT EXAMPLE OF THE GIGANTIC industrial development that roller-coasted up until the First and Second World Wars. Companies such as Harland and Wolff, the Sirocco Works, the Ropeworks, Short and Harland aircraft factory not only employed thousands, but were the largest of their kind in the world. The men behind these record-breaking enterprises were inspired by such men as Samuel Smiles who penned the Victorian classic *Self Help*. One of the author's own sons founded the Belfast Ropeworks Company and Edward Harland who developed the greatest shipyard in the world, was one of the author's model industrial leaders. The creative instinct, combined with an adventurous sense of enterprise, industriousness and commercial acumen, inspired those men even though it was shaped by a moralistic Victorian ethic that declared that it depended on your own exertions whether you succeeded or not, and this in turn had filtered itself into the bricks and mortar of East Belfast.

Ireland has little in the way of natural resources on which to build such industrial giants. But it has something infinitely richer.

It has raw energy, bloody-mindedness, brawn and brain. For, in truth, this was the colossus that shored up and drove the engine that made the name of Belfast synonymous with the building of the biggest ships in the world: constructing, fitting out and manufacturing the Royal Naval Fleet; producing the finest engineering hardware that was installed right across the globe; having the world's largest ropeworks whose products were known 'from pole to pole', whose raw material of hemp was sourced from Russia and Manila and sisal fibre and coir from the Philippines, India, New Zealand, Africa, China and South America. Such an industrial landscape produced a workforce who needed no lessons in geography. They knew the map of the world from the labour of their hands.

Belfast-built ships were berthed in every harbour across the globe, moored in place by Belfast rope, while the Sirocco Works was producing turbines, industrial pumps and all manner of heavy-engineering products that were exported to every developing country. Belfast-built aircraft and engines were already reducing the size of the earth. And all of it spiralling out of the 'sleeping giant' of East Belfast, as its inhabitants affectionately called it.

Such a celebrated industrial legacy could not fail to penetrate the thinking of the people who lived in its shadow. A fierce pride and sense of belonging was hammered, annealed and even branded into the skins of the populace. Generation after generation had grown up in these backstreets and worked all their lives in one of these industries. If they were cannon fodder to industrialization they hardly recognized it. These industries provided an assurance and certainty that was almost biblical. East Belfast was like a collection of inbred neighbourhood protectorates which, like the tribes of Israel, were tied together by a shared belief, aspiration, and a kind of inward-looking exclusiveness that saw itself as set apart.

These people created giants, and the giants nourished them, for they were a special people.

All this I learned slowly and sometimes by chance. My introduction to this new world was marked by the wailing siren that blasted out from the shipyard and the ropeworks. At five minutes to eight every weekday morning these hellish klaxons resounded through the street. It was a call and a warning. A call to the altar of the workplace and a warning of loss of pay or, worse, oblivion and the dole queue. Twenty minutes before this dread command, the streets were awash with men and women shuffling bleary eyed to their work. I hated the noise. It reminded me of some hideous monster.

It was another chance discovery that made my new home less strange and less scary. While helping to unpack boxes of goods brought from our old house, I found an old heavily bound book. It was full of faded newspaper cuttings with pictures of boats and yellowing photos of groups of workmen all staring rigidly at the camera. There was lots of writing too. All the workmen looked the same with their large cloth caps and scarves neatly folded beneath their chins. I recognized none of them and wondered why we had this book. For a moment, I fancied it was a forgotten family album I had never seen before. When I asked, Mother quietly informed me it had been my grandfather's scrapbook. 'Which grandfather?' I queried. Maternal and paternal grandfathers were two very different creatures in our house. They loomed out of the dark like ghostly godfathers. 'Your daddy's, of course.' 'But he's dead!' I exclaimed. 'Yes, and before you ask me anything else, you'd better talk to your father,' Mother concluded.

Over several nights, I learned much from that scrapbook. Into it, my grandmother, my dad and his brother, Uncle Arnold had written and pasted pictures and newspaper cuttings after my grandfather had died. 'Old friends of his just kept sending bits and pieces and we just kept sticking them in,' Dad explained. 'Your grandfather was a hard hat in the shipyard. That's him there. You see that small man with the bowler hat?'

I looked at the tiny black and white photos whose gloss had long since cracked like all the photos in the book and had begun to yellow. The figure who was my grandfather stood at the end of a group of men. He had positioned himself at an angle to the group and to the camera. The bowler hat sat square and solidly on his small round head. The photo was only about two inches square and because it was shot at a distance to accommodate the group it was difficult to discern the facial features of each individual. I thought my grandad looked a bit like a walrus with the great bushy moustache that curled down from his nostrils to his chin. He wore a dark suit with a waistcoat that buttoned high on his chest. His shirt collar was rounded and stiffly starched so that the folds of flesh on his neck rested on it. His face gave little away. It was a mixture of seriousness, impatience, pride and embarrassment. 'You can still see the shine on those boots of his after all these years,' Dad said jokingly, pointing to Grandad's stout boots. 'Spit polished them every night,' he continued, then became silent for a second before volunteering, 'Your grandfather was a kind of foreman or boss in the yard. That's why he is the only man wearing a bowler hat. That's one of the gangs that worked for him.' Then Dad's voice became conspiratorial. 'The workers never liked their bosses and some of them deserved it. There were some bosses who treated their men worse than animals. That's why they wore hard hats, just in case someone tried to drop a heavy hammer or something on their heads from the gantries!'

Dad explained about gantries and pointed out the different professions of men in other pictures, but it was lost on me.

Somehow I had got gallows and gantries mixed up in my mind. My eyes were fixed on my grandfather whom I never knew and the 'murderous' crew in the photo. For a brief second I conjectured how my grandfather had died. Was he slain by a careless hammer deliberately aimed? 'Was Grandad a bad boss?' I asked, too afraid to voice my thoughts. Dad looked at me and thought for a moment. 'He was a stern man, I suppose. He expected everyone to earn their wages. "Good honest sweat was worth its weight in gold, but worth more in respect," he used to say. He played football for the local team and was a very good player, and that earned him respect in return.'

With my apprehensions greatly eased, this glut of new information and images about my ghost of a grandfather excited me. 'Did he build many ships?' I asked. 'Lots,' smiled Dad. Then turning a few pages, he read from a list of ships' names, followed by tonnage and a year date. 'And look here. Do you see this one?' I looked at the name and line after line of neat handwriting and figures. Dad read out the words 'Royal mail steamer *Titanic*', and pointed to a picture of the ship. Below the image someone had written a collection of facts and figures about the length and width of the vessel. There were also figures relating to the size of the engine, boilers, and even the propellers. I didn't understand much of it but remember words like 'triple expansion reciprocating engines' and 'displacement' because I had never heard them before; more importantly, my father was unable to explain them to me, but I remember the sentence at the end of the catalogue of facts. It read: 'Foundered off the coast of Newfoundland half an hour before midnight on 14th April 1912. Loss of souls 1522. Now resting two miles down on the Atlantic Ocean floor.' Dad explained that people who drowned at sea were called 'souls' and, like the other words, he couldn't explain the reason for that either.

He turned the pages again to reveal another picture that showed the vessel in construction. 'Look how tiny those men are beside the ship. They're like spiders,' he said, fascinated himself. I looked at the image then asked him to turn back to the photo of my grandfather. Dad turned the pages again distractedly, explaining as he did how his father kept meticulous notes about all the boats he worked on. 'You see that gold chain on his waistcoat?' Father said. 'Well, it's a pocket watch and your grandad timed everything. I remember him saying to me before I went into the Air Force that understanding the importance of time was essential for order and discipline and those were things that would make me successful at anything I chose to do.' He paused for a moment before continuing: '"Everything has its own time. So there's no need to rush anything." He said that too. I think he was trying to put me off joining up.' He turned back to the book. 'I haven't seen this for years,' he mused as he looked at the pages, pointing to pictures or quietly reading some of the yellow newspaper cuttings. 'Lots of this stuff was sent from America by an old uncle of mine. Some of it was from friends of your grandad's who went to live in America. They had all worked in the yard together. Even after he died, his friends kept sending him stuff about the *Titanic* and your grandmother and your Uncle Arnold stuck them in.'

Dad paged through the book slowly, letting me look on. 'What does that say?' I asked, pointing to a newspaper cutting of the giant ship and workmen like ants scuttling about it. The article described the construction of the ship as a monstrous iron enclosure with enough scaffolding for the naves of half a dozen cathedrals to be laid end to end. Dad explained that a cathedral was ten times bigger than any church. I got lost trying to calculate how ten churches multiplied by six cathedrals could equal one ship. But when he read how at last '. . . the skeleton within the scaffolding began to take shape, at the sight of which men held their breaths', I stopped trying to imagine the size of the vessel and looked again at the picture of the ant-like workmen crawling through the colossal girders. Beside me my father was reading how 'It was the shape of a ship, a ship so monstrous and unthinkable that it dwarfed even the mountains by the water.' This talk of sunken ships, lost souls and skeletons had me intrigued. My mind was beginning to accelerate into the world of pirates and the world of *Gulliver's Travels*. 'Listen to this,' Dad said as he read from a cutting from the *Belfast News-Letter* published the day after the launch:

'It was a wonderful and awe inspiring sight and a thrill passed through the crowd as their hopes and expectations were realized. The ship glided down to the river with a grace and dignity which for a moment gave one the impression that she was conscious of her own strength and beauty and there was a roar of cheers as the timbers by which she had been supported yielded to the pressure put upon them. She took to the water as though she were eager for the baptism and in the short space of 62 seconds she was entirely free of the ways.' The newspaper report goes on to describe how the huge crowd showed their appreciation as 'the men on board took off their caps and cheered lustily after the launch had been consummated and thousands of people in the yard and on the banks of the river promptly followed their example. For two or three minutes there were scenes of great enthusiasm. The tugs which were waiting close at hand to convey the vessel into the deep water wharf where she will receive her engines sent up shrill sounds from her sirens, the ladies waved their handkerchiefs excitedly and the men shouted themselves hoarse. But gradually the noise of the crowd after the vessel had been pulled up melted away and the yard was left in the possession of the workmen who for months had been devoting their energies to the building of the mighty leviathan.'

'Your grandfather was there that day,' he said. 'He was only a young lad at the time, he said you could hear the ropes and timbers snapping like cannon fire. Then after most of the crowds had left he stayed behind with some other men. They all stood silently watching the big liner. Some of them whispered and some of them even cried a bit. Your grandfather said it was like being in church at prayer time only all the prayers and preaching in the world could not measure up to that moment.' Dad looked directly at me with a soft smile. 'That was the day your grandfather decided that he was going to be a shipbuilder. But he kept this book more like he was a captain filling in his log-book.'

Dad left me with the book. 'Put it away safe,' he commanded. I leafed through the pages looking for more pictures of my dead grandfather. I thought I saw him in a few of the photos but they were so small and the faces of the men were so tiny that I could never be sure. There were lots of newspaper cuttings and handwritten notes and some postcards and illustrations of the great ship. I remember some of them, particularly one of a young woman dressed in a flowing white garment with a wreath of flowers in her hair. She was standing in the foreground with the back of her wrist on her forehead, her other hand raised high against a Corinthian pillar. It was the classic pose of forlorn distress that was the stock in trade of leading ladies in the silent movies. In the background is a night-time scene of the sinking ship, its funnels plunged into the icy seas. A small lifeboat sits off from the disaster. Looming beyond the ship is the great, almost ghostly bulk of the iceberg. The scene is one of utter gloom and hopelessness but above the distressed ship a great radiant cross is glowing. The stylized mingling of religion with the theatricality moved me. I thought of the shipyard workers who I assumed were more used to swearing and shouting, standing with silent tears in their eyes as the ship first took to the water.

137

There was also a copy of an etching in black and white depicting Neptune sitting on the sea bed with his trident across his crooked arm. His hand was holding the sunken ship as though it were a toy. His other hand stroked his long flowing beard ponderously. He studied the toy *Titanic* quizzically, wondering what to make of it. High above him, the ocean is empty. A lone albatross skims low over the surface as if it is searching for something. There were lots more pictures and artists' impressions of the ship but they were sterile images of a lost grandeur and didn't raise my curiosity the way the emotionally charged postcards did. Inevitably the scrapbook disappeared, to resurface several times over the years, usually during one of my mother's periodic 'redd-outs'. Finally, like the ship that was its principal subject, it too disappeared.

During these *Marie Celeste*-like appearances I would read through it not so much for the contents but for the picture it gave me of my grandfather. Under the heading of 'Icebergs' there were hand-written notes alongside sections of newspaper reports. In his own hand he records that the icebergs were greater in number and further south than ever previously recorded. In another note he cryptically writes 'The White Foe' then beside it, 'one of the most wonderful sepulchres in all history.' I still recall reading reports describing icebergs as the most terrifying yet alluring phenomenon. Obviously sinking in the oceanic abyss surrounded by these towering frozen sentinels captivated him.

Perhaps my grandfather was a romantic, caught up in the fascination of the Victorian era with tales of crushed ships and frightening loss of life in the outlandish landscape of the frozen north. This was after all the generation that was reading *Frankenstein*, Conrad's *Heart of Darkness*, Coleridge's *Ancient Mariner*, Jules Verne's many stories set among ice and the ocean depths and Jane Eyre's reference to 'these death white regions'. It was the golden age of polar explorations, with reports of Arctic expeditions countered by Antarctic expeditions. Stéfansson, Scott and Shackleton were heroes who endured distress and defeat and were worshipped for it. My grandfather would have been a young man at this time thrilled by the sense of amazement and fear and the stories that surrounded these adventurers. Maybe to him they were more than exciting stories. After all, he had stood in the bowels of the great leviathan as it was being constructed. Maybe he had carried some of the one million rivets that held its skin together. In a small way, he too had been consumed by and was part of an heroic enterprise, unique in all the world. After all these years, even with his 'log-book' long gone, I am sure that he wasn't simply collecting material or creating his own sepulchre to the *Titanic*. I think he was, like the lone albatross in the postcard, looking for something. What kind of fate pulled icebergs and liner into that awful collision? And left, as Thomas Hardy described it, the sea-worm crawling through the wreck, 'grotesque, slimed, dumb indifferent'.

In other pages my grandfather had cut out whole hymns from a church hymnal. Here and there, pertinent words were underlined.

> Sin and guilt and death and Satan
> All against my soul combined
> Hold me up in mighty waters
> Keep my eyes on things above
> Righteousness, divine atonement
> Peace and everlasting love.

And again:

And when my talk on earth is done
When by thy grace the victory's won
Even death's cold wave I will not flee
Since God through Jordan leadeth me.

Then the poignant refrain:

Nearer, my God, to thee, nearer to thee . . .

I am sure my grandfather was not a religious man. My father confirmed that he never appeared to be to him, but that he never ridiculed those who were. So I can only conclude that the inclusion of these hymns suggests that the stern, time-watching foreman was as susceptible to collective sentiment as anyone else. But for a man who wasn't overtly religious, several pages contained sermons on the 'meaning of the *Titanic*'. Some were puritanical rants about the luxurious liner and its millionaire passengers, suggesting that tragedy was an act of God, a kind of recrimination for excess and materialism. In one such sermon, the preacher refers to jewels as the plaything of creatures of the deep. Others are more temperate and compassionate, seeing in the event great human sacrifice and heroism.

More curiously, the scrapbook contained many newspaper and magazine cuttings about the otherworldly aspects of the ship and its passengers. There are stories of passengers having dreams or premonitions before departure, which caused them to choose not to travel on the ill-fated ship. There are fortune tellers' warnings and records of people who had visions of disaster. My dad told me that many workers in the yard held superstitions about a ship's maiden voyage. He explained that my grandmother was a believer in spiritualism and had got my grandfather thinking about it. When

I pushed him on the matter, asking if my grandfather believed in any of it, he shrugged his shoulders and answered, 'I don't rightly know. He was the kind of man who didn't like mysteries. He liked answers. He was a craftsman, so everything had to fit neatly in place.'

From the many cuttings, most of them the handiwork of my grandmother, it was obvious the ship was freighted and overloaded with weird stories, superstition and the kind of psychic energy that would intrigue a young man with a curious and intelligent mind that demanded answers. I knew my grandfather hadn't much in the way of formal education but was, in my father's words, 'a voracious reader, who could add and subtract faster than a moneylender's clerk and could tell the weight or length of something just by looking at it. He had a craftsman's hands and an architect's brain.' But for all this, the scrapbook suggests a man compelled by the super- natural aura that surrounds the story of the *Titanic*. Maybe he was at a susceptible age and he sought to make connections between the spiritual deep and the depths of the ocean.

There were unbelievable stories of a cursed mummy coffin on board and even the intriguing story of a famous journalist who had been lost on board the ship yet had written about his last hours weeks before he sailed off in the *Titanic*. It is hard for me to understand what all this meant to the man who had meticu- lously collected and pasted these things into his 'log'. But if he was, as my father revealed, a curious man who disliked mysteries, then I am content to think that maybe a part of him wanted to believe in a reality beyond human consciousness and even the logic of science; a reality that would provide all the answers.

There were many more cuttings from newspaper reports, mostly of the tribunals of inquiry into the disaster. Occasionally a hand- written note would confirm that a particular item had been sent from America. One story stays with me still. A lifeboat captain points a gun at a terrified young boy who attempts to climb into a life raft full of women and children. 'You're a man,' he insists, and the boy retreats to the ship and obviously to his death. Manhood and self-sacrifice at the end of a gun puzzled my grandfather and almost one hundred years later it puzzles me. I wonder what that lifeboat captain remembers of his boatful of women and children. How emasculating was it for him as a survivor: an adult man condemning a male child to death, to save others and to save himself? The questions are interminable. They connect me with my walrus-faced grandfather in ways that I hardly understand. He seemed captivated by accounts of the final hours of the ship. Some cuttings described the starlit silence of the evening and the intense quiet. Some describe the cries for help from people struggling in the icy ocean or how the distress rockets lit up the faces of the passengers crowding the deck. These rockets not only illuminated the night but also confirmed their dreadful fate. I remember clearly, because I came across it many years later at university, an intimidating line by Emily Dickinson: 'First the chill, then the stupor, then letting go.'

Remembering these few photos of him and of the crews of men he 'captained', his necessary aloofness, his time-watching, his heroism on the football pitch and his 'log-book' which I suppose he must have kept for years, I try to get an accurate picture of the man but know that it can never be accurate. After all, the log-book was pasted and patched together long after his death and the event which it recorded. The 'otherworldly' references and newspaper cuttings may tell me more about my grandmother. So I am left to think that maybe he was only an apostle to the Victorian gospel of work. Maybe his conversion at the launch of the *Titanic* and its ultimate loss set the seal on his life. Maybe he wanted to refashion the world and to work off in every rivet and plate that he oversaw a guilt that was not his own. Maybe he believed that labour was equal to moral righteousness. And I remember how in those images of the yard, the men sit or stand, chest out, flushed more with pride than arrogance. They are knights – dirt, sweat and swearwords were their armour. They had their own code of chivalry. I like to think my grandfather tried to understand it and uphold it. At least, that's how I choose to remember him from those pasted pages and those 'yellowing, dicky-bird-watching pictures of the dead.'*

* Dylan Thomus, *Under Milk Wood*.

GHOSTS IN THE GLORY HOLE

THE TINY TRIANGULAR SPACE ENCLOSED BENEATH THE STAIRS WAS CALLED the 'glory hole'. Everyone in the street called the under-stair space the 'glory hole' and in every glory hole of every household you could unearth a family history from an assortment of old biscuit tins containing important documents like birth and death certificates, receipts, rent books, even old ration books. Other tins, like old tea caddies and tobacco tins, had their uses. Some were full of rusted nails and screws. Dad reserved his tobacco tins for his fishing flies. There were tins of assorted buttons and tins with handwritten herbal remedies, and recipes for making poultices to draw out the poison of boils and bee stings.

If my mother displayed little interest in organized religion, I am sure she maintained an unspoken reverence for the dubious orthodoxy of charms and cures that, she informed us when we were children, were contained in a certain witch's box in the glory hole. She had apparently been given this box of 'cures and curses' as she called it by an old woman whom she used to look after when she was a young girl. This old woman was very fond of my mother and, as she had no children of her own, she lavished attention on her. My mother returned this affection and would run messages for her and care for her when she was ill. The other children thought the old lady a witch and avoided her and her house. But for some reason my mother had taken to her and one day, shortly before she died, she handed my mother this battered tin box with the advice that it would protect 'her and hers from the quackery of doctors!'

Mother had a rudimentary knowledge of the medicinal qualities of some plants, as I can testify. As a child I suffered for years from boils and sties in my eyes. But the boils were defenceless against my mother's poultices. They were a real heady concoction of bread soaked in buttermilk and vinegar mixed with an assortment of leaves and flower heads and a thick dollop of honey from the bee comb. It never failed to work and I can still remember the stain of yellow pus on the bandage as she removed it from the infection after one of my sleepless nights. There was another tincture she used to dab on my eyes at the first sign of an infection. If I was distressed or in pain she might apply some balm or mix me a drink of hot milk infused with other ingredients and then tell me of a magic incantation I was to recite over and over to myself until I fell asleep. Such was the power of the witch's box that the spell never failed. The wound or the pain might be still there in the morning, but it was much reduced and I had slept peacefully in thrall to the magic words.

There was another, more powerful aspect of the witch's box. It contained curses! These were the opposite of healing spells and they were terrifyingly powerful. They could cause very bad things to happen to evil people; they could even make a sickness pass from a good person to a bad one. My mother comforted me when my growing pains were intense by telling me that pain could not live long in 'good people,' so my pain would go away. It was 'lost' pain that was looking for some 'bad' person and it had temporarily come to rest in me while it got its bearings. The real power of this witch's box was its implicit threat. If we had been misbehaving or disobedient my mother had only to threaten to bring out the box and she would soon cure the 'devilment' in us. It was enough: within minutes we had become cherubs and angels and all was in harmony in the household.

Maybe it was the presence of the witch's box that made the glory hole special. Everything one wanted to keep safely was put in the glory hole. Often I would fetch something for my mother or stash something away in it for myself. As soon as I entered I was always aware of the witch's tin box and as I hunted through raincoats, fishing rods, boxes of fly tackle and box upon box of long-forgotten bric-à-brac, mostly placed there by me or my dad, I was careful to avoid that tin box.

One evening, I inadvertently knocked the magic box off its shelf and I heard the tin clatter to the ground behind me. I stood for a few seconds in petrified silence. Part of me felt that if I survived the next ten seconds then all the curses in the box would come to visit me over the next few weeks. At the very least, my growing pains would overwhelm me and I would be left a cripple wearing callipers for the rest of my life or – worse still – I might wake up dead! The utter contradiction of the thought was lost on me. But I was sure some fantastical consequences were about to befall me.

I turned slowly, half amazed that I could still move, and looked to the floor. Before me lay the malevolent and magical contents of the box. The secrets of the witch herself, the smell of stale lavender hit my nostrils. Spread out before me was the oddest collection of witch's artefacts. An assortment of old photos and ink-block images of people who meant nothing to me. From the period style of their clothes, they must have been the long-dead relations of the witch woman. There were mass cards and biblical tracts; a collection of buttons all made from bone. There were cuttings of death notices taken from an old newspaper, now faded and barely readable. There were handwritten notes about the medicinal qualities of plants along with pressed flowers and leaves. Also a few small booklets entitled *Nature's Herbal* and the *Pharmacopoeia of the Forest*. The word pharmacopoeia scared me a little. Something told me it must be an old witch's word for 'curses'. Buried beneath all this was a neatly folded sheet of tissue. I opened it up to reveal a beautiful unfinished tapestry embroidered with silken images of birds which looked nothing like the street pickers or starlings that I saw every day and had even tried to trap.

For a moment these puzzled me: there was nothing very witchy about them . . . or was there? Anyway, I didn't want to think about it. If the witch herself didn't punish me from beyond the grave, I was sure to get a roasting from my mother. As I picked up the items, glancing briefly at them, the power of the box must have diminished. My fingers didn't burn and as I slid the box back on its shelf I was less afraid.

For a few weeks I didn't mention the incident and as nothing drastic happened to me that old tin box lost its hold over me. It contained no witch's power. It was simply full of an old woman's trinkets and fanciful memories of friends and dead relations. Such was my confidence that I asked my mother about the woman she had briefly cared for. Particularly why people thought of her as a witch. 'People say things they know nothing about.' As she said it, I felt that 'I knew it' feeling but said nothing. I was smug at the thought that Mother could never scare me with her threats of 'the witch's box'. 'But,' she continued, 'Agnes Richie held seances in her house and all sorts of people went to them. Old Mrs Richie could talk to the dead. You only had to bring her something that belonged to a dead person, like a photo or a tie or a hankie. She would sit with it for a while with her eyes closed then she'd see the dead person and talk to them.' Suddenly I wasn't so sure about the harmless, powerless box and the photos and death notices. 'You'd be surprised at the people who went to Annie's house, especially the men. It was the cats that made people call her a witch. She had about half a dozen of them. They used to sit on the back of the settee or on the sideboard and in her lap and stare at you. The cats' eyes were watching and staring at everybody who came in. Annie talked to them like people. They all had real people's names like Charlotte or Rebecca. One was called Mr Something-or-other and there was even one called the Reverend Doctor McLeish. Every one of them answered to its name and obeyed her every command.'

All this talk was making me very edgy and I asked nervously, 'Do you believe in ghosts, Mum?' 'No!' she answered, then, getting up, she continued: '. . . and I wouldn't have time to talk to them if I did'. 'Me neither,' I answered taking refuge in her dismissal. I wasn't so sure I believed what she said. Memories of the hanged sailor Da Silva came washing over me.

The old tin box had regained its power, if just a little diminished. When I went into the glory hole again I saw it sitting there looking at me like one of Annie Richie's cats. Whatever the truth about Annie Richie and her cats, Mother was the keeper of the box and the glory hole was its secret kingdom as much as I thought it was mine. For many years, anything my mother chose to do with the contents of this space was never questioned. She had the authority of the box and all the ghosts that resided inside it.

My mother never lost her impatience with all the junk and clutter that my father and I stored away in the small cupboard under the stairs. Things I was sure had been safely stashed away I later found had been long since cleared out. It was as if my mother had been overtaken by some uncontrollable need to purge the household. Often my silent anger and resentment was coldly dismissed with a remark like 'There's enough rubbish in this house' or 'There'll soon be no room for us all to breathe with all this rubbish everywhere!' 'Redding out' was like a fever to my mother. She had little time for sentiment or memory, and things had no significance for her: if they had no practical value, they were simply clutter and only fit for throwing out. Sometimes she went to extremes. A pungent smell of lavender and turpentine hung around the house for days when Mother was in her spring-clean madness. She was the only woman I knew who would spend hours on her knees hand-polishing the linoleum in the hall, stairs and landing. Our house had a permanent smell of cleaning fluids, disinfectant and carbolic. She replenished her cleaning cloths with ripped-up remnants of old shirts and vests. Cleaning cloths were the only clutter she permitted.

When spring arrived she flung open all the doors and windows to let in fresh air, but curiously she wasn't fond of fresh flowers. If someone gave her some as a gift or by way of a thank-you for a favour she would tolerate their presence only for a day or two. Yet she placed small posies of plastic or dried flowers comfortingly around the living room and parlour. Real flowers died: that was the problem. 'Dead flowers smelt,' she said, and for her, having them about the house was a way of inviting death into the home. 'There'll be plenty enough flowers on your coffin,' she would say if anyone ever suggested bringing wild flowers home from a day in the country. As a child I thought her words seemed hard, but there were times when she would redeem herself.

On a Saturday or Sunday morning in early spring, the whole family caught a bus out to 'the end of the line'. From this terminus we would walk for a mile or so along a desperately quiet country road until we came to a small hillside enclosed by long lines of blackberry bushes with the first buds of their creamy white flowers. The hillside was awash in bluebells. We climbed the gentle incline through this sea of lavender blue. Mother always seemed to be quietly smiling to herself.

There we would stay for hours, feasting on cheese and tomato sandwiches. Dad and my sister and I went walking through the lanes counting livestock and chasing baby rabbits. But Mother sat content on her blue lined hill oblivious to our curiosity or excitement.

At other times when we went walking along the small laneways that surrounded our holiday home near Groomsport she would remark how pretty the wild flowers were. 'Much nicer than wilting in a jar.' I didn't clearly understand it then but there was a hint of longing, perhaps even an edge of despair, to these moments of quiet rapture.

Being in the countryside seemed to slow my mother down; to drain all the frenetic energy out of her. But it was a temporary thing. Mother was no advocate of country living. If she had been offered it I am sure she would have refused. She was an urban creature who fed off hardship. She could only cope with the rough edge of life and the little victories that came her way because of it. She was a battler, a sort of street urchin who was helpless unless she was in the thick of something or making something better for someone else. Mother needed to be needed and a pastoral idyll would have suffocated her.

Inevitably, whatever store my mother may have set by a belief in rural superstition and magic charms or plants, it withered away and was forgotten. The healing qualities of plant poultices, the weird liniments made from rhubarb and other leaves boiled and strained through an old pair of nylon stockings disappeared from our house. The inhaling of noxious fumes from a basin of boiled plants to cure catarrh seemed to evaporate out of our lives and a new range of patented cures took their place. The old witch's box may have disappeared, but its place on the shelf was filled with California Syrup of Figs, Angier's emulsion, St Elmo's Fire and Milk of Magnesia which we pronounced, 'Magneeshy'. Then there was the cod liver oil, the viscous concentrate of baskets full of Seville oranges simply labelled 'Concentrated Orange' in a thick glass bottle with a cork top. And the smelly extract of malt which stuck to the spoon like it had been glued there. 'Malt extract', the label pronounced with threatening authority. It was a different alchemy, not a new one. A new set of quasi-scientific words and potions for an urban population that hardly knew where it had landed itself.

Neither did I. Mayflower Street was new territory to me and I sheltered in that tiny house, not wanting to leave. After all, I knew no one here. I hung about my mother's apron strings, I suppose not knowing what else to do. She had promised me that I should not go to school for the next two weeks, maybe because I had no pals and was in an alien place. I was left to absorb the world I had arrived in. Once a week, Mother walked me to a place called Bridge End. It was an area of shoddy sheds and locally owned factory developments that sprawled out haphazardly at one end of the bridge across the River Lagan which divides the city. If the weather was good, me and Mum would walk to the Bridge End along Newtownards Road which was full of shops. At the end of this road was a place where you could get a bottle of strong bleach for a few coppers. Some weeks after our arrival we discovered that we could buy the same bleach off a handcart at John Long's corner, ten minutes from our house.

John Long's corner was a junction point of several roads that met like an arrow point. John Long was the name of the chemist at the corner. So I suppose it was appropriate that one of the many characters who have stayed with me like sentinels marking my arrival should have his goods outside the chemist. His handcart was piled up with a dazzling variety of bottles. Some of the long and slim ones were fluted, others were squat and bulky with really thick necks. The empty glass looked green like seaweed, I thought. In the middle of them was a huge globular bottle encased in a wire cage surrounded by straw. 'Blee-each!' screamed the man behind the handcart as if he had just swallowed a bottle of the stuff. 'Brimstone blee-each!' he squealed to emphasize his wares. Mother always brought an empty lemonade bottle for him to fill. The great globular bottle would swing up and the fluid run out of its belly into our bottle. 'Smell that,' said the man. 'Strong enough to bleach the blackest soul.' He said this every week till I was bored. Then one day out of the blue, he announced that angels drank the stuff to make them go white. Mother dismissed this remark, suggesting that he might have been drinking his own brimstone bleach!

The bleach man was only one of those strange characters that I seemed to hone in on. I remember them less for themselves than for the noise they made. 'Oi-raw!' called the skin man who walked up the entry that separated the back of Mayflower Street from Heatherbell Street. The skin man collected household refuse to feed his pigs. He parked his tractor and trailer at the bottom of the entry and walked up the alley announcing his arrival. He grasped a mucky galvanized bucket in each hand and hardly said a word as the bolts were drawn back on our yard doors and all manner of food slops were emptied into his waiting buckets. 'Right, missus' was the most he might have spoken.

The ragman wandered up our entry whenever the notion took him. He sang and carried a basket in each hand. He was the best salesman I ever knew. He had cups, hideously embossed with flowers which he would give as a thank-you for whatever clothes were given to him. He was a charmer, for sometimes he would volunteer to read the teacups of the 'lady of the house'. I remember many back doors being opened with women waiting, cup in hand, for the ragman to read their future. Mother was one of them. And always he did it as if it was a coincidental payment for whatever she had handed over. My mother had a collection of cheap cups which the ragman had thanked her with, but the story of each of them I cannot guess at. There was always a pot of tea brewing before the ragman arrived.

Tommy, the coal brick man had a club-foot. He trundled his cart up the front street clumping it down every four houses or so. 'Coooal-breeek!' he called, then sucked on his Sherlock Holmes pipe. The neat square blocks of compressed coal dust steamed just like his pipe. Tommy's 'Coooal breeek' was just as efficient as a bag of coal and a lot cheaper. Everyone loved Tommy, who had one leg nine inches shorter than the other. He was skinnier than a scarecrow and wore a leather apron longer than my mother's. Yet he pushed his handcart full of steaming coal bricks from street to street in all weathers. Later I learned that Tommy kept a donkey in a small shed in his end terrace yard. But when the donkey got too old to pull the cart, Tommy pushed it and let the donkey retire to his shed. I used to go and feed Tommy's donkey dandelion leaves I picked up at the side of the street. Tommy and the donkey never seemed to get any older. One day the donkey was gone and everybody knew that the inevitable had happened but never mentioned it. Neither did Tommy. He simply club-footed his handcart up and down the streets for years calling out, in his increasingly croaky voice, 'Cooal breeek' as the squat blocks steamed and smelt of something between tar and soot.

Tommy could lift a line of a dozen bricks stretched horizontally between his hands and carry them from his cart, through the house and out into the back yard without straining and dropping them. His skinny frame belied a massive strength in his forearms. The coal brick stretched between his arms like a skinny black accordion and his hands blacked with dust seemed to have disappeared or melted into the brick. His face, too, had acquired a sooty mask. Only the whites of his eyes and the silver band of his Peterson pipe shone out from this black apparition that moved through our house every Thursday afternoon.

One afternoon when I walked past the gateway to Tommy's yard, I discovered him sitting on an old kitchen chair. It was a Saturday, and Tommy was soaking up the sun. His shirt sleeves were tightly rolled up to his shoulders revealing incredibly white skin. Instead of great muscular forearms, his limbs were hardly thicker than the legs of his chair. But his face was shining. I could hardly believe my eyes. He called out to me, 'Young Keenan, is it?' and beckoned me to him. He opened a small paper bag and proffered the contents to me. 'Bull's-eyes!' he said. 'Take some.' I stared for a moment at the black and white striped balls of boiled candy, then back to his face. I had rarely seen or heard Tommy say more than a pleasant but cursory greeting or remark about the weather. Tommy always remarked on the severity of the weather: Frosty out, coul' out, nippy out, freezing out or chilly out. Now I watched mesmerized as he gabbled on about what a 'decent' woman my mother was and how I seemed to be getting bigger by the week. It wasn't so much that the man was talking in full conversational sentences that held my attention, it was the black tobacco-stained stumps of his teeth flashing out of his scrubbed and shiny face as his lips moved. I had never seen his teeth before as they were always locked on to his pipe. His concise commentary on the weather hardly ever allowed his lips to move. I listened, gazing stupidly at the man, then took one of his bull's-eyes, and then a second one when he insisted.

'Thanks, Tommy,' I said and he smiled his great big black smile back at me.

I walked home turning the bull's-eyes in my hand. The thing was, the Tommy I had been talking to was the complete reverse of the 'black' coal brick man who limped through our house. It was as if he had been turned inside out! I told my mother about the 'new' Tommy I had discovered. 'He must have been scrubbing himself for days!' I exclaimed. Mother noticed my amazement and suggested that perhaps he mixed some 'brimstone bleach' with his soap and water.

A few other voices echo out of the backstreets of my childhood. 'Heron' Maggie screaming 'Aaard-glass-herns!' like a bronchial crow sticks out as one of them. She was selling herrings landed at the fishing village of Ardglass. Of course there were other women who called at our door selling needles and thread, or items of delph ware. But they came and went, leaving little impression. When a true hawker calls out the goods they are trying to sell it reaches right down inside you like an incantation. Caught up in this spell, you go to them. How Heron Maggie got her name I will never know. She looked nothing like a heron. Maybe it was the colloquial pronunciation of the word 'herring' which she sold. Maggie was a big-boned, big-breasted woman. But her stature seemed somehow to diminish under her long black shawl. She wore what looked like men's shoes without laces in them. When I asked my parents about this I was told conspiratorially that Maggie had webbed feet and that was the reason for the big shoes. I believed this; after all, with a name like Heron Maggie, why would I not? Mostly she wore her shawl over her head or else covered it with a headscarf. Her butcher's apron was covered in stains and scales. Mother never bought fish. She couldn't stand the smell of it, so I never got close enough to Maggie to see what her face was like. It was her keening cry 'Aaard-glass-herns' that hypnotized me. Sometimes it was mournful and beguiling, at other times sharp and incisive. Then there was the speed and careless precision with which Maggie cleaned fish. To me the way she filleted the fish was related to her calling voice. There was something curious and predatory about Maggie, just like the bird she was named after. I loved listening to Maggie and simply watching her, so much so that I often had to be trailed away from my vantage point. Mother would remark that it was no wonder she didn't buy fish for we would be there all day, or she would impatiently challenge me: 'If it was a choice between fish to bring home or Maggie, you'd choose Maggie. Then where would I go?' At first I was shocked at the proposal but I quickly forgot it. There was no choice to make. There was nothing motherly about Maggie but her cry called me to her irresistibly.

Maggie was a bit like Tommy's donkey. One week she was there and the next she wasn't. Or maybe we just stopped shopping where Maggie cast her magic. Her ghost passed on to another street hawker. Years after her disappearance, Tommy Trew visited our streets in his bone-shaker lorry. He too sold herrings along with all manner of market garden produce. Tommy Trew's call was different. 'Herns aloi, Herns aloi, the real Ardglass, the real Ardglass'. Tommy didn't have Maggie's magic, his cry was no incantation. It was slippery like the greasy fish lying in their boxes on his lorry.

The lorry roared up our streets, stopping every hundred yards and he would hang out the window and shout for the housewives to come out to him. He was small and stout and he smelt of sweat. Tommy had no mystery about him: he was in business and his business was making money. The kids followed after his lorry just to hang off the back of it as it drove off. For a while he roared at us. 'Go away a that we ya!' or 'I'll slap the ears off the lot of ya!' But then he gave up, we were there for the ride, not to steal his merchandise. He wore a leather bag around his waist with different compartments for halfpennies, pennies, threepenny bits, sixpences, shillings, florins and half-crowns. As long as his money and his merchandise were safe, Tommy was content to put up with our pranks. It was Tommy's call 'Herns aloi, herns aloi' that fascinated me. No one knew what the word 'aloi' meant and no one ever asked. It didn't have the same appeal as Maggie's incantation.

Every Saturday evening the newspaperman whose call 'Ooolster-sect-ardy' echoed in our small hall as the *Ulster Saturday Night,* a sister paper of the *Belfast Telegraph* landed on the floor. The delivery man's shout had the same ring to it as the medieval town crier who went about the village proclaiming 'All's well, all's well'. I had no interest in the newspaper but it meant that Saturday evening had arrived and that meant a feast of ice-cream mixed with lemonade, bags of crisps or penny bars of chocolate, while Mum and Dad watched the *Black and White Minstrel Show* or *The Billy Cotton Band Show.*

Television held no interest for me. Not like the brimstone bleach man, the skin man and the ragman or Heron Maggie or the coal brick man. They were the last remnants of an era that was passing away. They were mysterious, or even frightening. They seemed to come from another world and occasionally they entered into ours. They came and they went, from where and to where I never knew, but was forever curious about.

There is a story that many people would be familiar with. The story of how a mermaid came to live on the land and became part human. To this day I am sure Maggie was one of them and was a different breed of human. So was the ragman who read teacups in exchange for old clothes. Curiously, if he was ever given the clothes of a dead infant or child he placed them with great reverence in a separate basket. He was different and knew things we did not. Even

Tommy the coal brick man, with his black and white personas and his black and white bull's-eye sweets, had an air of magic about him. And there were more magical characters like the deaf and dumb knife grinder, the bread man who often gave me a 'sore head' bun every time I could recite him one of the commandments, which was a trial for me! The scrap merchants whose horse-drawn cart caused great excitement. They never spoke to us much, but when they did it was impossible to understand them. They had a different rhythm to their speech as they pronounced their words differently. 'Egyptians!' as an old woman from the bottom of the street called them. 'Give them what you like but don't let them across your doorstep!' she warned. The whole notion of Egyptians with horses in our street was better than the Saturday matinée.

Caught up in my enthusiasm, my mother told me about street musicians she had remembered. A fiddle player who sang a song called 'Bonnie Mary', the tune of which she could not remember. She said her favourite was 'Good Night, Irene' and she began singing the chorus. I was greatly surprised by this. I recognized the tune but didn't know how. 'I sang that to you when you were a baby and years later a little girl called Irene used to mind you and take you for walks. You used to cry to go home with Irene,' she teasingly explained. I still know the song and sometimes find myself absentmindedly humming it to myself in the lazy languorous way I recall it.

She also told me of a tin whistle player who played the instrument through his nose. Sometimes he had an instrument rammed into each nostril with his hands and fingers playing the tune. I was amazed at this and for some weeks, attempted to imitate this musician. But to this day I cannot understand how anyone can blow long enough through their nose to sustain a tune. 'Do you think he'll come back?' I asked excitedly. To which my mother could only answer 'O I don't know, son, his likes are long gone! Some of them were very special people and then there were some who were proper scoundrels.' Then she explained about the preacher who walked the streets 'like he was the Almighty himself!' The man had held a bible out at arm's length and wore gold-framed pince-nez spectacles perched on the bridge of his nose. He was forever preaching about how difficult it was for a rich man to enter the kingdom of heaven 'so he could coax a few coppers out of our purses', she exclaimed, then continued, 'and I am sure if I had got close enough to him I'd have smelt the inspiration of the power station on him!' The 'power station' was the local name for a public house famed for the potency of its cheap wine known as Blowy-Up. 'There was another one who played the accordion with one of his trouser legs rolled up to show off his false leg.' Then she laughed. 'There were many stories about just how he lost that leg though he wanted everyone to believe he had lost it in the war.' I never did see the one-legged accordion player, nor did I see the preacher she used to call the Pharisee because his far-seeing religious conviction was dubiously inspired by a night at the 'power station'. Equally I never saw the nasal-blowing whistle player but I waited for weeks wanting to see them. All of them took up residence in my imagination, and that was real enough for me. They were players in my street theatre and although they left the stage early, they are still hanging about in the wings, 'waiting to get in on the act' as they say.

BETRAYAL AND THE BIRDMAN

OUR NEIGHBOURS ON ONE SIDE WERE CALLED ROBINS. THEY HAD ONE daughter named Florrie. For whatever reason, Florrie had never 'flown the nest'. She was a grown woman when we arrived and she looked, spoke and dressed just like her mother. For many months I found it almost impossible to tell them apart. I never saw much of Mr Robins. He had to retire from work early due to some illness. Except for regular appearances of Mrs Robins and Florrie going off shopping together or occasional appearances of Mr Robins standing on his doorstep looking at the sky or sometimes tending his rose bushes, you would hardly know they were there at all.

The Robins house was always immaculate. It was the smartest, cleanest, shiniest house in Mayflower Street. None of the family in any way resembled the bird they were named for as all of them were tall and lean, so tall in fact that I couldn't believe the three of them would fit into the tiny terrace house. However, Florrie and her mother each had the energy of a robin and they spent most of it maintaining their nest at number 39. Mr Robins was a pigeon fancier. His bird loft was built over the outside toilet and coal shed that every house in the street had. Every morning I awoke to the sound of Mr Robins's pigeons. They made a warbling noise like marbles rolling backwards and forwards over a sheet of corrugated cardboard. In the summer time when all our windows were left open I would hear Mr Robins move about in the loft talking to his birds. His voice was low and his speech was slow, as if he was passing on some secret. They seemed to understand for they would warble back at him with the same soft modulation. One day I heard Mrs Robins tell my mother that her husband spent more time in his loft than he did in his house. On another day I watched him standing in the back entry that divided the streets. He had a basket that looked like a suitcase at his feet. Every few minutes he reached in and lifted out a pigeon cupped in his hand. With his other hand he spread the wings one at a time like a fan. He held the bird up close to his face and studied it. Occasionally he caressed its head with his index finger and spoke to it. The bird sat motionless in his hand listening and watching him. Then he stretched out his arm and with the slightest flick of his wrist he released the bird. For a few seconds the creature seemed lost in the air and flew around giddily. Eventually the bird found its bearings and landed on the roof of the loft where all the other birds from the basket would join it. I was intrigued by this ritual. Many times Mr Robins saw me watching him from my bedroom. But he only looked at me briefly.

Mr Robins was a bit off, I thought. He spent so much time up in his bird box on the roof that I was convinced he had forgotten human speech. For more than a year I never heard him say anything more than 'morning, missus', or 'hello' if he happened to be in his garden when my mother or father were coming or going. I don't think he ever spoke to me once in all that time. But I knew he saw me watching him.

One day Mrs Robins lost her door keys and asked my mother if I could climb over the yard wall and let her in. Mother was happy for me to help and I was over her wall in seconds. It was like another world. The outside WC was housed under the loft and against the yard wall and beside it was the coal shed. Between this and the rear wall of the house there was a space of some six to eight feet where people generally kept their bins and yard brushes, mops and buckets and any other things that could not be accommodated in the glory hole. But not in the Robins house. Mr Robins had housed this area with its own door and window replete with lace curtains. Everything in the yard was tidied away with precision. The limewashed walls were spotless; even the clothesline which stretched the length of each yard in the street had been neatly rolled away out of sight.

I sneaked a quick glance through the curtained window and saw shelves stacked with all shapes and sizes of boxes and bottles. There were neatly stacked books and magazines, all of which were about birds and bird-keeping. And pictures of birds on the walls, but they were not racing birds – they were images of bird carvings and paint-ings of medieval sciences with birds in them. There were drawings of ancient lofts that looked like churches, and gods and goddesses with avian familiars. It was a bit spooky.

I slid back the bolt and opened the yard door. Mrs Robins and my mother came in. Immediately Mrs Robins remarked on how tidy and smart it looked but said that the way Mr Robins had enclosed the place left little room to do anything else but come and go. 'Sure he spends all his time here.' Then she chuckled and continued. 'It suits him, sure he can sit on the lavatory, fry sausages in the pan and watch his beloved birds come and go all day long!' Given the size of Mr Robins and the tininess of his yard, such a feat was just impossible, I thought. Mrs Robins pointed to the shed and declared, looking right at me, 'He calls that the chemist shop and the library and no one but himself ever goes into it.' I went red with guilt imagining that Mrs Robins had seen me noseying into her husband's secret den. 'God alone knows what he gets up to in there. If I ever die suddenly one day, you'll know he poisoned me!' I was surprised by our neighbour's good-natured talk about her husband, and mentioned it to my mother. 'Ah well, I'm sure she gets little enough conversation out of him and she was glad of the company. She has few enough people calling on her!'

Though his wife's humour did lend a little more sympathetic humanity to her husband, he remained a mystery to me. A man who, I imagined, either spent hours concocting strange recipes or else sat in his aviary conversing with the birds! I had come to accept the fact that Mr Robins was going to remain a silent curiosity living next door. So I was surprised and even a little afraid when the man popped his head up from his roses one day as I was coming home from school and asked, 'Would you like to come and look at the birds?' And that was the day I discovered the big secret about Mr Robins. He was related, very, very, distantly, through his birds, to Noah!

The detail of this emerged over several weeks, after my first visit to the inner sanctuary of the bird box. We entered it from a fold-away ladder that ran up the wall of 'the chemist'. This took us, via a trapdoor, into an empty compartment right in the middle of the loft. At each side of this were sliding doors that opened directly to the birds. On one side were the old and mature birds and on the other, young birds, some of them newly hatched.

I could hear them moving about restlessly as the trapdoor closed and Mr Robins slid back the door into the mature birds section. As he eased the door open, he spoke in a soft, gentle tone as if soothing an infant. Then he ushered me in, whispering me to be quiet and move slowly. I didn't admit to him that I was a little afraid. But the easy tone with which he spoke to the birds coaxed me on. I suppose I expected the whole place to explode with terrified birds flying willy-nilly in a panic, but it was the opposite. A few birds fluttered from one perch to another. Some positioned themselves on the long beam that marked their entrance and exit. But they were not trying to make a quick dash to escape. They huddled, unafraid, as if to make room for us. Mr Robins picked up several of the birds in turn, naming them and describing their various skills or personality traits the way a parent would introduce his children. 'Most people have got the wrong attitude to birds,' he whispered. 'You see, these fellas really love the company of humans. I could sit here for hours and talk to them, like I was reading a fairy story and they'd sit there nice as you like and listen to every word. I'm nearly sure that they can read your mind. Once they get to know you they'll give you their undying affection. There's a real big bond of trust between a man and his birds. If you love them, they'll love you back ten times as much.' All the time he was talking he would interrupt himself to say hello or stroke one of the birds. He had only to hold out a hand to a particular bird and it fluttered on to his fingers. 'Birds are the only creatures you can give complete freedom to and they will always, always return to you. With other animals you can never be 100 per cent sure. But with a bird you can be absolutely sure. That's how much they trust you and love you.' He placed a beautiful grey bird in my hands. 'See what I mean about people having the wrong attitude. She's not a bit afraid of you. Feel how still she sits and look at the way she's watching you. She loves you already!' The bird studied me without blinking. Its weightlessness amazed me. In my hands it was wholly at my mercy, yet it was I who felt helpless and awed.

After a few more minutes we entered the other compartment. The younger birds were a little more excitable but calmed instantly as their keeper spoke. A few birds in a box were only beginning to put on feathers, yet Mr Robins knew which was which and who was likely to be the most agile. 'In another few months this fella should be able to fly 40 miles an hour or more in a good head wind.' Mr Robins gabbled on for several minutes but what he was saying was lost on me. Much of it I couldn't hear. He had got into the habit of speaking softly to reassure his birds and there was a primitive rhythm to his voice that sounded more like bird-babble than human speech. As he descended back into the 'chemist' my eyes were drawn to a framed print hanging on the wall. It was a picture of two avuncular monks sitting at a wooden table in what I suppose was an orchard, and in the background was a large, oddly shaped structure. It looked like a pyramid with the top cut off. The upper elevations of this structure were full of neatly cut, regular holes. Pigeons were flying in and out and several were roosting in it. The two monks at the table obviously had something to do with this ancient aviary. One held a bird in his hand in the exact manner I had watched my neighbour handle his birds. The bird's wing had been splayed open and both men were surveying the creature studiously. Two or three pigeons had perched at the other end of the table where a handful of crumbs had been thrown. Mr Robins noticed my interest. 'Don't make lofts like that any more and you wouldn't see any men like them around here. In the olden days the monks used to keep hundreds and hundreds of birds. Even the Romans had dovecotes that could house up to five thousand birds!' It was obvious that he marvelled at this. 'You see, back in them days people didn't have enough feed to keep too many animals alive through the winter. Most of them were slaughtered and the meat was salted to preserve it. Couldn't have been very tasty after a few weeks. So all the rich people kept pigeons for fresh meat.'

I wasn't sure whether it was my curiosity about the 'religious' picture hanging in the shed or the talk of Romans and gigantic aviaries or even the idea of pigeon meat which was a revelation to me. But, this tall, skinny, quiet man was transformed. When he told me a few weeks later about how he was related to Noah I was convinced that up in his bird box above the lavatory and the coal shed was another world. Mr Robins was the keeper at the gate.

The story about Great-Great-Great-Great-uncle Noah was not so far fetched and the logic of it was very simple. You see, before the Flood, Noah filled the Ark with a pair of every creature he could find. Then the Flood came and drowned every living creature except those on board the Ark. So Noah had the only pair of pigeons in the world. 'Dove,' Mr Robins told me, was a fancy name for a fancy pigeon. Anyway the pigeon returned with the olive branch and Noah knew the Flood was receding. And so it follows that every living creature is descended from Noah's Ark. Noah's pigeons were the Adam and Eve of every bird in his loft. Noah had bred, fed and trained his birds to return to the Ark just as Mr Robins had with his pigeons in the back yard of 39 Mayflower Street. Now if all the pigeons in the world were descended from the birds on the Ark, so were all the people. Thus Noah was Mr Robins's great-great-great-great-grandfather! It was as simple as that.

This was only the beginning. On my visits to Mr Robins, I picked up fragments of geography and history that I would have to wait years to be introduced to in school. In fact there were things I learned from being with Mr Robins that I would not learn from anyone else. Dad had once told me about pigeons being used to carry coded messages during the First World War. But this was not half as fascinating as the idea that the ancient Egyptians and Greeks used pigeons as message carriers. In a place called Mesopotamia, which was two thousand years older than the worlds of the Greeks or Romans, pigeons were worshipped as messengers of the gods.

Every house had at least one or two clay figurines of these birds placed on their roof in the hope that good news would always come to the occupants. 'No wonder everybody believes angels have wings,' Mr Robins declared. I picked up these odd pieces of history at random, for Mr Robins would toss them out the way he scattered corn for his birds.

For a while I thought he must be very clever like one of the people on *The Brains Trust*, one of Dad's favourite TV programmes. He certainly read a lot. There were copies of *The Racing Pigeon* and the *British Homing World* everywhere. Lots of books about birds in general were neatly stacked in his 'chemist' and on shelves in the living room. Later I found out that he never read them from cover to cover. He just picked through them and he liked illustrated books best. One day I found one of these books open at a page with a black and white photo of a statue in the British Museum. Underneath were the words 'Astarte, goddess of love with the pigeon as her symbol'. The statue looked more warlike than loving. I never asked Mr Robins about it. It was just another of the quirky things that I discovered and that made the man so interesting.

Before school taught it to me, I also learned my geography up in that loft. Sometimes I learned more than I was later taught! My Protestant schooling studiously avoided the history or geography of the south of Ireland, but bird men, like their birds, did not recognize any borders. The racing schedule of the Ulster Federation listed names like Katesbridge, Gormanstown, Arklow, Wexford and Skibbereen. Mr Robins would point out the places on the map. At other times he would talk about a place called Pau in the Pyrenees, Rennes in France, and places in Belgium and the Shetland islands. He would tell me how he used to listen to the weather and shipping forecasts and try to gauge his birds' progress as they returned from these places. 'Birds love human companionship, that's what brings them home and you are never closer to your birds than when you are waiting for them to return.' It was obvious that Mr Robin's affection for his birds was overwhelming. 'Racing over great distances can be very hard on a bird, especially if the weather is rough. So you have to really butter them up when they come home,' he told me. 'A little bit of glucose baby food in their water or else rice soaked in honey and dissolved in water then fed to them for a few days will build them up.' Over the weeks I learned about turning their feed corn in the sun, adding a little salt to cabbage, and the secret of 'green water'. Apparently any water in which green veg has been boiled and then left to cool should be given to the birds once a week. 'It purifies the blood and helps prevent the spread of disease. You have to look after the blood. Disease will fly through the birds like a lit match in a haystack. It's not easy to bury the bloodlines you have established over the years.'

I was beginning to understand why his shed was called 'the chemist' or sometimes 'the surgery'. There was something more to his story about burying dead birds though I didn't know it at the time. One evening Mr Robins was explaining to me the finer points of a good bird. He held one of his pigeons in his outstretched hand. 'She shouldn't tip forward, you see. A deep-keeled bird whose breast-bone is too great a depth from its backbone makes the bird too square. It needs a long keel that sweeps with a gentle curve towards its tail.' As he spoke his hand ran from the bird's throat, down over the breast and out to the tail feathers. 'These birds really have to be tough to fight against fog and rain and clouds that slow their progress. Strong head winds and even electric storms can totally disorientate them. Remember, they navigate by the sun. So they have to allow their brain to develop. Birds are the smartest of all creatures. Sure, they can practically talk to you. You see this bit –' he said, pointing to the spongy honeycomb-like material above the beak: 'Well if it's not a bright clean white colour, you've got a sick bird. A dull eye is the same. It's a bit like dog with a dry nose.'

Mr Robins conveyed all this information in his slow, almost inaudible way and when he had finished he paused for a moment, then said with great earnestness, 'The thing is, your birds have to be watched all the time. You have got to be with them and observe them constantly!' There was something about the way he delivered that final instruction. Usually he just gabbled on half to himself and half to the birds, allowing me to pick up whatever interested me. I rarely questioned him. But something prompted me to ask: 'Why don't you race them any more?'

'Ah, these aren't racing birds, son. I gave that up a long time ago. They are all high-flyers. They never fly too far and can pull a few fancy tricks and I can always keep my eye on them.' I noticed he had taken to addressing me as 'son' quite often now. At first it was 'young lad' or 'young Keenan'. Only occasionally did he use my Christian name, Brian. Sometimes I felt that he was half in and half out of the world when he was speaking, but when he said 'son' I felt he really wanted to communicate something. But whatever it was, he left it hanging in the air. A week later I learned why from my father.

Mr Robins had originally kept his loft at the end of one of the allotments that ran along the bottom of our street. A river flowed through it with clumps of young sycamore growing along its banks. 'It was a good south-facing location with all the clearance in the world for birds to come and go. The river, trees and the line of allotments would be a clear marker to a returning bird,' my dad explained. 'So why did he move it?' I asked with curious interest. 'Ah that's another story and if I tell you, you are not to ask him about it.' 'OK,' I said, wondering if I really wanted to know.

Dad explained that Mr Robins had been keeping racing pigeons there for many years and had a much-respected reputation amongst other bird fanciers. One morning he had walked down to feed and clean the loft only to find the birds wheeling about the allotment and some of them on the ground. This was highly unusual. At the loft he found feathers all over the place and several young birds dead inside. There was no sign of anyone having broken into the place. Such a thing was unheard of. But there were several scratch marks that the intruder had left as it made its escape. At first he didn't know what to think. Some of the allotment owners who arrived after him were equally shocked. Some suggested it might have been a fox – but that was unlikely, as some of them kept chicken coops at ground level and any fox would have gone straight to them. It was assumed that the culprit was a cat; probably more than one. However, there was no way someone's cat could have got into the loft, and cats are solitary creatures that do not hunt in pairs.

The only conclusion that everyone could agree on was that someone had deliberately tossed two cats into the loft for some utterly perverse reason. The realization of how the catastrophe had happened only deepened the sense of shock. The men who owned the allotments all knew one another and often checked with Mr Robins about the progress of his birds during a race. Often they sat and watched the sky with excitement, waiting to spot a returning bird.

'You see, when something like that happens the birds are never the same. It's like they have been driven mad with fear. They leave the loft to escape and will not return because they now associate their home with fear and death. It's like it changes the character of the birds and it changes the relationship with their owner. Sometimes the younger birds can be retrained but not with the same owner or the same loft. With the older birds it is useless, and because of what has happened they are useless as racers also. Most of the other breeders won't buy or even want birds that have been damaged in this way. They rarely mix with the other birds in a new loft and usually never breed. Sometimes if they do lay eggs, they don't look after them.

'It was a terrible thing to happen. Mr Robins had had some real champions which everyone wanted to buy or breed from. It took him many, many years of careful breeding to achieve and it was all wiped out in a few hours for absolutely no reason. They never found out who did it, or why. People talked about it for months. Poor Mr Robins, there was nothing he could do. The next day he gave away the youngest of his birds to other breeders who wanted them; most took them out of sympathy. The rest he had to have destroyed. He didn't go near the loft for weeks. Then one morning, very early, he went down to the allotment, knocked it down and then burned it. It was a long time before his friends in the pigeon club could convince him to start up again. That's why he keeps exhibition birds now. But he never goes to the pigeon club and he never shows his birds. Florrie has told your mum that you're the only one in years he has brought into his loft. Maybe he's making an apprentice out of you.'

I don't remember how I reacted to the story. I suppose it shocked me and then it passed. I never did say anything about it on my subsequent visits. I was still a boy, only newly learning about these birds. I was not an adult who had bred generations of birds. I could imagine how Noah would have felt if someone had burnt down his Ark full of animals before he had released them.

Mr Robins kept this tragic past to himself and continued in his own haphazard way to explain the world of birds to me. As he pointed out the differing acrobatics of the tipplers, rollers and tumblers, I thought of my model biplanes and thought too that maybe Dad would help me build a loft. Mr Robins had hinted that he would give me a few starter birds. Mother of course vetoed the idea before I could get enthusiastic about it. Dad was taken by the proposal. I knew he would enjoy the birds as much as me. Mother also knew it but her phobia about birds inside the house was even more determined. It was irrational, and there was no point in arguing.

The roller is about half the size of a racing pigeon and can turn over five times in a second. I stood many afternoons watching the birds and tried to count the number of rolls in a second. It was impossible. These aerial acrobats were mostly white in colour but I had a favourite. It was called an Orlik. The Orlik is like a small eagle in flight. When it is flying it looks like a circling crescent. It was not its flight pattern that drew me but its unique colouring: deep red with white tips on its tail and flight feathers. Watching these birds fly I knew why I preferred them to the racers. It was simple. You could watch them without the worry of where they were. They could entertain you in a way racers could not. They had skill and unconscious artistry where the racer had stamina and an unfailing mental compass. It was a bit like the difference between the biplane and the warplane. They had different purposes but for me it was the high-flyers every time.

I had learned much from these pigeons so I suppose it was inevitable that I should get my first lessons in the art of seduction from them. I used to watch the males 'blowing their crop' and parading themselves in front of the females. The hens were not coy and would walk slowly and seductively to entice the cock. When the hen is aroused she will follow after the cock, relentlessly inviting him to 'beak', an action in which the potential males stand head to head with the female, ringing each other's beak in opposing circular movements. If this doesn't convince the cock, the lady does not give up, and she makes a stroking action along the back of the male's neck. 'They can strut about and play hard to get all they like, but the hens have it all worked out. They know their man and sooner or later he gives in.'

I remembered Mr Robins's advice that you have to 'observe your birds constantly', and I never tired of watching this ritual. Just to illustrate how amorous these birds could be, he pointed out that it was even possible for two hens to mate. 'A male and a female will always produce two fertile eggs, but both hens in a particular mating will produce four eggs all of which are infertile,' he informed me. If this wasn't strange enough, I also learned that both sexes produce 'milk' in their crop to feed their young. I was too young to be interested in girls, so I absorbed all this surprising stuff with no embarrassment. Girls were a few more years down the line but, even so, I was becoming dimly aware of why the lascivious-looking Astarte, goddess of love had a pigeon for her symbol!

My casual apprenticeship with Mr Robins spread itself out over a couple of summers. As I said earlier, Mr Robins looked nothing like the bird he was named after. Yet as I look back on those years I see how, in a curious way, the man did resemble the birds he looked after. With his long skinny angular form, his round bald head and round glasses with thick black frames that made his eyes look enlarged and staring he could have been a giant scaldy! A scaldy is the young bird before it puts on feathers. At this early stage they are terribly vulnerable and totally dependent, and these were characteristics that my birdman displayed in his own retiring way.

Over those few years, the relationship between us was naturally petering out. Mr Robins had told my dad that he was getting too old and too arthritic for climbing up and down the loft ladders and as his eyesight was getting worse he couldn't see the birds when they were flying. He had reduced his breeding programme. 'They are just an old man's fancy, Jack. I'll keep a few, I suppose, just to keep me going.'

When I had long ceased calling on the birdman, and when he had reduced the numbers of his birds drastically, keeping only a few of the very best for breeding purposes, something happened which severed the connection between us. I was about twelve or thirteen at the time. My mum and dad were planning to take us to Carlingford Lough, a long inlet of water right on the border between Northern Ireland and the Republic. It was an annual day out for many families from our neighbourhood. But it was more than a day out for us. 'We're going smuggling,' Dad whispered conspiratorially.

Well, it was smuggling but on a very small scale. At that time the respective economies of the North and South of Ireland were very different. Everything was cheaper in the Republic of Ireland. Everyone in the North knew it and took advantage of it regularly. There were customs men and custom posts. But no one paid a penny in customs. There were more back roads across the border than there were customs men to patrol them. These 'unapproved roads' were marked on every map of Ireland I ever saw. So if you wanted to smuggle anything by car or lorry you simply looked at the map for an unapproved road and went about your business. Of course, those who did not have the luxury of transport were not to be outdone. They piled on to buses, travelled to the small town of Warrenpoint, reloaded themselves into an open boat, crossed the lough, bought what they wanted and sat in the pub discussing their contraband with the rest of the family smugglers then sailed back to Warrenpoint, usually with more than they could carry.

Naturally, I didn't know about this and believed we were off on a great risky adventure. Omeath, in the Republic, was a tiny place with a few shops, a couple of pubs and a smattering of private houses. But every summer the outlying fields were full of tents and open stalls selling everything that you could think of. It was like landing in Jack and the Beanstalk land. There was a boisterous carnival atmosphere about the place. It was a real fun family day out, with the added attraction that everyone was a smuggler! On the return journey, the smugglers were in high spirits because of the booty they were bringing back and the amount of alcohol they had consumed. Alcohol was half the price in 'Beanstalk land'.

So we shipped back across the lough, our boat set low in the water with its burden of drunken smugglers and their endless bags of cheap goods. There were bags of butter and of bacon, giant slabs of cheese, parcels of meat that would last a month. Carton after carton of cigarettes were lashed together and looking like builder's blocks. There were bottles of spirits and cases of beer, bag after bag of neatly folded clothes and underwear. Transistor radios and records galore, boxes of toys and tools. The boat looked like Santa Claus's sleigh. Everyone on board was wearing leprechaun party hats like Santa's helpers. All it needed was a team of dolphins or magical swimming deer to drag us across. Boat followed after boat. It made me think of the pictures of the lifeboats in my grandfather's *Titanic* book. I watched all this in amazed silence. No one knew what I had and I wasn't about to tell them just in case we got stopped in mid-water by a customs patrol boat. I didn't know if there were such things but I was keeping quiet. I had a gun wrapped up in the coat folded across my knee!

Mother and Father had a big row about this before we left Omeath. Mum was determined that it wasn't coming home with us. 'Ah, for God's sake, Minnie, it's only a pellet gun. I'll put up a target in the yard for him or better still, we'll go down to the river in the allotments and he can shoot rats, or Maurice will take him rabbit hunting when he goes!'

As they argued more I said nothing. The rifle looked just like rifles in the movies. It was real, after all. It fired tiny bullets called pellets. I had never really thought of killing anything with it – I just wanted to have a real gun. In the end, my mother relented. The gun was purchased. Dad showed me how to break the barrel and he slid it into the arm of his coat, folding the jacket around it. 'Carry that over your arm so no one will know. I'm keeping the tin of pellets. We don't want any gunfights with the customs men,' he warned, winking at my mother and sliding the tin of ammunition into his pocket. 'Why don't we buy some tins of shoe polish and put the pellets in there with some polish spread over the top of them. No one will know what it is!' I suggested excitedly. Dad smiled and Mum scowled at him. I was taking this smuggling business very seriously.

When we reached the other side it was like a comic version of an invasion scene from the *World at War* series. People were hoisting their bags up to waiting friends who would walk a few yards, leave the bag down and come back for more. Everywhere people were hauling bags of goods, shouting and panting under the weight of their contraband. One man shouted to everyone else, 'You're all a bunch of smugglers and thieves and I'll be reporting the lot of you to the police in the morning' as he stumbled along with bottles of spirits hanging out of his coat pockets, bucking under the weight of his own bags. Everyone laughed. But I kept myself off to one side walking as fast as I could without seeming to be in a hurry. No one, I was convinced, knew of the gun draped over my shoulder under my father's coat. I shielded my secret weapon nervously and never spoke a word to anyone the whole way home.

I never did shoot any rats at the river. Mother forbade me from taking the gun out of the house. I did go hunting with my uncle Maurice and he explained that the gun was too short range, the pellets too light for rabbits and that it would be better for birds. 'That's a crow killer you have, Brian,' he informed me. I tried shooting at a few crows but never hit them. Maurice explained: 'You have to hide and wait for them. Birds are clever. They know a gun when they see it.' Dad pinned a target to the back door and in no time I became quite the marksman. But I tired of it. A rifle, after all, was not meant for indoors.

For months I had to make do with showing the gun off to my friends; they were all very envious and I played up to it, making up stories about the number of rats, rabbits and crows I had killed. They were highly impressed, and when I told them I had even wounded a fox and that it got away before I could reload, they were doubly impressed. Like most liars, I never thought my imaginary marksmanship would catch me out. But it did, with more profound consequences than I could have ever imagined.

One day, while I was showing off my gun, one of my pals challenged me. If I was so good a shot why didn't I show them? I told him that I was not allowed the gun outside the house unless I was going hunting with my uncle. 'It's too dangerous,' I said coolly, relieved at my mother's prohibition. 'Well why can't you shoot out the window at those pigeons on the other roof?' he demanded. I was caught and didn't know what to say. I looked out the window and was relieved to discover that the pigeon was not one of my neighbour's. It was an ordinary 'street picker'. 'It's out of range,' I said, beginning to panic. 'No it's not,' my friend insisted. 'You told us you shot plenty of things further away than that. Go on, shoot it or else you are a big liar.' He was right: that's exactly what I was. But I didn't like hearing it and I didn't like being told it. And most of all I didn't like everyone knowing about it. Possession of the gun had given me some kind of status but now that it was being challenged it was either me, or the pigeon.

Slowly I slid down the sash window in my bedroom and silently eased the barrel of the gun out. The frame of the window provided a perfect resting place. The pigeon, perched on the roof tiles some fifty feet away, was oblivious. I delayed taking aim. Then delayed again, desperately wanting the bird to fly off. 'Go on, shoot it,' whispered one of my friends. They were all staring at the bird in hushed anticipation. Joe who had threatened to expose me as 'a big liar' was jealous of my ownership of the gun. Joe was the best runner, best football player, best climber. In fact, Joe was best at almost everything . We all did and played whatever Joe wanted us to. In comparison I was mediocre at everything and I was jealous of him. 'Give me the gun and I'll do it,' he said.

I was cornered. If he shot the pigeon instead of me, I would lose the prestige the air rifle had given me. It wouldn't matter that I would still own the gun. Joe would be 'the best' again, and I would be worse than mediocre. I would be the big liar who was afraid to shoot a mangy old street picker. Already I heard the taunts ringing silently in my ears. Any time I was seen with the gun, my friends would begin chanting that I was a 'scaredy cat!'

I couldn't bear it. I couldn't bear the fact that they were right. I was a 'scaredy cat'. I had never killed anything and that I was about to do just that scared the life out of me. I couldn't just deliberately miss the bird. I had boasted about what a great shot I was and could even prove it by hitting the target Dad had made for me. But this was different. This was murder. I turned away from my friends' gaze and stared along the barrel fixing the pigeon in the V of the sights and fired.

I watched the pigeon start into the air for a few feet – then it seemed to stop in mid-air before dropping recklessly out of sight.

My pals behind me were ecstatic. 'You got it, you got it!' they chanted. Even Joe was excited, and he was the first out of my room to find the dead bird. I slid the gun back under the bed and followed them. I was amazed that I'd hit my target and was also delighted that my secret was safe. Whatever status the rifle had given me, shooting the bird elevated me even more. Everyone was talking excitedly about the shooting. I was last out of the house and they were calling me to hurry. Their admiration was intoxicating and when Joe came up to me, his face beaming, and said 'I never thought you would do it. You're frigging brilliant!' I was stunned. Here was the lad who was always 'the best'. The local hero of our four streets telling me I was brilliant. I wanted everything to stop right there. I didn't want to find the dead bird. I just wanted everything to stop.

We found the lifeless pigeon in the next street. It was a scrawny, ugly creature but that did not lessen its impact on me. I wanted to get away from it; I didn't want everyone in the street to know I was responsible for its death. I didn't want anyone to know. Joe picked it up and looked for the entry wound. He was showing off. We were all afraid of the dead bird, me most of all, but Joe was displaying that he wasn't afraid. 'Do you want it?' he said, thrusting the feathered corpse towards me. I recoiled and he laughed a loud, mocking insinuating laugh. 'Leave it and come on,' I said. I could hardly hear the words as I spoke them. I turned and walked away. There was nothing else I could do. Joe reclaimed his mantle and I walked away, defeated.

For the next few days, I didn't think about the pigeon. The whole incident was completely forgotten about by my mates in a few hours. There was little fun to be had from a dead bird. It was as if it had never happened.

About a week later I was in my bedroom again going through my collection of comics to see which I could swap. They were kept

179

under my bed along with the rifle and an assortment of toys. I pulled the pile of comics out, glancing at the rifle. I recalled the incident of the previous week and immediately dismissed it. As I stood up I looked out through the window. There was another pigeon standing a few feet from where I had shot the first bird. I watched it for a few moments, then set the comics on the bed and dragged the rifle out from under it. I broke the breech and loaded the pellet. I slid the window down, just as before. I kept thinking to myself that no one would know, and anyway I would probably miss. That last shot was a lucky one. A small voice inside me told me to leave the bird alone. So I waited until the forbidding voice could hardly be heard. 'Do it , no one will know,' said another voice, and yet another reminded me that my uncle Maurice had said it was a 'bird gun'. I waited until my head was full of convincing voices. 'Go on,' they were all saying. 'It's only an old street picker probably riddled with disease. Go on, put it out of its misery.' It was like all my friends were there again, admiring me and my gun. They all thought I was brilliant and a great shot.

I slowly eased the barrel out the window and rested it once more on the wooden frame. I tried to line the bird up in my sights but it was busy walking back and forward along the ridge tiles. I watched it and was becoming breathless by the minute. Nervously I hissed under my breath for it to stand still. I remembered how the last bird had suddenly ejected itself into the air and I imagined the pellet had entered its body. Then how it seemed to fold and awkwardly fall to the ground. 'That's the way the old Sopwith Camel pilots did it, firing off rounds from their Browning machine-gun at the enemy. That isn't a bird over there, that's the Red Baron,' I told myself.

Suddenly the target stopped moving. I repositioned my body to give me a direct line of fire. The bird waited, making occasional jerky movements with its head, but its body remained motionless. Brian, barrel and bird were in a continuous line of flow. 'Easy peasy,' said the voice inside me.

'Brian Keenan!' shouted a voice from the yard below. 'I do hope you are not shooting pigeons. My God, you should be thoroughly ashamed of yourself. Wait till your father hears about this.'

Mrs Robins looked up at me from her tiny back yard. She had obviously come out to hang some washing. I fell away from the window as if I had just been shot instead of the pigeon. To be caught red handed in the act of murder was bad enough, but by Mrs Robins of all people . . . 'What if she thinks I'm shooting her husband's birds, what if she tells Dad, what will I say?' The voices inside me were not so supportive now. My invisible confederates had taken flight, scared into oblivion by Mrs Robins's bitter voice. I was frozen to the floor where I sat, my hands sweating, and the rifle had become a snake that was about to sink its fangs in me. I wondered if that was what the last bird felt when I shot it. I felt sick and wanted to throw up.

After a few minutes I pushed the gun back under the bed. I remained in the room for half an hour or so. Batman and Robin stared up at me accusingly from my pile of comics.

'Well, I could always deny it. I could say that she must have seen me with a rolled-up comic trying to swat a fly,' I said to myself. It sounded plausible. Then a dozen other excuses welled up inside me, each more implausible than the last. When I finally emerged from the room, I brought the sick feeling with me. I felt I was in the biggest trouble I'd ever been in and I hadn't even shot the bird. I could hear myself desperately trying to convince my parents that it wasn't any of Mr Robins's birds. 'It wasn't, honestly, I swear it wasn't,' I could hear myself pleading over and over again. But it didn't matter. I was still a killer.

Incredibly, nothing happened though I sweated blood for days. Mrs Robins had obviously said nothing. I avoided her and her husband every time I saw them. I even took to going out through the back door in case Mr Robins was in his garden. If I saw Mrs Robins talking to my mother, I delayed coming near the house until she had gone into her own. Effectively I went into hiding for something I didn't do.

There was one thing I did do. I never again poked the rifle out the window or even so much as looked at a pigeon on the roof. To this day I am still not sure if Mr Robins knew about my guilty secret. The relationship simply closed down. I never visited the loft again and was too embarrassed to try. Perhaps Mr Robins thought I had lost interest in the birds and deserted him. He died about eight months later. Guiltily I watched the funeral procession from my parents' bedroom. I imagined what his remaining birds might be saying as they tumbled and performed a last roll of honour.

Mr Robins knew he was dying What if I had, for a short time, become his surrogate son? Maybe someone to whom he could leave his beloved birds and who would care for them as he had. If it was so, then my seeming uninterest must have been a big disappointment. On the other hand, if he did know about the pigeon on the roof, he would probably have been as ashamed of me as I was of myself. If he thought the pigeon was one of his own I am sure he would have hated me for such betrayal.

The thing that bothers me most was that my actions would have seemed to him as ugly and heinous as that of the person who threw the cats into his pigeon loft. I dread to think that my action would have made me that person for him. I will never know. I choose not to dwell on it. A little twinge of guilt remains and I do not want it to get any bigger lest I start to wonder if the thing I didn't do in some way made the man give up and hastened his final years.

Betrayal and the Birdman

Well, Mr Robins, descendant of Noah, pigeon fancier and breeder of champions and avian acrobats, I don't know if it was because of you or something I used to watch my father do, but every morning without fail I feed the wild birds wherever I happen to be.

THE SABBATH RITUALS

THE SUBJECT OF MY RETURNING TO THE CHURCH AND EVEN SUNDAY school, NOW that we were in a new neighbourhood was briefly discussed and even more quickly resolved. It was entirely up to me, my mother said: if I wanted to join the other kids then there was no reason why I shouldn't. But it was a half-hearted option. After all, I was no wayward son that needed to be received into the arms of the waiting Church and the way my mother declared that I was old enough to make up my own mind suggested that she was doing a Pontius Pilate job on the issue. She had long since washed and dried her hands of the Church.

Dad had no more interest than my mother. He did confess that in his childhood he had attended Sunday school, though like myself he did not have to endure it for long. He remembered that one of the teachers there was a Norwegian who had somehow come to live in our 'new' part of the city. He was a strong fundamentalist and an Orangeman. When he started talking about Jesus and the Bible, his thick Scandinavian accent and his urgent evangelism had my father totally lost. But he did remember the Norwegian walking in the 12th of July Orange procession. He said he always wore a kind of vest under his orange sash with quotes from the Bible written in big bold letters on his chest declaring 'You must be saved in the name of Jesus' and on his back were equally bold words about the dire consequences of damnation. He stood head and shoulders above all the other men and 'the silver insignia on his sash were shinier than your mother's brasses,' Dad said. I was intrigued by the image of this great big Norwegian marching head and shoulders above everyone else and preaching the Gospel in an accent so thick and incomprehensible that no one could understand it. Dad called it Double Dutch. That had me really confused. Why did a Norwegian speak Dutch to children who only spoke English? Dad laughed at my perplexity and told me not to worry about Double Dutch or Sunday school as he hadn't, and there were things he learned that Sunday schools couldn't teach. When I questioned him on this he looked at my mother as if seeking approval. He then began a list of his childhood escapades that clearly revealed him as an unsuitable student for Sunday school, and as someone who cared little for any impending damnation that the big Norwegian insisted on proclaiming.

According to my dad, Sundays were days of sheer devilment. 'It was like the devil himself had created this day specially for us to get up to no good and thoroughly enjoy ourselves at the same time.' Dad smiled to himself before explaining his devilment. He and his childhood friends used to climb into the allotments about half a mile from his home while their owners were off at church, and steal eggs from the hen boxes that many of the allotment holders kept. There was one particularly nasty allotment owner whom all of his friends disliked. He was forever complaining about kids playing near his house and some people even claimed that he poisoned their pets. No one could prove it but no one had anything pleasant to say about the man. He, in turn, returned their feeling with his own generally unpleasant demeanour.

On a piece of ground next to the allotments he kept a few goats and chickens and had made a gateway from his allotment to where they grazed. On occasions my dad and his mates would leave the gate open, allowing the goats to come in and start devouring everything on the allotment. Then they hid to watch the old man's anger and confusion when he discovered what had been done. Most Sundays, they raided orchards, went hunting badgers or tried to net wild birds that they could sell to men who bred them with canaries.

This Huckleberry Finn image of my dad pleased me greatly and I had to agree that his Sunday adventures were far more interesting than sitting in Sunday school. I wondered if he ever teased the big Norwegian and if there were any other characters like him. No one, he assured me, ever made fun of the man. But there were other foreigners who came and went in my father's neighbourhood. He remembered Dutch engineers who were brought in to help in reclamation work alongside the shores of Belfast Lough, which was only a few miles from his home. He talked of riding on old sand barges between the shoreline and Dufferin wharf in the shipyard with his dad. He recalled many foreign workers who came and went. 'None of them had much time for religion but most of them had a very radical view of things,' he said. One character that fascinated him was simply known as 'Big Red the atheist' and as my dad put it, 'Many things were said about the man, but few people really knew anything about him.'

He did know that Big Red had been a sailor in the days of steamboats and sailing ships. 'A man who had been places the rest of us never knew existed – and maybe they didn't!' Father smiled. 'He was a fearless character who was afraid of nobody or nothing and he got roaring drunk whenever he had the money to do so. But he bothered nobody and he could sing sea shanties all night long with a big booming voice that had a melody all of its own. No one ever made fun of the Big Red either and few people ever chose to debate his opinions. Some called him a communist or a socialist. Some even dismissed him as being a bit mad in the head. But the only ones who were mad in the head were those halfwits and fanatics who would argue with him about his gospel of the "labouring classes", as he called it. And every one of them went off with their tail between their legs. There was more than a few men like the Big Red. Your grandfather used to call them free-thinkers. But Big Red was special. He had the hand of an artist. He was a skilled cabinet-maker who could carve wood into meticulous patterns. He was famous for the little sailing ships he could make which he had put into bottles. He was also something of a tailor and could sew better than a lot of women.' Dad stopped and thought for a moment before continuing. 'People liked Big Red not because he was bigger and smarter than them. The way he talked about the working man was very impressive!' I got the sense that he was remembering things as much for his own benefit as for mine. When I asked what became of the man, he said there were probably lots of stories and very few of them with any truth. 'He just disappeared,' Dad explained and the way he said it suggested that he was as curious as I was.

I liked the idea of the Big Red and even the Norwegian and I thought of them as being a bit like Desperate Dan from the *Dandy* comics. That idea was only occasioned by their size. Yet they were not only bigger, they were different from other men. Dad told me that the streets he grew up in were inhabited not only by the Dutch workers but by people from the North of England and Scotland. Dad liked the strangers primarily because of the way they spoke. But as he grew older it was because of what they said rather than their manner of speaking. The influence of these immigrants stuck with my father for a long time. If my grandfather used the word 'free-thinkers' to describe them, Father chose to speak of them as being more radical than the local men. I'm sure he valued their radical world view more than he knew.

But to my great sadness those characters had gone, as were the sand barges with their billowing red sails. Most of the allotments were gone, and the fields where he had hunted wild birds and badgers. Because Dad grew up on the outskirts of the city where the countryside was his next-door neighbour, and my mother grew up just across the railway line from him, the country remained in their blood – Mother with her poultices and cures and Father forever bringing home injured animals.

Industrial expansion had pushed the country far away. The ship-yard, the aircraft factory, the engineering works, the ropeworks all needed workers; and workers needed homes. The countryside that my parents knew was now just another urban area laid out with rows of streets, roads, shops and public houses. We didn't need immigrants with their odd way of talking and thinking, for the country folk came tumbling into the city to grab up the work. Everything got smaller and tighter and enclosed. The people who grew up in these streets began to look inwards, not outwards.

What took root was a new set of territorial and tribal loyalties and they supplanted the old rural values which were neither radical nor visionary in the way my father would have understood. But it did speak about destiny. These backstreets were part of the empire and its industries were its backbone. Blood sacrifices had been offered to secure it on the battlefields of France and those who led this new industrial dispensation were determined to imprint that sense of destiny where and whenever it required reinforcement. Its effect on me was, at first, submerged and subtle like all enforced doctrines.

Noticeably there was no St Barnabas dominating the streets. The nearest big church was a few miles away, surrounded by the leafy avenues of the professional classes. The houses and gardens that made up this wealthy enclave were fairytale like. Three of them alone would have swallowed up our whole street of fifty houses. St Donard's where my father's name is supposedly registered as 'missing in action', stood like a bastion at the entrance to this upper-crust world of doctors, barristers, teachers, business owners and, weirdly enough, a piano, singing and elocution teacher. Such finery was obviously not suited to the likes of us who came from further down the road and who had little hope of joining the ranks of 'our betters'.

Practically every street corner in the area where I had come to live contained a mission hall. Evangelical and Pentecostal churches seeded themselves through the backstreets of my youth like a virulent rash. On any Sunday you were never out of earshot of hymn singing. Every one of these gospel halls had a piece of scripture emblazoned across the doorway or else framed behind glass or hung on the outside walls. They were dire warnings and implications about being 'saved' and 'getting right' with Jesus. The consequences of not doing so always hinted at a hideous time in eternity. There were many echoes of the old Norwegian's scriptural vest which must have made him feel at home. These quotations never declared outright just what the 'judgment' would be. Hint or suggestion screamed at you in bold block capitals from the tiny church walls. This had the effect of reinforcing a sense of declared belonging. You were either 'saved' and part of the elect or you were 'damned' and 'outcast from the fold'. In a crude sense this meant that if you were born and bred in the working-class areas of the Bible belt of East Belfast, you were a 'Prod' (Protestant) and proud of it.

Needless to say, I never went into any of these establishments though I was curious about those who did. The women always wore hats and the men carried bibles as big as lunchboxes. The congregations came and went from their churches, all of them marked by a collective expression of inertia; even their body movements seemed languid and lifeless. Mother remarked that a good dose of syrup of figs would do them more good than all the communion bread in the world. She added that 'people who are interested in other people's sins either have too many or none of their own, in which case church is the right place for them!' To me, the sound of the hymn singing seemed as turgid and chilly as the small dark halls it came from and the people with their air of well-scrubbed piety only hung about the church for a few minutes and then they were gone. It was as if they had shared some secret and didn't want to expose it or themselves to the scrutiny of the street.

If he didn't have to work, Dad could be found early on Sunday morning before the rest of us were awake bent over the ironing board in his vest and pyjama trousers. He was happy to iron his own shirts, delicately damping the collar and cuffs with a solution of water and powdered starch. 'A Windsor knot demanded a starched collar' was his motto. He was so meticulous that he would stand in front of the mirror sliding the two ends of the tie up and down across the back of his neck until he got the lengths of the thinner end and the broader front piece just right, so that the bottom of the tie would just touch the waist of his trousers. If for some reason this perfect measure was not achieved after the tie had been knotted, it was rapidly removed and replaced by a new one. A 'Windsor' should never be attempted twice with the same tie, as the first attempt would have left it so creased that a perfect flowing triangular knot could never be obtained. First, it should be pressed again under damp brown paper and left to sit for ten minutes. My father explained that a proper dress shirt should be comfortable or it would never be smart, and he showed me how I should be able to put my index and middle finger between my neck and the collar of the buttoned-up shirt without choking myself. It was an absolute must that a Windsor knot was worn only with a cut away collar. Not all these sartorial rules were rigidly laid down. They were simply something I should know, like the skill of tying shoelaces.

A pair of clothes brushes came out from a box in his wardrobe only on Sundays. With small neat flicks he would brush down the jacket like a pony he was grooming. Then he would lay the trousers out on the ironing board, unfold a sheet of brown paper over them, splash the paper with flicks of water from a bowl, and iron a perfect crease. It wasn't vanity or flamboyance with him: he had no idea of personal elegance. He simply wanted to 'do the job right', as he said. I suppose it was a ritual hangover from his days in the RAF and I have a sneaking suspicion that he joined this branch of the armed services because, amongst other reasons, the uniform was smarter.

However, his fastidiousness fell apart when it came to 'doing up' his cuffs with cuff links. He was utterly hopeless. He could pick his way through the thousands of wires in a telephone exchange box, and strip the plastic coating of the finest copper wires with effortless speed and precision, but he could not manage cuff links! For the most part they remained in their box for funerals, weddings or 'the Twelfth', that curious time in the calendar when Ulstermen affirmed and celebrated their Protestantism.

Those of us sinners who shunned the offer of salvation got through Sundays as best we could. The day seemed to crank itself down on all of us with silence and tedium. There was an air of obligation about Sunday, which many people referred to as the Sabbath, and there was something rabbinical in the air. It was full of don'ts like an invisible addendum to the Ten Commandments. The Sabbath was not for reading newspapers or watching TV. Even the radio was switched off in many homes. Playing records was a minor abomination, as was playing in the park and there were many more 'do nots' on this holy day of restriction. However, they were for the 'holy Joes' and didn't mean much in our house.

If the weather was fine we would walk up the leafy avenues of the rich and Mother would admire their well-appointed homes. I enjoyed these walks. Sundays were accompanied by a sullen quiet that descended on the streets where I lived. But in the big wide tree-lined avenues the quiet had a different quality. It was peaceful, not oppressive and sometimes it felt strangely fragile and precious. But if we went to the country for the day this fragility seemed to seep away and then Sunday became special. It was as if we had not only left the streets behind but had stepped out of time altogether. The leafy avenues held echoes of that timelessness: they had become temporal passageways that flicked open for a few hours on a summer Sunday.

Sunday afternoon strolls and bus rides to the end of the line where the country began were the exception rather than the rule. Mostly me and my mates hung about the shop at the corner of our street and listened in wonder to the older lads who had left school and were apprentices in the shipyard or engineering works. That was another rite of passage that awaited me; to be entered into the ranks of apprenticeship was the first rung on the ladder of manhood. But their stories did not convince me, or entice me. In fact they scared me off – their shipyard was not the one I imagined my grandfather having worked in.

We gathered at the street corner outside Joe's shop which sold everything anybody wanted and if you couldn't afford it he simply wrote it up in a big notebook and you paid him when you could. Joe never opened on the Lord's Day and all us fallen angels hung about his shop front listening to the lads who now were working men. Their stories were full of bravado and bluster, each trying to outdo the other. They all smoked with great style, arguing about the best brands. There was one kind of cheap cigarette for work and another for Friday and Saturday night. Girls liked fellas who smoked flashy cigarettes. When they boasted about their weekend exploits I listened intently, my churning stomach full of anxiety. They talked about drinking, dancing, fighting and 'lumbering' girls all in the same breath. Occasionally they would turn and look at their reflection in the window of Joe's shop and slick back their Brylcreemed hair like they were all Elvis. One of them had this special way of grooming. He would comb back the side of his head with his left hand, smoothing down what he had combed with his right, then he would swiftly comb back the hair on the top of his head. That done, he slid the long-tailed comb into his back pocket or breast pocket and then he showed his style. He looked straight on at his image in the glass for a second or two, then ever so slightly inclined his head to the right, then flipped it, with an equally slight movement upward, and paused to peruse himself. In one move-ment he slowly dropped his head as the fingers of his left hand eased deep into the folds of combed-back hair and re-emerged pulling his hair over his forehead. The effect was to leave him with the sides of his head slicked back in greasy comb lines while the hair at the front tumbled down over his forehead in a mess of waves and curls. He would look at himself again then make a comment about the girl he picked up at the dance the previous night. That invariably led to a litany of stories from his mates about their own sexual exploits. There was talk of the number of love bites they had left on some girl's neck, how far they got, whether they had groped real flesh or only handled 'it' through their partner's clothes. Being allowed to rub your knee between her legs was a sure sign that she was going 'to give you it' later. But getting a girl to put her hands between your legs was a sure sign that you knew what to do with girls. All this sexual activity happened either up an alley at the back of a dance hall or cinema.

I was dumbfounded but tried to remember all the moves for future reference. It was all very worrying. First you had to get the groping order right. Then you had to ensure you had a steel comb with a long skinny handle which could double as a knife. You had to make sure other fellas saw it as you combed your hair so they would know you were 'tough as fuck!' Then there was all the drinking and smoking that had to be done, especially with the right kind of quality cigarettes, and also you had to have a fancy Ronson gas lighter or one of those flip-top wheel and flint lighters like all Americans had. Your trousers had to be tapered to show the right amount of shoe and you had to order a suit, hand made from Burton's. The list of prerequisites seemed endless. There was a way to dress, a way to drink and a way to grope a girl, and they were learned outside Joe's corner shop on the Sabbath! These life sciences had all the importance of the biblical tablets handed down to Moses, and me and my mates fretted over them more than any lecture handed down from the pulpit.

It wasn't only anxiety about my forthcoming sexual adolescence that bothered me. After all, I could simply avoid all that by avoiding girls; the idea of my future apprenticeship concerned me more. I couldn't just decide not to work. Becoming a tradesman and having 'served my time' to acquire such hallowed status was what every boy was supposed to aim for. In the ethos of East Belfast, becoming an apprentice was a sure sign that you were on the road to a secular salvation. It would give you status and provide a firm foundation for your adult life. Acquiring a trade in a place like the shipyard was another badge of belonging and most of my mates accepted this idea without much question. I was not so sure; and the Sunday afternoon sessions outside Joe's shop confirmed my unease.

I listened to the lads who were already serving their time in the yard. To me the word 'yard' related to the tiny back yard of our house. I knew the shipyard was much bigger and its hugeness scared me. One of the lads, Geordie Little, boasted that he worked in the biggest shipyard in the world with an army of over 40,000 workers. Many a morning I had watched fragments of this army scurry off to work in their navy boiler suits and donkey jackets. In the faded photos my grandfather had kept, the faces that stared back at me were in some way familiar, and I could imagine stories about each one of those anonymous men. The workers I witnessed slouching off to work each morning were a different breed. Maybe it was the uniformity of their clothes: the navy and black overalls and jackets erased individual characteristics. And when Geordie spoke about the continual ear-splitting din that echoed throughout the miles of dockland, I thought not of an army of working men but of beetles scrambling through the great hulks of half-finished ships, just like the picture in the long-lost scrapbook.

Geordie explained that it took him 'months and months' to get used to the noise. When he first entered the shipyard the over- whelming noise had made him feel smaller than he actually was. 'You had to get tough real fast, because everybody shouted at you and you couldn't tell whether people were asking you something or telling you something or were just being nasty old bollocks because they didn't like the look of you!' For months Geordie explained how deafening it was and then revealed that it was only when he began shouting back at people that he stopped being afraid of the place and, more curiously, that he also stopped hearing the dreadful noise of the place. Geordie's solution to the problem of communication was simple: as everyone shouted, the only way to know what they wanted, if indeed they wanted anything, was to watch their face. If you didn't like the way it looked at you, you simply shouted back, and walked off. 'Once you learned to shout back people left you alone,' he said knowingly. 'There are some old fucking bastards in the place that just love trying to frighten the shit out of new apprentices but you soon get to know them so you stay out of their way or ignore them until they spot some other new kid to torment.' Such language was not fit for the Sabbath but outside Joe's shop on a Sunday anything was permissible.

The more I listened to Geordie and the others brag about the hardships of the yard, the less I was enamoured of it. The yard had its own disciplines and internal codes of conduct which you had to abide by. There were invisible boundaries you did not cross and unwritten laws that you dared not break. Coming to terms with these things was not submission so much as affirmation of confraternity and belonging. But the image clashed with the romance I had built up around my grandfather.

The hard industrial ethic combined with bullying and bragging in the stories of Geordie and his mates and I wasn't sure it was something I was up to, ready for, or even wanted to be part of. Geordie confirmed this in his own unconscious way. I noticed that if he was talking about his weekend conquests the burning cigarette would be held at the corner of his mouth. But when it came to stories of work, he smoked his cigarette down to the butt. He adopted a curious way of holding this last half-inch of cigarette. His right hand would be turned inward in a loose claw with the butt held reversed between his index and middle finger, the lit end almost burning his palm. Obviously there were two ways of smoking: one for womanizing and one for working. One was open for anything it could get its hands on and one half closed, like a defensive fist.

BRANDS FOR THE BURNING

IAN PAISLEY WASN'T MUCH OLDER THAN GEORDIE AND THE OTHER apprentices, Billy Hoey and Sammy Stothers when he arrived in Belfast, but he had apprenticed himself to the Gospel, and the worldly ways of Geordie, Billy and Sammy would have been anathema to the young firebrand teacher who became Pastor of the Ravenhill Evangelical Church, a tiny side-street gospel hall just across the Lagan that marked the gateway to East Belfast. It is said that at his installation as pastor another Salvationist preacher prayed with the congregation that God would give his young servant 'the tongue of an old cow'. The old preacher knew well that a cow's tongue could be as sharp as a razor and saw in the young Paisley 'a brand from the burning' – a young preacher whose colourful imagery and religious invective would surely have skinned alive any sinner and left him standing shivering and pitiful before the throne of the Almighty.

But it wasn't only individual salvation that the evangelical preacher pursued. Like his master, he cast his nets wider, for he was after bigger fish. With the zealot's enthusiasm, he set about to root out Protestant apostasy and redeem the backsliders from the road to perdition. There was but one truth for all men and that was the literal word of the Bible, the holy scriptural truth. Those who didn't believe it were liars and charlatans in the service of Satan. Chief amongst them in Paisley's perverse hagiography was the Pope, the arch-fiend and Antichrist, the old serpent and idolater. Those who followed him were at best to be pitied – but were nevertheless to be purged.

But the preacher was not a lone voice crying in the wilderness. There were many who found comfort and assurance in his sermons. The power of his sulphurous tongue lashing out vituperous condemnations bewitched them and held them in thrall. It uplifted them and made them feel like the chosen people of God. Paisley once famously declared: 'God has a people in his province, God has a purpose for this province and this plant of Protestantism sown here . . .' He wasn't quite clear on the specifics of this purpose, but it was enough. It gave a scarifying religious legitimacy to that sense and need for belonging. It also fuelled a plague-like sense of exclusion, and of hostility towards anyone and everything that did not belong that worked itself out in slogans painted on the gabled walls of the streets I had come to live in. No Surrender, No Pope Here, Up the Queen and Fuck the Pope were a kind of shorthand endorsing the street myths that grew up around the Fenians, Taigs and Papist bastards who were beyond the pale. This 'other side' lived under a cloud of utter delusion. To some zealots, they were waiting like a pack of hyenas to bring down 'this province and plant of Protestantism,' as Paisley defined his homeland. To his followers 'Those who are not with us are against us,' became a battle cry and it brooked no dissent.

I was told that you could spot a Fenian a mile off, but no one explained how. 'You know them by their eyes,' I was told but what was the dead giveaway in their eyes? They were unclean, had homes like rubbish tips and they lived like pigs. If you kissed or even touched a Catholic you'd be diseased. The mass was devil worship. The Virgin Mary was a harlot, and consequently so were all Catholic women. And so the list went on, becoming more scatological and obscene. It is amazing how perverse the imagination can become when it is given some kind of sanction, however dubious. Even the Pope had cloven feet and had a tail under his robes, like all priests. Nuns wore black and never married because they had sex with the devil and no one wanted them after that.

All this adolescent fantasizing washed over me for two reasons. My parents dismissed it and warned me against listening to such nonsense. I am sure they were quietly anxious about stories I might have heard but was too afraid to repeat. When I asked my mother what a 'Jezebel' was she rounded on me, demanding to know what I had been told about 'Jezebels'. When I sheepishly explained that someone had described one of our neighbours as a Jezebel she ordered me never to use that word about anyone, no matter who they were. 'You weren't brought up with a foul tongue in your head, so don't be repeating the muck that comes out of other people's mouths.' With that commandment the matter of the Jezebels was closed for good.

The second reason why I am sure those curious and colourful stories did not affect me much was the unreality of their claims. I never saw any nuns, or priests. I didn't know much of what happened in the mission hall in the next street, never mind the black mass that took place in a Catholic church. I had nowhere or no one on which to hang these stories so they came and they went, curious and confusing but as insubstantial as smoke in the wind.

Those intimidating slogans painted on the gable wall at the top of our street were insubstantial too. Because I passed them every day they faded into the brickwork like ghost writing – except when they were newly painted each year and the Fuck word rebounded

off the wall and into my face: the Pope was fucked and so were
Fenian gets. The words 'Queen and Country' were elevated like a
holy oath and Ulster blocked out in red white and blue was equated
with nirvana. 'Ulster will fight and Ulster will be right' bequeathed
heroism to the 'Loyal Sons of Ulster'.

To me, these were no more than words on a wall that came and
went with the seasons. All I wondered was when they were painted
and by whom. They seemed to appear magically overnight. The
occasion which brought out all this slogan writing and fertilized
the stories about Catholics was the imminent approach of the 12th
of July, a date sacrosanct in the calendar of Protestant Ulster. I loved
this time for the spontaneous buzz of activity it brought about. It
was a festival that excited everyone. As kids, we thought we owned
the place.

Union Jacks were hoisted at every house, bunting was strung
across the street. Some streets, more caught up in the fever, erected
arches across the street entrance and hung portraits of the Queen,
along with images of William of Orange and quotations from the
Bible and from Lord Edward Carson, the founding father of the
state. Kerbstones for miles around were painted red, white and blue.
The good fairy waved her magic wand and everyone went mad.

The big event for us kids was the building of a giant bonfire
which we all called the bonefire. From the beginning of June our
neighbourhood was as animated as an ant colony. Every kid spent
every daylight hour collecting material for the 'bonefire' which
would be set alight on the night of the 11th of July, as late as possible,
when it was dark.

For weeks, gangs of youths would descend on any open ground
where trees might grow and would hack them to pieces with blunt
axes and rusty carpentry saws. We would drag the severed branches
through backstreets and along main roads to the site of the fire.

When we weren't chopping trees, we trawled the neighbourhood knocking on doors and demanding 'anything for the bonefire'. Right up until the eleventh hour on the Eleventh night, this ant army of youngsters would be on the move, shouldering old wardrobes, beds, mattresses, rotten back doors, sideboards, car tyres, fruit crates, orange boxes – everything and anything that burned. We were soldiers and warriors caught up in a great campaign. The towering mountain of timber and other combustibles was a kind of gigantic talisman we worshipped and guarded. Ultimately we would sacrifice it all to the fire God. To us it was no child's play: this was very serious business. We were commandos on a mission. It was life and death stuff.

But soldiers had to survive, and when we were not collecting wood or standing guard over 'the boney', we would be knocking on doors asking 'A penny for the Pope'. The Pope was, of course, a scarecrow creature made up from old clothes stuffed with cardboard and rags. None of us knew what a Pope looked like, except maybe that he dressed in white. Very rarely did our Pope dress in white. Cast-off working men's clothes were a long way from surplices! The only thing that declared our mannequin held holy office was the crudely painted plaque hung across his chest stating simply 'The Pope'.

One year, one of the kids from our boney stole a hat from the school nativity play which he insisted looked just like the Pope's hat. It would obviously help to make a very impressive guy and should enable us to collect a lot of money. I am not so sure how much money our Pope and his hat made us, but to this day I wonder at the young boy who had the foresight to steal the hat from a Christmas play, keep it hidden away for six months, only to hawk round the streets and finally burn along with the papal effigy on top of a bonfire.

One of the doors we knocked on always brought the same response. As four or five of us stood around the effigy, which we usually wheeled around in a pram to demand money, this man's response was always the same: 'No red socks and no rope, no penny for your Pope!' It was easy enough to put a noose on the Pope, but red socks were rarely available. It was worth the effort, for then the man would throw silver sixpences into our collection box. One time I overheard him mumble something about thirty pieces of silver and when I asked what he had said, one of my friends answered 'Who cares!' as they gloated over the silver shining among the copper coins and brassy threepenny bits. 'That man hates the Pope better than anybody,' one friend declared. 'Sure he's given us a half a crown and more!' Our Pope made his rounds of the streets several times before he was hoisted with great gusto to the top of the huge pyre to await his roasting.

The papal collection was mostly spent on fish and chips with enough salt and pepper and sauce to marinate the back of your throat instantly. Lashings of lemonade and occasionally bottles of beer were purchased to ease the digestion and soothe the stinging vinegar. Cigarettes, matches and candles were stocked up on. The small change went on potato crisps, sweets, chocolate, and frequently comics.

The important thing about every 'boney' was the huts that were erected from the jumble of broken furniture, old doors and anything else that could be used to create an enclosed space, most often at the edge of, but built into the tower of timber. They were fabulous places, rank with the smell of damp wood, old sofas and mattresses. We lit them up with penny candles and paraffin lamps, creating a cavern which glowed a golden yellow in the dark mountain of firewood. As the weeks passed our hideaways took on the odour of greasy chips, tobacco, stale beer and wet clothes. The hut was furnished from the household debris that we had been given: even old, faded photos of the long-dead relatives of people we didn't know were hung in their broken frames about the makeshift walls.

These provided shelter but they were also a kind of guardroom. There was incredible rivalry between the streets about who would have the biggest 'boney' on the Eleventh night. Raiding parties were sent out in the early hours to steal their neighbours' firewood or, more spitefully, to set alight their fire before the appointed hour. So these huts housed a round the clock gang of lookouts and defenders. The weaponry to ward off any attack was frightening: old rusty axes and claw hammers, brush poles with kitchen knives bound to them and wielded like bayonets, studded belts, bicycle chains and fearsome catapults with a ready supply of small stones (or occasionally marbles) were all held at the ready. So consuming was the need to protect our great heap of timber that we were permitted to stay out all night 'on guard'. There were innumerable skirmishes with the other streets. But it was more to tease and challenge than to destroy.

If ever there was a benign meaning to the term 'dens of inequity', then the 'boney' huts were it. Things happened in these dens that could happen nowhere else. Here the warriors learned to smoke and swear. Girls were never allowed to stay out all night. In their absence, the older lads boasted about the girls they had lumbered or groped. The female anatomy was discussed in great detail. Most of the lads knew little or nothing but spoke like learned professors! There were long debates on whether some of the boney money should be spent on dirty magazines like *The Naturist*. Great games of dare were dreamed up in the candlelight and had to be carried out by a specific time. Failure to do so meant being barred from the hut. Cards were drawn to determine which unlucky character had to face the challenge or be ostracized from the brotherhood of the den. Orders were given on who should raid the allotments. Decisions were taken on who would be deployed to distract the attention of shopkeepers while the others helped themselves to whatever they could get their hands on. Instructions were given on how to bring a fight to a quick conclusion and ensure that no one would want to tackle you again. The details were gruesome and involved everything from ramming a pencil into your enemy's ear to stabbing them in certain parts of the body with sharpened aluminum-tail combs. There were explanations of how to make a knuckle-duster from a rolled-up newspaper and threepenny bits or how to make 'fighting shoes' by packing the toe space of shoes with wet newspaper wrapped around ball bearings. 'Sink your boot into somebody's balls with a pair of these and ya won't have to worry about them getting up for a week at least.'

So it went on; the fascination with the human torso seemed endless. Whether it was male or female, it was all about muscle and conquest. Inside the mountain of wood, a testosterone tornado was spinning and raging. When that particular fire went out there were plenty of other stories to fill the long cold night. Stories of family problems that would never have seen the light of day but for the confessional of the 'boney' hut. There were funny stories and sad ones. There were amazing ones. On the nights in the ramshackle room at the heart of the great fire pile they were somehow sanctified. It was a special place away from the world where you could learn forbidden things, use language that your mother would cut your tongue out for, listen to incredible stories that the atmosphere of the hut made real. Here we were utterly free from all constraints. In the hut, you could be bad, bold and utterly disgusting; but more than that, you could be heroic. It was a real place of belonging.

Then came the eleventh hour on the Eleventh night and the atmosphere was fraught and electric. Everyone came and circled

the waiting fire. Children in pyjamas, babies in blankets clamped
in the arms of their parents. Old folks brought chairs to sit on.
Men and some women spurred on by alcohol sang and danced and
we, the kids who had tended, protected and even found sanctuary
in it, crawled over the waiting pyre stuffing paraffin-soaked rags
into it. We poured gallons of the stuff around its tattered petticoats
and then torched it, to the hysterical roar of the gathered street. It
never failed to ignite. Massive plumes of black smoke bellowed into
the night sky which by now was glowing red from all the other
fires burning across the city.

As a young boy, I wallowed in this occasion, oblivious to what
it meant. I had no time to worry about symbols. I loved the sheer
exuberant freedom of it all. By inclination, I was a quiet kid; toughness or aggression frightened me. This childhood characteristic
made me stand out from my contemporaries. But in the weeks
approaching the Eleventh night I was a warrior, wild and free and
savage. I was one of them. I distinctly remember standing on top
of the woodpile as it was set alight beneath me. I could hear the
crowd scream for me to climb off quickly before I was engulfed. I
looked down at them for a moment: they seemed far below me
and their anxious voices almost inaudible. I was near the top of
the flaming mountain and didn't want to come down. I was more
intoxicated than the drunkards or the dancers below me. I climbed
higher and the roaring of the people rose with me. Up past the
Pope himself I went, disappearing and reappearing from the smoke.
I didn't know what I was doing or why. I was aware of the flames
and could feel the wood collapse as the timbers far beneath me
charred and turned to ash. People were still screaming for me to
come down while some of my friends cried out, 'Go on Keenie, top
it!' encouraging me to climb to the summit of the bonfire. Maddened
by the atmosphere, I grabbed the Pope by his collar and dragged

him upwards with me. The crowd yelled even louder at the insanity of my daring. Up I went with the Pope to the very pinnacle, where I planted him to the noisy delight of the crowd below. 'That's right, Keenie, make him suffer!' shouted someone.

I looked down and slowly took in the upturned faces. I knew most of them, yet suddenly felt I didn't know any of them. I felt something like raw resentment and anger. Then I felt real panic and confusion. It was a sense of the danger, but it was combined with a sense of being empty. 'Fuck the Pope!' I shouted but the smoke caught my throat and my eyes were stinging like they were bleeding. I panicked again. I couldn't see my way down. Then I heard a voice calling out from an upstairs window, pleading, 'Brian Keenan, get down, oh please, Brian Keenan get down now, quickly.' I recognized the red hair and then the face of a girl called Ann who lived in the next street to me. I fancied her but never had the courage to do anything about it. Without hesitation I leapt down the piled wood. At the mid-section I jumped off the fire and on to a yard wall, ran along the top of it then shimmied down at the opening for the back door. Someone shouted that my ma and da were on their way and I'd better clear off before they arrived. I was in a dilemma. I wanted to go and see red-haired Ann who had got my hopes up by her display of anxiety. But I knew I was in big trouble. I had to get back home before my parents returned: that way I could tell them the fool on the bonfire wasn't me, and they would believe it. I was too sensible and shy to be a mad hero, much less a Protestant one dragging the Pope to his final immolation.

The next morning, the streets looked and smelt like the aftermath of an air raid. The fire had become a huge crater of ashes. It lay smouldering. One or two kids tossed some left-over timber on to it. The streets were silent. All the blinds were pulled. It was as if the place had been evacuated. All my heroics of the previous evening had blown away too. However much my antics may have excited the crowd of onlookers and even encouraged the red-headed Ann Moore to see me in a new light, it never went much further. For a few weeks we exchanged lingering glances, each waiting for the other to break the impasse, but it never happened and I quietly crawled back into my shell of reserve.

The thing was, I never plucked up the courage to pursue my instincts with girls mainly because I wasn't popular with the boys. My lack of popularity wasn't because of anything I did or even said. It was how I looked. I was one of those unfortunate kids who had a very big and very prominent set of front teeth. That set me apart and earned me nicknames such as Bugs Bunny, Ratso, Fangs and Vampire Face. Mostly I learned to accept or ignore it. But the nicknames had side-effects. I was never picked to play on the five-a-side football team; in fact in any team sport I was begrudgingly the last person picked. Indeed, I never developed enough enthusiasm to be competitive or to join in at anything. Sometimes I might hang about briefly, waiting to be invited to take part in some group activity but most of the time I was happy with my own company. It was only occasionally that the name-calling was vicious, and usually this was some bully at school whom I didn't know but who seized on the opportunity to inflate his ego by demolishing mine. With my street friends the nickname was applied out of habit and usually without any malign intent. I learned to live with it and for the most part, I didn't hear it. That is, until puberty came creeping up and the subject of girls began to take up more and more of my pals' conversation. Now it wasn't simply the nickname but the stigma associated with it. 'Who would want to kiss you in case you bit their lip off!' The laughter and the expression of mock horror on the faces of my accusers was more hurtful than the names, but I never showed it. I acquired an invisible shell about myself that protected me but from which I occasionally found myself looking out longingly.

I am sure my mother was aware of my predicament for often she would repeat to me how 'sticks and stones may break my bones but names will never hurt me'. Sometimes she was a bit more blunt: 'You don't mind what they say for there's not a half-ounce of brains between the lot of them!' At other times she really let loose. 'Every time they say something, you just tell them you can't hear what they're saying because of the dummy-tit sticking out of their mouths.' Some of her put-downs were even more robust but she reserved these for older boys. 'You just tell him he should change his nappy more often for his mouth is full of . . .' She always omitted the last word and looked me knowingly in the eye. I rarely took her advice, as I tended to shy away from confrontation. The one occasion I did use the retort about dirty nappies I remember well.

It was a Saturday night and one of the older lads from the next street made some cutting comment about my appearance, ending his snide remark about my inability to get a girl with a line from 'Little Red Riding Hood'. 'Oh boy! What big teeth you have.' Everyone tittered at him and looked at me. The youth was an apprentice some five or six years older than me. Most of us only knew him to see. Somewhere in my head I was thinking that he didn't know me enough to be making fun of me, and then I heard my mother's words coming out of my mouth: 'Away home and get your nappy changed, ya big lig, for you're talking shite!'

Instantly there was silence, followed by a burst of loud laughter. I was frightened by what I had said to my tormentor more than I was of him. I turned to walk off as brazenly as I could, expecting the big lad to come running after me and give me a severe kick in the backside and a scalp across the head. But it never happened. The laughter that was turned on him held him back. I could hear him call after me, 'Go on, you Goofy-faced wee bastard!' Whatever Pyrrhic victory my defiance had given me, I never repeated it. Everywhere I saw him I avoided him. So in the end, he really had the victory.

However, my childhood isolation was not only conditioned by my buck teeth. I suspect that the fact that my father was on 24-hour call-out to work added to it. And my sister was eight years older and not much interested in my childhood world. Mother was a fighter, not a talker and I hadn't the temperament for any solutions she might offer. In any case, I am sure that in working-class families the quality of parent–child communication was very different from today. Adults and children didn't talk about things. That's the way it was, and you got on with it.

Quite often, on a Saturday my dad would take me to the cinema in town: the one that showed only Disney cartoon features. I hated cartoons. Their forced unreality and childish slapstick bored me. Dad on the other hand adored them and laughed heartily at the characters' antics. If it was his way of showing me that Bugs Bunny was no fool and probably smarter than the whole Disney menagerie, then it didn't work for me. Disneyland was pathetic and I suffered it in silence.

Afterwards we would go to Woolworth's where Dad would buy his favourite sweets – a bag of liquorice Pontefract cakes and a few bags of different kinds of nuts. Then it was off to Smithfield, an enclosed street market that was more like a corner of Casablanca. You could buy anything in Smithfield. All kinds of people from all over the city came here. It was a world unto itself. Packed to the rooftops with second-hand furniture, memorabilia, record and book stalls, antiques, curios, and oddities of every description stood waiting in this treasure house. I suffered the Disney movies just to be brought here. Every week there was loads of new stuff to look at.

Dad and I always went to the place that sold the war memorabilia where the shopkeeper looked like a cross between a gypsy, Shylock the Jew and a retired hit man from the Mafia. A marked foreign accent added to his allure. But he never smiled, and he scowled slightly if you refused to pay his prices. Then it was off to the bookshops. Dad always bought a few second-hand paperback westerns or war stories and let me choose some comics. I liked *Creepy Worlds* or some fantasy stories for their sense of another world and their fabulous illustrations.

Music flowed inside the big shed-like structure that housed the market – Lena Horne, Nina Simone and Mahalia Jackson poured their heart out alongside R & B masters like Muddy Waters, Sonny Terry and Brownie Magee, Ray Charles, and Booker T. For me, Sonny Boy Williamson's moody harmonica outshone everything. The names of the musicians and the music that backed their songs added to the fantastic otherworldliness of the market. Many years later, I realized that my father brought me here mainly because I didn't play much with the other kids at the weekends. But I knew that he liked it here too. Though he never said it, I just knew.

Anyway, I was happy in my isolation. I had no sense of being lonely. Nor did I seek companionship much. I was happy with our dog, Rex, which I had selected from an RSPCA kennel. It took me weeks to cajole my mother. Neither she nor my father could understand why I insisted the dog must come from a dogs' home. Dad called it a 'bitsa' dog as it had the look of a creature that was made up from bits of different creatures. Still, I liked it and it loved me and that was enough.

As I look back on it, I see my shyness and chosen isolation as a place apart for me. A timeless space where the imagination flourished, and, like the images from my comic books, it was a magical vacillating inner space jam-packed with characters from imaginary worlds. Occasionally, on Sunday afternoons, I would sit and try to copy the landscapes of my fantasy comics on the remnants of old wallpaper rolls that my mother kept for covering our school-books with. I suppose I was like my dog. A bit of a mixed bag. A young boy who lost himself in drawing pictures of other worlds, who listened entranced to Nina Simone singing her haunting version of 'Strange Fruit' and who was shy of girls when all his mates were experiencing the first flush of testosterone. Sports never interested me. I was happy enough not to be picked to play.

It is hardly surprising, then, that I should have slipped through school almost unnoticed. I enjoyed learning new things but hadn't much enthusiasm beyond that, except for books. I liked reading and was far ahead of the rest of my class; for me, it was a way not to be bothered by the rest of the world. So it is odd that my first introduction to real books should be a reluctant one. I was around nine at the time and attending Avoniel primary school. For no reason at all my teacher, Mr Burnison called out across the class, 'Well, Keenan, I think it is time you went and got yourself a proper book in the library!' The announcement at first stunned me, then I felt myself getting smaller with fear and embarrassment as my classmates turned and stared at me in prolonged silence. The library in my school comprised an old Welsh dresser which stood at the end of the upstairs corridor, next to the classroom of the kids who were in their final primary school year. Only they were allowed to use the library. I had another two years to go before I would be in that class. So this singular honour of inviting me to access the 'library' should have encouraged me. It was quite the reverse – I had enough problems being singled out for my appearance without this. Mr Burnison ordered the class to be quiet and get on with their work while he called me up to leave the room and visit the library. I skulked up the aisle, my face on fire.

I looked up at the twenty-seven books that made up our library. There may have been more in the cupboards in the corner section; I didn't know. 'Well, Keenan what do you fancy?' I strained to read the titles on the book spines. The Welsh dresser looked colossal and I felt as if this great altar of words was about to fall down and crush me. Part of me wished that it would. While I stood staring, the teacher brought over a chair for me to stand on. Up close, the books looked like bricks. 'Come on, Keenan, we haven't got all day!' Burnison's soft voice encouraged me. I wished the day would disappear. I dreaded walking back to the classroom book in hand. I felt like a condemned man. The teacher might as well have been asking me if I had any last words for the world! The titles on the spines were a blur. But one did stand out: *The Call of the Wild* by Jack London. Nervously, I slid it from the shelf. The dust jacket was faded and worn but there was an image of a dog standing proud in a snowy landscape, lit up by a big moon, and in the background a shadowy forest at the edge of which was a shadowy pack of wolves with vicious yellow eyes. I suddenly thought how dad's name was Jack like the author's and though the dog on the cover looked nothing like my own, I liked the look of it. It stood defiant and proud even though it wasn't a wolf.

I climbed down off the chair. The teacher glanced at the book. 'It may be a little difficult for you, Keenan, but it's a great adventure story. Try it, and see how you get on.' As we walked back I began to understand why the books had looked like bricks. The one in my hand felt so heavy. When we entered the classroom again, I saw all my friends' faces look up at me. Their eyes looked just like the wolves'! Sheepishly I went to my seat. I shoved the dead weight of the book quickly into my bag and fixed my eyes on the page in front of me, repeating the seven times tables like a magic spell that would make the moment vanish.

On the way home a few lads made some remark about being teacher's pet and some others put their hands over their eyes as though they were looking through binoculars. 'Booksy Bugsy,' they hissed laughing at my demeanour. But it evaporated quickly; as far as they were concerned, I was welcome to my books. It was too much like homework to them.

I left the book for some days before taking it up, and when I did it was no longer a dead weight in my hands. It swept me away utterly. Every day for several weeks, I was lost in the author's freezing wilderness. The story of the mongrel Buck incited a frenzy in me that other books rarely have. Buck was an odd creature, part St Bernard and part sheep-dog, who lived an indolent life in northern California. But Buck's life was changed for ever when he was stolen and sold as a sled dog. He endured brutal beatings and extreme hardship. From the jaded heart of civilization, Buck is tossed into the terrifying heart of the primordial world. He learns to survive the freezing wilderness, to devour raw meat, to kill and to be forever alert even in the deepest recess of sleep. But Buck learns more than the means of survival and he becomes more than a superb sled dog and a loyal companion. The howls of the wolves he hears at night burn deep into him. After savaging and killing men who murdered his master his only refuge is the wilderness that fosters his wildness. Buck finally runs with the wolves and becomes the pack leader. Every night, in my sleep I could hear old Buck howling across the frozen snows.

As the weeks sped by I cared little about the fun my friends were having and I cared even less about the name-calling, or that I was excluded from many of their games. They could play football if they wished. They could go and rob orchards or draw up plans for stealing chocolate bars and orange juice from the corner shop. Such dangers were tedious to me and if they likened me to idiot cartoon creatures, I refused to hear them. Even if it hurt me! But their jeering was an echo, for I was far off in another place. While they were kicking a football or stealing apples from a tree, I was running at the head of a wolf pack in a wilderness that made back-garden orchards seem like toffee-apple land. Many years later, when I read C.S. Lewis's 'Narnia' books, I thought that his wilderness behind the wardrobe was another toffee-apple land. Even Lewis Carroll's Wonderland was a frilly fantasy that I couldn't abide. *The Call of the Wild* had got into my blood in ways that even then I didn't understand.

A decade later as a young man of nineteen, I re-read Jack London's masterpiece more in love, this time, with the author than his creation. And I underlined these words:

> There is an ecstasy that marks the survival of life and beyond which life cannot rise . . . And such is the paradox of living. This ecstasy comes when one is most alive and it comes as a complete forgetfulness that one is alive . . . and it came to Buck, leading the pack, sounding the wolf cry, straining after the food that was alive and that fled swiftly before him through the moonlight.

It's almost half a century since I picked up that book. Sometimes I think it picked me. But I have been running after Buck and scenting that ecstasy ever since.

ON THE ROAD

I WAS TEN WHEN MY YOUNGER SISTER ELAINE WAS BORN. I DON'T remember much about the event except that our house seemed to be constantly full of neighbours. It didn't bother me much as I could escape to my books and comics. I had acquired quite a few from my Saturday visits to Smithfield market. Amongst them were a few 'Biggles' books, *The Famous Five*, *Black Beauty*, *David Copperfield*, *Kidnapped*, *Treasure Island*, and several more, all of which I have long since forgotten. Except, perhaps, Robert Louis Stevenson's works, *The Adventures of Huckleberry Finn* and *Tom Sawyer* and *20,000 Leagues under the Sea*, but they all came second to London's Arctic tale. The exception was *Moby Dick*, and that masterpiece still sits on my bookshelf. It so impressed me as a child that for a short time if I was confronted by any problems I would contemplate what Queequeg might advise me to do. It wasn't like an imaginary friend, more a point of reference that I had chosen to personify in Queequeg, the exotic harpooner from Melville's book. I was so captivated by this character that I drew elaborate designs on my wrists which I secretly chose to believe were magic symbols tattooed by the strange seafarer himself. It was a child-hood affectation but I still believe it had some real magic in it, for those inky bracelets made me immune to whatever might be troubling me. However, they never lasted long. They were too obvious and too inexplicable, and in any case my mother's carbolic soap made short shrift of them.

Elaine's arrival into my world of frozen wastelands and great black heaving oceans happened, as I viewed it, coincidentally. I remember my mother coaxing me to feel the baby in her tummy. The slight movement under my hand as she pressed it to her swollen stomach did nothing for me. I knew she wanted me to make some connection with the child that was to be my brother or sister, but I didn't want to be bothered and was even a little frightened. It wasn't the invisible creature that was moving around inside her, it was the intimacy that my mother longed to share with me. My ten-year-old world was being invaded by a creature I couldn't see and emotions I didn't understand.

For months after the baby's arrival I ignored it completely. I didn't resent it: it was simply nothing to do with me. My dad loved the baby. He would nurse it and talk to it. He would tickle it and even hold the baby to his shoulder with one hand as he shaved his face with the other. He sang it the song that I had learned to skip to. His affection for the child overflowed into the house. As if that wasn't enough, people came to visit and talked about babies for hours. When they weren't talking, Mother and Brenda would be off for long walks with Elaine and her pram. At least they understood that I wanted nothing to do with these walks. So, they left me to my own devices. A key was hung on a piece of string behind the letterbox of our front door, so that I could come and go as I pleased. They knew I was happy enough on my own but insisted I should go to one of our neighbours if I needed anything. I never did either go to the neighbours or need anything. What they thought I would do, sitting alone in some designated neighbour's house, was beyond me.

Dad, it seemed, was oblivious to my total unconcern about the new baby and we stopped going to Smithfield market together. It wasn't sudden; our visits just seemed to peter out. Anyway, Dad had taken to watching football on Saturdays and asked me to go with him. It was pointless. I knew nothing about the game and cared less. So, once I had declined his offer two or three times, he never bothered asking again. We had long since ceased going to the Cartoon Cinema together. I was glad of that, given that I had been a cartoon character in the eyes of my friends. If 'Goofy' or 'Bugs Bunny' wasn't good enough to play football with them, I didn't want my dad hearing me called by my nickname on the football stands.

The other important thing that happened after Elaine's arrival was that the wooden bungalow we had holidayed in each year was to be pulled down along with a few others nearby. I adored the world that Balloo opened up to me. I loved the fishing, the mushroom picking, carrying water from the well, my nights sleeping on the veranda, the hours scouring rock pools with my dad, and the animals and birds that only he could find and bring into the musty warmth of the wood house. Knocking down the bungalow amounted to demolishing a significant part of my childhood. Balloo was fairytale country and adventure land rolled into one. But it was more than that. The yearly visits to our bungalow were like the marks that I was never able to make on the bedroom wall. Balloo marked my growing up. I could remember being carried on my father's shoulders to the farm when I was barely able to walk, going on torch-lit safaris at night. Listening to the adults' conversation through the wooden walls. I learned so many things at Balloo. It was a special place and it was going to disappear. I spent sleepless nights trying to work out how we would get enough money to buy the old house or build another one somewhere else. Not being able to sleep on the old couch or the veranda depressed me. For many weeks I was inconsolable.

My books and comics created their own compensations. It was about this time that I made a big decision about my future. Maybe it was the high seas adventures of *Treasure Island* or the heart-stopping suspense of the story of the great white whale. Then again, perhaps it was the legacy of my grandfather the shipbuilder and my father's silent and mysterious love of water. At the age of eleven I determined that I wanted to become a merchant seaman. It seemed the only realistic route out of this mundane world to another, more colourful one. One day I told my parents of this momentous decision. My mother smiled, asking me, 'Wherever did you get that notion?' I couldn't answer her as I didn't know. My dad fell silent and gave my mother one of those looks that you know is an exchange of unspoken knowledge of some kind. He said no more about my chosen profession and neither did I, though I continued with the idea into my teenage years.

In the introduction to the copy of Melville's book which I have had for many years, the Victorian reviewer writes: 'Does the imagination not rather spring from some great restriction such as the whiteness of the whale – whiteness which strikes more of panic to the soul than that redness which affrights the blood.' In an unconscious way, my own world was set about with restrictions and loss. Things that I loved and enjoyed were closing down around me and only the wild extremities of my imagination would set me free, and carry me beyond any restrictions. My increasing shyness, as many saw it, had little to do with loneliness or isolation; it was something other than this. I had learned to create a fascinating inner space packed with imaginary characters from imaginary worlds. I never felt lonely. Quite the contrary. If my head was too much in the clouds, I was happy for it to be there. Maybe that was the reason for my mediocre performance in school, or maybe school was another mundane reality that I found no place in. Whatever the reasons might be, I was one of thousands of children who failed their eleven-plus exam and was consequently earmarked as a failure and consigned to a secondary school system whose best hope for its pupils was a place in the shipyard or a factory, or that they would disappear into some regiment of the British Army where any spark of individuality would be extinguished like an irritating fly.

So off I went to big school with my mates. We were all dressed in black blazers, grey flannels, grey shirts, a tie with diagonal orange, white and black stripes, and shiny black shoes with soles that looked like they had been cut out of car tyres. I walked the last mile from the bus terminus through the neat redbrick semis, then up through an area of parkland. Kids seemed to be flocking from every direction, hundreds of them, all dressed exactly the same yet every one of them strangers. I remember thinking then how my father had explained to me why birds flock together, flying willy-nilly in great bunches at the beginning of autumn. The assembled multitude of young boys in black blazers moving inexorably towards the fearsome fate of the big school seemed just like a flock of birds made restless by seasonal change. Then I thought of swarms of flies on piles of cow dung. All the strange faces about me revealed the same anxiety. They were filled with dread and thinking, 'Oh shit!'

The first few weeks in Orangefield Boys' Secondary Intermediate School did not lessen my anxiety. The regime of moving class with each subject and with having six or seven teachers was confusing enough, but the fact that all of them wore a long black gown over their normal clothes added an air of fearsome authority to them.

Our English teacher in that year was a certain Mr William Cummings, forever known as 'Wild Bill'. Though he was tall and solidly built, his bald head made him look less than wild, but his demeanour more than made up for that. Mr Cummings never spoke; he roared orders. Everyone was simply referred to as 'You boy!' And when Wild Bill arrived in the classroom his entrance was more like the clumsy landing of a big bony vulture. He roared out for silence and then surveyed the room with a steely eye. Every one of us bowed our head, determined not to attract his attention. I couldn't bear his loudness. Everything was commanded. But it was more than the noise. Wild Bill kept a cane, taped at the striking end with layers of sticking plaster to ensure that the skin was never broken. His justice was summary and he applied his cane with a steely stare. The welts he left on many a hand testified to the pleasure he took. Fortunately I was too terrified of him ever to incur his wrath. But I felt it every time he punished someone else.

Wild Bill was a character but not much of a teacher. Most of the time he asked individuals to read aloud from whatever book he handed out and obviously he determined from my reading that he would not have to bother much with me. I was never more grateful that I had read books when others were playing games. One book he handed out to the class was Kenneth Grahame's wondrous *Wind in the Willows*. At first I thought it a childish book full of animal characters which were nearer to the cartoon characters that I loathed than they were to the brutally realistic animal protagonists of Jack London. I hid myself behind the book as a means of defence from Wild Bill's tyranny and later as an escape from the boredom of his class. The otherworldly atmospherics of the river bank and the rich characteristics of Ratty, Mole, Badger, Mole and Toad were a far cry from Wild Bill's torture chamber.

I adored Toad's irrepressible wildness and his utter incapacity to understand the social mores of the world he inhabited. He was the irrepressible outsider who was really a very likeable individual but who had no interest in ordinariness or decency. Toad was compulsively and madly wayward. If there was an animal who agreed with Oscar Wilde's words 'I live only for pleasure. Pleasure is the only thing one should live for', then Toad was it. Ratty, solitary by temperament, secretly admired Toad and wanted to be more like him. But he was protected by rules and regulations from such romantic inclinations. Badger may have been less repressed than Rat, but was altogether too innocent to be headstrong, which could not be said of Mole who simply dithered about in cautious indecision. Wild Bill of course was like none of these. Sometimes when I tried to think of an animal that would properly represent my tyrannical English teacher my imagination would not let me get past one of those fat boars that charged and snorted out of the pig boats at the docks. Wild Bill had neither the interest nor the ingenuity to teach the subtleties of the characters in the book. It is only because I still keep a copy and have re-read it since that I remain fascinated by it. If a classic is defined by its capacity to create an imaginary self-contained world that can endure through several childhoods, then *The Wind in the Willows* achieves that with me even if it was originally a means of escape from a very real terror.

Sometimes when I was at the river that ran alongside the allotment at the bottom of our street, I tried to imagine Toad and Ratty, Mole and Badger. But it never really worked. The river was filthy and full of all manner of rubbish. It smelt in the summer. Although there were rats and even toads to be found a mile or so upstream, the proximity of houses, roads and urban noise made it impossible to make the imaginary leap, though in the fright-fevered classroom of Wild Bill, I made the jump easily.

It would be easy to assume from the antics of Wild Bill that the school was a scary place. It was to a retiring twelve-year-old, and also it wasn't. The school had been constructed following the 1947 Education Act. Free post-primary education for every child up to the age of fifteen was the promise of post-war years. It not only carried with it the assurance of adequate education as a means of social reconstruction, it also threw up vision. Educators who caught hold of the promise applied it in more profound ways than the legislators envisaged.

John Malone, the principal of this new school was no Dickensian character and Orangefield Boys' Secondary Intermediate School was not a Dickensian invention, even if some of its staff might well have been the product of that writer's imagination. John Malone was known as 'The Boot'. He had an air about him that belied the acronym. Certainly he was austere. His presence in a corridor silenced us immediately. He seemed to flow down those corridors in a state of reverence. 'The Boot' always wore an immaculate black suit, white shirt and perfectly knotted tie. He was also bald, but not like 'Wild Bill'. His baldness was like a tonsure and the remains of his silver hair shone. He was never seen without his black cloak and his shoes – or boots, as I assumed they were – shone too. He emitted radiance, respect and silence but was altogether different from the rest of the black-cloaked acolytes who made up the staff.

John Malone embodied vision, and a strength of personal belief that I have rarely encountered. His ideas on education were radical and they were underlined by a sincerity that made them profound. On several occasions in my school career I was counselled by 'The Boot' and always found him a great listener. That was his unique quality: he understood what you were saying and the way you were saying it no matter how inarticulately or angrily you expressed it. Above all, there was a gentleness in his austerity that was absolutely convincing, because it was absolutely honest.

The man really valued the talents and, more importantly, the potential of every child in that school. I was one of over fourteen hundred pupils, and 'The Boot' knew every one of us by our first name. When John Malone asked a boy in the corridor 'How are you getting on, John?' that boy felt like he had been blessed: not only because 'The Boot' knew his name, but because he listened to the answer and responded to it. Intellectually he would not comprehend the notion of children as failures. And he gathered like minds about him. He had a staff young and enthusiastic enough to carry the dead-weight teachers that the school had inherited from the existing system. There were many teachers who merely tolerated John Malone's liberal and sometimes radical idealism, accepting it with silent begrudgery. Their view of their pupils was simple: 'Shut up, do what you are told, and don't dare question anything.' And to reinforce this dictum, they always had a cane at the ready. Thankfully such backwoodsmen were in the minority. When he could, John Malone chose staff who valued not only their profession, but also their pupils. They encouraged questions, arguments and debate. Education was not a blackboard with chalk marks that we had to copy or learn off like battery hens. The best of them dispensed with such limited perspectives: they blasted a hole in the blackboard and dragged the world in through it. They gave those of us who had the capacity a taste for something greater than the bureaucrats in the civil service had devised for us. The layout of the school said it all. It was mechanistic, like the minds in the Department of Education that thought education was merely a formula to produce factory fodder. There was a corridor for science, a corridor with woodwork and metalcraft workshops. Beside them, a room laid out for technical drawing. The corridor beside the science rooms was given over to art, while opposite that were the English, geography and history rooms. Two lonely music rooms lined the other corridors at right angles. At the far end of the school were two changing rooms and a large gym. Outside, the school was surrounded by football, rugby, cricket and hockey pitches, all undergoing construction. This plethora of sports grounds was to be shared by two other schools, a girls' secondary school and a mixed-gender grammar school. At the centre of this complex was a dining hall to serve the three 'systems' of education. All it served really was a pathetic educational apartheid. They were the curds and we were the whey. Everyone believed it except John Malone and his cohort of radical young teachers.

Many years after I had left school, I was reading a copy of a lecture given in honour of John Malone. In it the author Maurice Hayes cites a portrait of Miss Crane sitting in her mission school in *The Jewel in The Crown*. 'Perhaps the only excuse any of us have to be here is to be conscious of the duty to promote the cause of human dignity and happiness . . . with an obligation to not look afraid, not to be afraid to require a personal grace, a personal dignity, as much as she could of either, as much as was in her powers, so that she could be a living proof of there being, somewhere in the world, hope of betterment.' It could have been a pen portrait of my headmaster, only it fell short. 'The Boot' didn't simply believe in an aspiration to betterment. He did believe that education should lay down a personal route map for every child that would allow them to achieve and become whatever they strove after. Where Miss Crane might reflect on happiness, 'The Boot' pushed it further. Happiness was about authenticity and engagement with the world. If this meant challenging worn-out prescriptive notions about where we were headed in life, then so much the better.' The Boot' was ready to arm us with whatever intellectual and emotional ammunition we required. Such ideas were revolutionary in the prevailing educational thinking of that time but 'The Boot' was ethically and morally a deeply Christian man who was committed to the mission he had set himself. I have made much of John Malone, because without him tenaciously pushing and developing his inclusive vision many kids like myself would have disappeared through the cracks, as they say. When I arrived at the big school Goofy, Bugs Bunny and all the rest of the retinue of nicknames arrived with me. Only this time there was a bigger audience to hear them and ultimately take up the nicknaming. I retreated further into my shell. I put my head down in class, did what I was told and effectively disappeared off the educational radar. I didn't play any sports. Woodwork and metalwork bored me. I liked the precision of technical drawing and enjoyed algebra and trigonometry for some reason. I learned absolutely nothing in art class as the time was given over to craftwork like binding books or working with clay. Obviously the idea of making apprentice tradesmen out of us all was not to be limited to metal and woodwork. I suppose I slipped through my first years as an able but uninspiring kid. In those years, I can't say I enjoyed school or even that I didn't. I just went because that's what I was supposed to do, and every week day I did what I was supposed to do.

Every Monday morning my mother gave me five shillings to purchase five dinner tickets, which I had to exchange every day for a hot meal at the dinner hall. It took me about six months to realize that I could do better things with five shillings. If I added to that a week's worth of bus fares, I would have something to make my visits to Smithfield more interesting. Dad rarely took me there now, and maybe that was one of the reasons for my own secret escapes on Saturdays. I don't know why or how it came about, nor do I even recall the first time it happened or where I went, but it became a major part of my weekend for a long time after.

I suppose it was a chance thing. A momentary impulse which, once acted upon, could not be stopped. I think it was one of those Saturdays when everybody else was doing something. There was a second-hand shop on the Newtownards Road where you could exchange comics for a few coppers. Dad had gone to watch football and Mum was busy with our new baby. I didn't want to be about the house with her and Brenda. Neither did I have much interest in the Saturday matinée at the cinema any more. I had my five shillings, plus several days' bus fare, which I kept in the box under my bed where I stored my comics. I had quite a varied collection and knew the bookshop would be happy to exchange some of them for me. There was a big pawnshop on the way to the bookshop that seemed to do more business than anywhere else. I had been to it several times with my mother, usually at the start of the school year to buy cheap shoes and 'mutton dummies', a very basic canvas and rubber gym slipper. That was when she had cash. On other occasions she obtained a Provident cheque from Billy the 'Provident' man. With this cheque she could buy my complete school uniform and clothes for the new baby. Every week Billy from the Provident would arrive at our house at 6.30 p.m. and Mother would pay him seven and sixpence towards the cheque. It was a form of moneylending and our house, along with everyone else's, was furnished on the Provident. The pawnshop fascinated me the way Smithfield did. There were things in the window that no other shop had. Some weeks before, I had noticed a fabulous harmonica there. The silver plates in the top and bottom were elaborately carved and beside it was a fancy leather case with a handsome silver clasp. There was a blue and white cardboard box embossed with a design that looked the same as that on the instrument. On it I read the inscription 'Alabama Blues Harmonium Company'.

I was unable to forget the mouth organ. I remembered the name of the harmonica player that I heard in the market at Smithfield. Sonny Boy Williamson. I was too young to know anything about music but Sonny Boy's mouth organ music was frenzied, magically inventive and always caught me up in its rhapsody. I had learned from the back of an album cover that as a boy the musician used to walk about with half a dozen harmonicas stuck in his belt. That impressed me. I fancied myself wandering around with this gleaming instrument hanging out of my back pocket – it would be better than any dagger-edged steel comb! And when I blew my harp people would really take note. I was so carried away by the idea of me and this mouth organ that I even began to make up names for myself. I don't know what made me think of it but one of them was 'Licorice Lips'. It had something to do with the fact that Sonny Boy's real surname was Rice and that his music wasn't blues, it was black and he was black.

I stood outside Geddis's pawnshop that Saturday admiring the gleaming harmonica. I knew the money in my pocket wouldn't be enough to buy it, but I had to know how much it was. Inside the shop I stood at the long wooden counter. 'Yes sir?' asked the pawn-broker. However intimidated I may have been, the way he addressed me made me cocky. 'How much is that old mouth organ in the window?' I asked. The pawnbroker looked down at me, then answered, 'Seventeen shillings and sixpence.' My heart sank. My head reeled. I would have to starve myself for the next six weeks at least! The man reached into the window, lifted out the instrument and proffered it to me. 'Try before you buy!' he urged me. 'No, no.' I said, stumbling over the words in panic. 'I just wanted to know how much.' The man smiled, then said knowingly, 'The man that owns it will be back for it before you have time to buy it.' He paused for a moment then added, 'He always plays a few bars of "Goodnight Irene" when he brings it in. Just so as I know it's working.' He leaned forward and said in a half-whisper, 'Doesn't like to leave it without saying goodbye, I suppose.' Then he winked at me and returned the instrument to its spot in the window.

I left the pawnshop dejected. I could always buy another one, I told myself half-heartedly. But I knew it would never be as special as this one which had come all the way from the Alabama Blues Harmonium Company. Then I wondered who owned it and always said goodbye to it by playing 'Goodnight Irene'. I remembered a photo I had seen of Sonny Boy. He had a tiny wispy growth of hair extending from the point of his chin and he wore a black beret. His hands were huge with long bony fingers. I wondered what my mysterious harmonica owner looked like. I half knew the tune of 'Goodnight Irene', and knew that Sonny Boy would never play it the way I had heard it sung. The mystery man who owned the Alabama harmonica, how did he play? Where had he learned? Behind all these questions I was starting to believe that because the song 'Goodnight Irene' was, in a way, my song then maybe the harmonica could be mine also! I looked at my small hands. I was thirteen. I think I knew from reading a record sleeve that Sonny Boy had been playing since he was five. Even then, I thought, his hands would still have been bigger than mine.

I was standing at the roadside waiting to cross with my comics in one hand and my dinner money in the other. I didn't know it, but I was standing at a bus stop and just at that moment a green double-decker pulled up beside me. Green buses were country buses and the sign on this one read Holywood, which everyone pronounced as Hollywood. Without thinking about what I was doing, I stepped on and climbed the stairs and sat on the front seat. Hollywood was in America, but I knew where I was going wasn't America. I knew it was somewhere miles from the city. What I didn't know was how far, or why I had stepped on the bus. 'Fares, please,' said the conductor. 'Where you going, son?' 'Holywood,' I said as that was all I knew. 'Single or return?' 'Return,' I answered. 'Half return, ninepence,' he said as he handed me a pink ticket which he had punched with a pliers-like instrument. I handed him a shilling from my dinner money. He returned an octagonal three-penny piece and walked off with the coins in his purse making a muffled rattle. I looked at the ticket. At least I could come back from wherever it was I was going.

I don't remember much about that first trip. The place was new and strange. I found my way to a small yachting harbour which was at the end of a long sweeping promenade. There was an old wooden pier going out into the sea. There was also a sign on it which said; 'Danger, Pier liable to collapse'. I disregarded the warning, confident the pier would bear my weight, and walked to the end of it. I could see the land on the other side of Belfast Lough. I had never been over there, I thought. I walked for a long time along the promenade, then climbed fences and walls to remain near the sea. I stayed there for what seemed like a long time, just walking and looking.

Then I remembered that I didn't know where to get the bus back to the city. Nor did I know what time these buses ran. I didn't panic but I did feel a little irritated. I had only just found this place and now I had to leave it. Reality, I felt, was tedious and time-consuming. It was like learning passages of scripture for homework. First Samuel, chapter 21 verses 1–6, and so you rhymed off the verses, mispronouncing the name of Ahimelech and not knowing what hallowed bread was, nor why the men kept themselves from women or why their vessels were holy. So you learned it because you had to, and you repeated it word-perfect except for Ahimelech and it was done. You never understood any of it or even why it was necessary. In a completely unfathomable way getting the bus home was as useless as learning scripture! I came home several hours later. No one was too interested in where I had been and I didn't tell them, principally because there was nothing to tell.

Later that evening we were having our occasional Saturday night treat, tumblers of lemonade with a ball of ice-cream dropped into it, bags of crisps and bars of chocolate. 'Do you know Holywood, Dad?' I asked. 'Sure,' he answered. 'It's about eight miles away unless you mean Hollywood in America which is much further.' 'Have you been there?' 'That depends on where you mean. I have never been to America but I have been to Holywood. Why?' I was silent and was about to say 'no reason' when I found myself asking 'What's after Holywood?' Dad began to rhyme off place-names then got up and left the room. When he returned, he had the road map he always kept in his working jacket or his van. He spread it out and his finger moved from Belfast down to Holywood. 'From here it depends which way you want to go.' Dad started explaining places on the map. 'Is this something to do with homework for school?' he asked innocently. 'No,' I answered. 'I've just got Bible verses to learn!' 'Best leave them till Sunday,' Dad said laughing. 'So why do you want to know about all these other places?' he asked again. 'I don't know,' I answered honestly. 'I just wondered!'

It was some weeks before I ventured off on another expedition. I am not even sure where I went. It seemed to be another unplanned thing; a spur-of-the-moment compulsion. I had gone back to the pawnshop to see if the harmonica was still there. I was unable to get it out of my head. I had already decided that it was mine and that eventually I would somehow acquire it. Another part of me hoped that if I kept going to see it I might meet the man who owned it. I fantasized that if I could tell him how important it was he might give it to me. If not, maybe he would teach me how to play it. I was sure my dinner money would cover the cost of these lessons. The lure of the mouth organ was incredible. With that mouth organ I just knew that my life would change. I stood at the pawnshop window staring at the harmonica. It was in a different place but it was still there. I would have done anything to get it. The impossibility of possessing it was crushing me. I turned to walk home and as I was waiting at the roadside to cross over a bus came towards me. I recognized the place-name on the bus from Dad's map and hopped on, knowing my dinner money would get me there and back. I liked the idea that only I knew where I was going, even if I didn't really. I repeated this bus-hopping intermittently for several months. I didn't have any reason for it except that the word 'hobo' had lodged itself in my head. I liked the sound of it and I loved the idea of it. Occasionally, if I spotted somewhere interesting *en route* to the bus's destination, I would get off as near to the place as I could on the return journey. I rarely stayed long at the places the bus took me to; I simply wandered around looking for something to attract my attention. I liked railway stations, old cemeteries and bridges and rivers. I think I really enjoyed the journey. I liked to be moving. Usually I was the only kid on the bus and this made me feel special in a way. Sometimes I had weird notions that I was the only person on the bus who was really moving, and everybody else had somehow stopped!

These sorties into the countryside came and went, but they always began and ended with me standing at the pawnshop looking at 'my' harmonica. If I could never have it, it seemed to have become a talisman or good luck charm. If it was in the window waiting for me then all was well with the world. Of course, there were times when the weather did not permit bus trips. Then I would go alone to Smithfield just to look at things and sometimes at people. All the time I was absorbing classic blues and jazz without understanding any of it. It made me feel like I was keeping faith with Sonny Boy and my mouth organ. It was a world of its own and I had become one of its residents. One day, a small-holder who recognized me from my frequent appearances in the place called me over. 'Here son, mind this place for a few minutes. I'll be back in ten minutes or so,' he said, and off he went. I felt pretty important being left in charge. The man never knew who I was except that I was one of the habitués of the place. He was only selling old furniture and odd pieces of bric-à-brac that no one would think of stealing but by choosing me to look after his things he had accepted me into the colourful confraternity of the disciples of Smithfield. The thing about Smithfield was that you didn't have to buy anything. You could own everything.

I hardly got to know 'Old Robbie,' the man whose stall I had looked after. He died some months later. I remember him sitting amongst his pile of old furniture and second-hand clothes crouched over a smelly paraffin heater. On the side he had painted a note to himself: 'Turn off before you go Robbie'. 'Did you ever forget?' I once asked him. 'No fucking chance, son, everybody here makes sure to ask me if they see me leave.' I could well understand why. Robbie's corner of the market was a virtual tinderbox that, once lit, would have engulfed the whole place in minutes.

He told me, one day, that he hadn't sold 'as much as a broken stick' for over a few weeks. 'Times are tight, all right' he acknowledged, then he tapped his index finger lightly against his nose and winked at me. 'There's an invisible name written on everything in my shop. I can't see it but I know the buyer the minute I see them. Everything sells, son, in its own time, everything sells.' I smiled to myself at Robbie's grandiose description of his corner as a 'shop'. It had neither door nor window. It was no more than a covered laneway piled high with cast-off rubbish. But Robbie made it a treasure house. If anyone stopped to look at a chair or an old roll of threadbare carpet, Robbie looked up casually at them and said, 'Do you see that chair? Do you know who sat on that chair?' Or, 'Do you know where that carpet came from?' Few people waited to hear the end of Robbie's story, but he continued telling it just for the sake of telling it. He never appeared bothered one way or the other if he sold the item or not. Why should he? According to his own dictum, 'Everything sells in its own time.' I knew he was right, but I didn't want him to be right. I didn't want my mouth organ to be sold to anyone but me.

When I was told my fourth form English teacher was to be Mr Ashe, I was hardly encouraged. Ernie, as everyone called him, was a PE teacher who taught English to the junior classes as a secondary subject. The man had close-cropped hair on a balding head and sported a goatee beard. His head looked like a billiard ball and the way his beard accentuated his mouth when he spoke made you think of a goldfish gulping food. His body was short and stocky like a ten-pin bowling ball. So he looked the part as a PE instructor but was much less inspiring as an English teacher.

I could not have been more wrong. In the year I had with Ernie Ashe I changed from a shy and competent but academically unremarkable pupil to someone who not only read books but who would discuss and debate their relative merits and flaws with unabashed assurance. Ernie revealed to me the simple, logical but usually unexplored truth that reading was about writing. Everything else, including all the schools of philosophy, all the religions, all the histories and every idea that made men discover the universe, existed because someone had written it. Words were a source of reciprocal magic. They had power but the writer was the alchemist that infused them with it. Words were his magical potions and by the way he put them together he could create illusions, foretell the future, discern fools, discover untruths, reveal hidden truths and illuminate the world. Writing could enable the blind to see and could give speech to the dumb. It could set prisoners free and raise up nations and it could take the writer to worlds that he might never visit.

Language was the stock in trade of prophets, philosophers, priests and even plumbers. It didn't just make the world go around: it created the world. But the big secret was that language was created by men. When God spoke to men he used words. Moses saw the moving finger write and in Ernie's eyes the emphasis was on the word 'write'. The Gospels weren't simply 'handed down' – that wouldn't do for Ernie. They were written down by men. Writing was inspired manual labour! It was the judicious but imaginative selection of words put together in a way that they take on a life of their own. When you put a certain combination of words together on a page it could catch fire. Words had a secret code that kept changing. If you knew how to use it, you could remake the world.

Obviously this collected wisdom of Ernie Ashe was not delivered all in one go. It was an acquired wisdom that was doled out in dribs and drabs, most of which went over the head of my classmates. But I was hooked right from the start. However, just being told these things wasn't enough. Language read or written was a labour which, properly nourished, could become an art and an inspiration.

Ashe threw out the syllabus that required his charges to learn certain poems and know certain books, for he knew that literature might as well be written on toilet paper if that was the way it was to be taught. Learning was about discovery, and Ernie set out to take us to strange places.

I remember a class where he read us pieces from Vance Packard's *Hidden Persuaders* to illustrate the power and deviousness of imagery. This developed into discussions of Nazi propaganda. Ernie was subtly introducing morals and ethics to thirty-five fifteen-year-old boys whose moral sense was being overshadowed by a developing testosterone count that made them more interested in the girls' school twenty yards away. Perhaps to counter this he read parts of *Catcher in the Rye* and Molly Bloom's soliloquy, which shut everyone up! He even brought in a copy of *Playboy*, declaring, 'This is not for looking at, this is for reading' and then began to read a long section of political criticism from an article by Norman Mailer!

He knew that practically everyone in the class hated books so he handed out newspaper colour supplements so that we could examine the world beyond the girls' netball yard. He made those of us who showed any spark of interest analyse what an author might be saying. He encouraged us to challenge the work. Could it be written better? Why did the author create the characters he did? He taught me a lesson about reading that I still employ. 'As you read a book, Keenan, try and see it in a different way. How would it work as a film or a play? How would you write dialogue to say what the author is trying to say?'

Maybe because I dreamed a lot and was given to creating my own fantasy worlds long before I arrived in his class, I took to his enthusiasms with relish. Ernie was quick to pick up on this and he encouraged me. Soon my essays were being read out to the class every week and Ashe, like the teacher in primary school before him, was giving me books of his own to take home. One of them was Maxim Gorky's *Mother*. I noticed that it had a stamp on the flyleaf denoting that it was issued by a special literary society in Moscow to promote the 'Literature and politics of the Soviet Socialist Republic'! To this day, I don't know if Ernie was a member of a proto-communist cell. I am sure he wasn't. Ernie's attitude to language was that it didn't belong to any ideology.

His attitude to poetry was similar. It could be a warrior's axe, an assassin's dagger or the archangel's flaming sword. Poetry, I learned from Ernie, was the 'powerhouse of language'. He wanted me to read poetry before anything else. 'That's where the secret code is, Keenan, crack it and everything is possible.' We did two classes of poetry every week. The rest of the boys hated it but I adored it. We covered some of the great English poets – Keats, Coleridge, Auden and others – but he also introduced Swahili, Russian, South American, French and Irish poets, and every other nationality he could lay his hands on. Ernie's English classes were, for me – though perhaps I didn't know it then – transcendental. A few hours every week he busted open the word box and language came spilling out.

I fell in love with Dylan Thomas and one day after reading some of his work and the poetry of Roger McGough and Brian Patten, I declared, 'I could do that'. It was a bit of cockiness on my part but Ernie's reaction nailed me. Looking straight at me, with a soft voice he said, 'You know, Keenan, I really believe you could.' Whether it was the way he said it or my over-active imaginative response, it was as if he was reaching down inside me and pulling out someone who was hiding there.

So I took up the challenge, knowing that I had a mentor who would support and encourage me. Ernie never failed to do just that. I can still hear some of his advice. 'Describe what you feel as well as what you know. There's a completely different kind of dictionary in the emotions. You need to study that.' On another occasion: 'The gap between one word and the next can be a millimetre or a mile. Mind you don't get lost. The surest way to get lost is to start showing off!' Then he made the startling revelation: 'If you can't find a word, make one up!' I was shocked at this audacity. 'Somebody had to invent them thousands of years ago, so why stop now?' That day was one of the most memorable – the sheer fun of it. The whole class began inventing new adjectives for everything they could think of. That day his dictum about 'words being powerful magic' really came into its own.

There were other teachers like Ernie Ashe. Sam McCready was

one of them. A tiny figure of a man who stood about five foot tall with a nose that Shylock or any Roman Caesar could have coveted. Some of the pupils referred to him as the Leprechaun or Titch McGeady. But he was a towering giant in the field of drama. Up until his arrival, our school plays were limited to the elite world of Molière's costume dramas; to me they were irrelevant, but classy pantomimes. When Sam took charge of drama, everything changed. Molière's stagy world was blown away and the gritty collision of religion and politics in Bernard Shaw's *Saint Joan* and the plays of O'Casey took their place. I don't know how he did it but Ashe convinced me to take part. Sam duly took me under his wing and made an actor out of me. If Ernie Ashe believed words were magic, Sam McCready performed magic not only on the stage but in me. Within a matter of months he had transformed me from a quiet lad, who was afraid of the rough and tumble of his contemporaries and who spent hours in his room composing poems, to a big-part actor on the stage in a youth drama festival in Dublin performing in the world première of Milton's *Paradise Lost*, set to the music of a varied collection of rock bands cut with scores from classic composers.

It was all very heady stuff and I was revelling in it. Spurred on by Sam, I was reading plays from the classical Japanese Noh theatre and even tried to write one in this ancient style. At the other extreme, I tried to write a short play based on Steinbeck's *The Grapes of Wrath*. It never saw the light of day but it did exercise my overheated imagination for weeks. At the weekends, when the other lads in my street were off to the pictures or trying to get a girl, I was going to watch *The Royal Hunt of the Sun* or attending rehearsal classes with the Ulster Youth Theatre. It was a short-lived affair. I think my thick Belfast accent couldn't make the elocu-tionary leap that was required to sustain any thespian notions I may have had. However, this dabbling at the edges of the theatre was opening up new worlds and new ways of seeing and expressing things. My long-held desire to become a merchant seaman was retreating; already I was in mid-ocean floating on a sea of words and drifting far away from the streets I grew up in. This intellectual 'growing away' was not a sudden, life-changing thing. It was part rebellion, part adolescent self-assertion, part attention-seeking and part hunger to discover a world that was more interesting than the world I was presently living in. All the makings of an angry young man! But the seeds of this were sown years before I came into contact with Malone, McCready and Ashe.

ACROSS THE GREAT DIVIDE

IF THERE WAS ONE WOMAN IN OUR STREET WHO WAS LONELY, IT WAS Mrs Price. she wasn't just the loneliest woman in the street but in the whole neighbourhood. Mrs Price had two children, John and Dolly, and all the family were Catholics. The only Catholics for miles around. I think I only ever saw Mrs Price a dozen times in my life at most, usually either coming or going out of her home. I never saw her in the shops, on a bus or even walking along a road. I never saw anyone other than the woman and her children enter or leave the house. The Prices had no friends, and no relations, it seemed. Their house looked the same as anyone else's but no one had ever been inside it. Everyone in the street knew they were Catholic but that was all we knew. The Prices never spoke to anyone and no one spoke to them. John was older than his sister and was about my age. I used to see him arriving home from school each day. He was always alone. When he went in, he stayed in. The only other times I saw him he would be playing inside the tiny garden that fronted the houses. As we never saw the family they were mostly forgotten about. They didn't register because nobody cared enough to be curious about them. They were Catholic, and that was enough. As kids, we didn't care because we didn't know what a Catholic was and we had no reason to ask.

By the time I was sixteen I had little interest in the Protestant and Catholic divide. I was reading Jack Kerouac, Albert Camus, Jean-Paul Sartre and Dostoevsky and was too hung up on my own adolescent angst to be bothered by such insignificant nonsense. In truth, I hardly knew what I was reading or what it was doing to me. I suppose my choice of books was a bit like my bus journeys. I never knew where I was going or why I had suddenly jumped on a bus. Albert Camus's classic novel *The Plague* was almost like a bible to me. I was reading about the plague of Nazism while all around me another plague was spreading and poisoning everything it touched. Sectarianism and its hideous spoor was taking root across the city and turning neighbourhoods into ghettos. Newspapers, politicians and preachers all fed on it with stupefying repetition. It arrived in our street with more virulence than in others around us because it had focus for its wrath. The Price family was as easy target.

I was drawn to John Price. Not because of any noble gesture or anti-sectarian motivation. Most of us didn't see the contamination spreading, or else we chose not to care. But it was in amongst us. I think it was the Catholic boy's 'otherness' rather than his religion that drew me and I am sure his isolation mirrored my own. When he walked along the street to his home his eyes were always cast down as if he didn't want to see or be seen by anyone. It seemed as if he was enclosed in an invisible capsule. Often I said 'hello, John' to him from across the street. His eyes caught mine for a moment and he returned the greeting then turned back into his own world. The distance across the street was a matter of feet, but it might as well have been an ocean. The thing was, I didn't know how to cross that divide and as I was the only person who had ever acknowledged him I am sure he was as confused as I was. It was as if we were throwing ropes to one another but the current that ran between us carried them away before we could catch hold. As John was rarely seen in the street there was little opportunity to try again. In any case, by the time June and July came around and the rest of us were off school, the Price family were rarely seen. When every street was a hive of activity in preparation for the Orange celebration, the only Catholics in the area pulled their blinds and bolted their doors. Every time my pals saw their Catholic neighbour, they would chase after him, taunting him with abuse. John walked slowly on to his door, never running and never answering them. If I was with them, I refused to join them. I remained silent or shook my head obviously, signalling my refusal to be part of their pack. I know John saw it but it never seemed enough: I desperately wanted him to know that I hated what was happening.

I could never tell for sure what he thought until one day when I rounded on the lads for attacking him. It wasn't physical but the words they slung at him were so barbed and vicious that they might as well have been beating him with batons. 'Ah shut your mouths the lot of you, away and leave him alone,' I spat at them. They turned to me in shock and silence, unsure what to do about this traitorous outburst. Then they moved towards me. 'Bugs Bunny the Fenian lover!' someone said. It seemed to have sparked something. They were spoiling for a fight and they knew I was the least physical kid in the street. They could physically attack me the way they couldn't with the Catholic lad, because he was so different and because they didn't know what that difference meant. They were almost afraid of him, and that fed their rage and hatred. But they knew me. They had played with me for years. I was their friend even if I had buck teeth and read stupid books. Suddenly I was very afraid. I knew that in their minds, beating me up would be more satisfying than hitting a Fenian. I tried to brazen it out.

'You're all big hard men when there's six of you!' It didn't work. Joey, the ringleader charged at me and pinned me by the neck to the wall. 'You think *you* are a hard man,' he hissed. It felt like something I had seen in a hundred gangster movies but it wasn't funny. Joey's action meant that he could not pull back and the others were watching, relishing what was to happen. 'Kick his balls in,' someone said excitedly. Another friend urged Joey: 'Go on, knock his teeth out!' They were all salivating, except me and Joey, who had me by the throat. My own throat was dry with fear and my assailant's eyes were desperate with indecision. Then from nowhere another voice began chanting, 'Proddy dick, proddy dick, your ma can't knit, your da can't go to bed without a dummy tit.'

It was John Price standing at his gate. The rhyme he was chanting seemed terribly childish and his head was tick-tocking, metronomically, as he spoke, the way you do when you are singing to babies. My pals turned from me and stared at the Fenian in disbelief. John Price stared back, repeating over and over again his ironic invective. My so-called pals were dumbfounded. They did not know what to do. I had no such confusion and walked off, knowing that any indecision on my part would ensure that the worst happened. Before I reached the safety of my own house John had disappeared into his and my friends were left squabbling amongst themselves. It was July again and the Eleventh night was approaching.

Something was happening in our streets that was malign and ugly. The innocent enthusiasm that had been part of my growing up had gone. I used to enjoy the excitement of this time and the exuberant mastery we had of the streets. They were our kingdom, we made our own rules and broke everyone else's. We smoked and blew smoke-rings in a flamboyant disregard of the warnings about stunting our growth and going bald before we were thirty. Inside our huts we swigged at bottles of beer and whispered about sex like we knew it all backwards. We were swearing worse than any trooper, but above all we were building the biggest boney in the neighbourhood and everybody would come to look at it and know that it was us who built it. We were the toughest, roughest, strongest fuckin' boney builders in all of East Belfast. There was no one like us and there never would be! Our boney was not simply a huge pile of rubbish. It was our protector. Inside that huge hive with its warren of huts, we were shielded from the approbation of the adult world.

It was the habit on the Eleventh night for people to move through the streets visiting one bonfire after another. It was a social occasion where families from the whole neighbourhood celebrated. There was a warmth that had nothing to do with the heat from the fire. It was little more than a celebration of the fraternity of the streets but it was wildly liberating and simultaneously assuring. Parents and children, neighbours and relations all joined in. But this world had been contaminated. In a fistful of years the atmosphere had changed to something nightmarish. The streets were still dark and full of anticipation. People moved through the burning grounds on rivers of alcohol, their mood blacker than the streets. From the tiny kitchen houses, record players blared out 'The Sash' and 'The Billy Boys' whose lyrics rang out, 'We're up to our knees in Fenian blood, surrender or you die, for we are, we are the Billy Boys.' The evening was consumed in the marching tunes we were to hear the next morning. Anti-papal slogans filled the air and out of the darkness, ecstatic voices called out bloody calamity on Catholic papists, Pope worshippers and every Fenian fucker that ever lived or breathed.

The Prices boarded up in their home for a band of drunken

revellers always stood across the street from their house chanting 'Holy Mary I am dying, just a word before I go. Set the Pope upon the table and stick a poker up his. Holy Mary I am dying just a word before I go . . .' When they tired of this they took up some other Orange anthem. They sounded like a choir of hellish hyenas. Then they would go off, as if they had done their bit for God and Ulster. Not a light flickered, not a living thing moved in the Price household, but that distracted no one. This must have been the longest night of their lives and it was getting longer every year. I found it hideous and sickening. Maybe I felt guilty because I too was a Prod, but mostly I felt angry. Something had been stolen from my world and what was left they could keep. I was holding on to what those years as a bonefire soldier had given me – wildness and freedom, fearlessness and equality. If they wanted to 'fuck the Fenians', well fuck them too!

I am sure this mood of adolescent petulance was picked up by my parents but the events on the streets were not something that was talked about at home. They were just something that happened. To engage in any discussion about their legitimacy or morality only gave credence to the worst aspects. My father was wiser than me; whether he recognized my confusion, I don't know. But I remember this story. He didn't tell it as some kind of moral parable. He just told it on one of those nights he came home from the pub. He had a smile on his face as he told it.

The pub my dad drank in every weekend was on the corner of a road that demarcated the only Catholic ghetto in East Belfast, known as the Short Strand. It was a collection of Victorian terraces and kitchen houses exactly the same as the others around it. Why this segment of streets came to be inhabited by predominantly Catholic people can be easily explained by historians. But my father cared little about that. The pub he drank in was owned by a Catholic and most of the staff there were Catholic. Everybody knew it and every man that drank in it didn't care a monkey's fart about it. My father was one of those sons who would have corrected John Donne and stated that every pub is an island entire of itself and a safe harbour for anyone. They were islands with their own rules and regulations. They didn't need to be stated: yet no one ever questioned them.

Dad was a member of the Orange Order, and as was his habit on a Friday he called in at his local pub after work. The next day was the 12th of July, when the lodges of the Order would march through the city in a triumphalist display. He had a cardboard shoe box under his arm and set it on the counter while he opened his pay packet. One of his drinking pals stood beside him. 'A big biff, two bottles of brown and twenty Roselawn tombstones.' Sean the owner called out, knowing what the order would be. Up came a large glass of cheap fortified wine, two pint bottles of Guinness and a pack of Park Drive. Cigarettes were referred to as Roselawn tomb-stones as Roselawn was the name of the local cemetery. Dad fumbled a pound note out of the brown envelope as 'Duckie' his pal downed the 'big biff' in seconds and gestured for Sean to replenish his glass, which he did as effortlessly as Duckie had drunk the previous glass.

'New pair of walking shoes?' asked Sean loudly, knowing that the Orange parades were always referred to as 'the walk'. Dad nodded. The publican asked to see the shoes and admired them when Dad opened the box and handed them to him. 'Tidy bit of work there, Jacky, but I'll tell you something for nothing: you'll be crippled before you reach the field!' he commented, bending the toe of the shoe upwards. 'The field' was the end destination of every Orange procession and that's exactly what it was, an open field in the coun-tryside on the outskirts of the city. Here the marchers rested and lunched or listened to speeches about Protestantism, politics, loyalty

and the enemies of Ulster before walking back to the city again.
'What size are they?' Sean asked and when he found out that Dad's
new shoes were the same size as his own he immediately proposed
that my dad should allow him to wear the shoes for the rest of the
evening, 'by which time they'll be well and truly broken in'. Dad
and Duckie looked at one another for a moment then smiled. Sean
smiled with them and winked, 'That way, you can all say I did my
bit for the Orange Order and that's a big deal for a St Anthony's
altar boy.' And he stepped out of his own shoes and into Dad's. For
the rest of the evening he walked up and down the bar and backwards and forwards between tables serving drunks. At the end of
the evening he handed Dad back his shoes remarking that he had
put up a few miles on them. 'All the fight is out of them now, but
I'll bless them for you if you want?' He knew he wouldn't get an
answer.

I don't think Dad ever saw any moral or meaning in the story. He
enjoyed telling it because it was a way of bringing the camaraderie
of the pub home with him. I loved the story because it mocked
the self-righteous bitterness that was coming to be associated with
this occasion.

I asked my father once why he was in the Orange Order. He
looked at me for a while as if he was never sure of what to say to
me because he was never sure why I had asked. We rarely spoke
together much in my teenage years, so when I asked him something it puzzled him. That's why, I suppose, he sometimes gave
puzzling answers, as if he was trying to shorten the gap that was
growing between us. 'People join things for all sorts of different
reasons. Sometimes it's tradition, sometimes it's something that
runs in the family, sometimes it's to show comradeship with your
friends and sometimes it's about principle, standing up for what
you believe in—' I interjected, 'Like a union, Dad?' He thought

again. 'In a way yes, and in a way no. Unions are about work and wages and the welfare of the working man. But the Order is about our culture. It's got to do with the kind of civic and religious liberties that tell you who you are.' I knew we were getting into deep waters and Dad wanted to be out of them before we both sank. 'I know what you're thinking, son,' he continued, 'but it's as I said: people join things for different reasons. Some people don't really know why they belong and they are the ones who are loudest at protesting what they are. People who shout loudest are usually the ones who think least.' Then he decided to bring the thing to an end. 'You'll understand it all when you're older, though I think you probably understand it in your own way.' The manner in which he said 'in your own way' stopped me from pursuing the matter. It was as if he was half acknowledging that the gulf between us was best left alone. My father was never an overtly demonstrative man. He could never be called wilful and if he was in any way wise it was primarily because he was tempered in his judgements. Dad's talk about the Orange Order (of which he later became a Grand Master) surprised me. He had broken a code of silence: he was giving me a warning like an old lion fending off the challenge of a younger male.

As I look back on that time and try to see the son my father saw, I am sure he was in part disappointed, confused and, ultimately, resigned. My prodigal nature had made me the son who had chosen not to follow. Yet I was so like him, choosing to live in my own instinctual way which I mostly hid from the world. I am sure he sensed it but didn't know how or why to question it. He knew our worlds were separate. That knowledge, if even he accepted it, must have caused him some hurt and a sense of loss. And if there was a measure of unspoken anger in his explanation I am sure it was because he was warning me about challenging things before I could stand on my own two feet in whatever world I was creating for myself. Even now, I am still undecided whether standing on one's own two feet also means standing alone. My father was more resolved about this. He accepted as much of the world as he thought was needful; the rest he left for others. He may have been a member of certain institutions but I don't believe he was ever a follower. He liked the company of men, but I never found him macho. Comradeship was important to him but allegiance was something he could never give unquestioningly. For the most part, he kept those questions to himself.

By the mid-1960s there wasn't much to keep me at home and there didn't seem to be much outside that attracted me either. I was in those awkward years, when the world seemed all out of focus. I was restless and discontented, without any reason. The move to the big school had increased my circle of friends and now I spent less and less time with friends from the streets around me. A distance had grown up between me and my parents. Elaine was the apple of my father's eye and he seemed to have more time for her than anyone else. He still went off on Saturday with his mates or sometimes to the pub and he was in the pub every Friday night after work. Sometimes he and Mum would go out together on Saturday nights. Dad was no longer on 24-hour call-out. It was his new, very settled routine that increasingly allowed him to go to the pub. He always came home in 'good form' but it was rarely reciprocated. Rows between my parents were becoming regular and increasingly bitter, especially on my mother's side. I found them very disturbing and dreaded hearing his key turn in the door on Friday night. I knew what was going to follow. The rows would hit fever pitch with the two of them hurling abuse at each other. It was hysterical and terrifying at times. What made it more scary was the fact that they seemed oblivious to us sitting in the room with them. Usually it would end with Mother dressing us and storming out of the house trailing us behind her. We would go to my Aunt Freda where we would stay for hours before returning home. Apart from the noise of my father's snores, the house was always silent. For days after, the atmosphere was sickening. There was silence and tension like the place was ready to explode – which it usually did the following Friday.

I hated these occasions and sat in stony silence throughout them. I hated my mother for her sickening hysteria and I hated my dad for coming home 'half-cut' each week. I didn't know who to blame. So I blamed them both and simply stared at the floor intensely until I couldn't hear the noise of their arguments any more.

At the beginning of these rows I always looked upon Dad as the culprit and I hated him for the way he treated my mother. During this time I had taken to sleeping with a knife under my pillow. It was similar to the knives I had watched the butcher work with the night we came to view the house. I didn't know why I did this. I was sleeping downstairs in a small room between the living room and the scullery and because everyone else slept upstairs, I reasoned, any intruder would find me first. My anxiety about this intruder spilled over into my dreams. The knife under my pillow offered me protection from the unknown intruder and from my dreams. I am sure now that that was a convenient excuse worked out by my rational mind. The real reason for my nightmares and the imagined intruder was those bitter hysterical rows I witnessed. Nearly every week I thought I could switch off from them but they crossed over my psychic defences only to manifest themselves in my sleep.

On one occasion when the screaming and shouting had gone on for hours, I had been in my room reading comics. I thought I was safe and was happy to be out of their way. But the walls offered no protection and my safe room became a torture chamber. I couldn't bear it; nor could I leave the house, because I would have to walk past them. So I slid the big butcher's knife from under the pillow and positioned myself behind the door. Sooner or later my father would come in through the scullery to go to the toilet out in the yard. I would stab him as many times as it took to stop the noise. Fortunately my older sister Brenda discovered me and chased me back to my room, chastising me for being 'so stupid'. But I wouldn't let her take my knife. The nightmare and reality had almost become one and the same thing ... and I still needed my knife! Yet, even if I did want to kill him, I pitied him the next day. Neither of my parents was speaking. Dad was left to make his own meals. He slouched about the house still feeling waves of resentment and anger from the previous night. He didn't know what to say to us and I was fearful that he would speak to me. For that would mean taking sides, and I wasn't on anybody's side. On these mornings, he looked so different. He seemed smaller and his face was more angular. He was a stranger and he tried to avoid looking at us as much as we tried to do the same. Both of my parents appeared lifeless, as if they had murdered a bit of each other the night before and couldn't face up to seeing what was left. Dad looked mortally wounded and also mortally sick of it all. He looked like a corpse.

Slowly my sympathies turned away from my mother because of the constancy and visceral nature of her attacks. In one sense, I didn't really blame my father for staying with his mates. Who would want to come home to this madness? In the end I stopped hearing them or seeing them even though the conflict raged in front of my face; the see-sawing of my sympathies had drained and numbed me utterly. Switching myself off happened automatically. It was as if I had developed an inbuilt early-warning system. I could feel the storm gathering so I went silently into my air raid shelter.

Some time later, I was reading D.H. Lawrence's *Sons and Lovers.*

I could hardly believe what I was reading. My mother and father were not Walter or Gertrude Morel but their domestic conflict seemed to reflect what I grew up with. Neither was I Paul Morel, the son in the story, nor did I sympathize with the author. In fact, the emotional echoes I picked up from the book led me to sympathize more with my father. I did not hate him in the contemptuous way that the son in the book hated his father. My mother's deadly hostility to my father was excessive and irrational. He was not hostile until provoked, then he had his own demons to contend with as well as my mother's. But I am sure my mother always began it. Sometimes I felt she hated his very existence. I am sure, at the height of her hysteria she hated the fact that she had ever loved him at all. I never knew what caused this change in my mother. She was never demonstrably affectionate with my father, or even with any of us, though we never doubted that she cared for us. It was my father who was the playful one. If he was ever affectionate with her in front of us she would smile at him, her eyes glowing with a mock warning. But when they argued, the menace in her eyes was terrifying.

The trajectory of my sympathies took years to develop. From a passionate concern for my mother and equally passionate dismissal of my father it slowly turned towards affection for my father, as he really was more sinned against than sinning. Long after these rows had become part of family history I was still angry with my mother. In the end, she seemed to have got over her hostility. I am sure she neither loved nor hated him, but it wasn't like a prolonged truce. It was more as if the constant conflict had wearied her. We were older now and she couldn't indulge in the hysterical histrionics of storming off into the night with her children in tow. In a way, I suppose, her feelings for us must have confused her. We were hers so she loved us – but we were his too!

I am not sure that she ever knew of my shifting allegiance. I never spoke to either of them about it. I dammed the whole thing up for years. I could never understand where it all came from or why it petered out when it did. It left me with a load of divided loyalties, resentment and unresolved confusion. All this added to the normal anxieties of adolescence and made me look outside the home for answers to everything.

PURDAH

MY FATHER DIED SUDDENLY, WITHOUT ANY ADVANCE-WARNING ILLNESS, when I was in my early thirties. By that time I had acquired a life of my own, making occasional sorties back to the house in Mayflower Street. I had noticed my father ageing. His shiny black hair was grey and receding fast, and his eyesight had gone the way of his hair, disappearing to wherever eyesight goes. Thick brown-framed glasses were constantly on his face. There was a quality of quiet about him; an air of resignation rather than acceptance. The thing that struck me most was his size. I was convinced that age had shrunk him in his last few years, as if living had been a process of erosion. Only his eyebrows had resisted and they grew in thick black tufts. I once joked with him that he wasn't really losing his hair it was just moving down his forehead. I wanted to say that his bushy brows reminded me of his own father's moustache but something stopped me. Perhaps I shied away from making a connection between the living and the dead. Talking to my father about his dead father was something neither of us had done with each other for decades. The idea seemed awkward.

An air of loneliness surrounded him. Maybe that's what enclosed him in his curious quiet. I remember on a few occasions calling in to see him in his local pub. He always stood in the same place at the corner of the bar, away from all the bustle, as if surveying the place from somewhere entirely outside it. He never noticed me walk across to him. It wasn't until I stood beside him with the usual 'How ya doin'?' that he seemed to know I was there.

Dad had always drunk with the same three or four friends. Now he stood alone watching over the empty space. We often talked about his mates. They had all died within a few years of each other. Dad often remarked that he was 'the last man standing'. His use of this battlefield image didn't really strike me then but the quiet that hung around him was an indicator of internal conflict. Invariably he talked about his own dying, but it was always indirectly. He spoke about 'his number being called' and the fact that he wanted to be cremated rather than buried. When I dismissively remarked that he would soon be reading the death notices in the *Belfast Telegraph* every night just like my mother, he said that he really wanted to 'go before her'. I never questioned him about this; I didn't want to pursue the conversation. There was something in the way he said it. It was affectionate and serious. My dad could cook and clean, he could iron his own clothes, he could even sew better than my mother. His statement wasn't made out of fear of being unable to look after himself. It hinted at loneliness, the dread of coming home to an empty house, of sleeping and waking up in the same emptiness every day. He wasn't being morbid or seeking attention. There was a sense that he was preoccupied and that he didn't want to talk about his thoughts. They just leaked out in these throwaway remarks.

He spoke about taking early retirement and buying a new car so that he could take the kids to places. The kids were his grand-children and it was as if he was planning his last few years with them. I tried to dissuade him from retiring but in his view the 'package' that came with it would keep my mother financially secure even if he died before her. He was always trying to place his death in relation to others. 'People retire to live not to die, da,' I remonstrated with him and there was an air of coldness, cynicism and finality about his answer: 'As long as you've got something to live for.' Dad was rarely cynical even when he was joking. His remark demolished my small advice and I knew I couldn't ask him what he meant.

There was a lot of thinking going on in my father's head but he had no mates left to share it with. He stood in his lonely corner with ghosts. On occasions when he mentioned dying to my mother, she dismissed it with the words, 'What are you talking like that for? Sure you're not dead yet.' When I think back on it now, a quarter of a century later, I'm sure my father knew that he was going to die. It's a feeling I have. I just know that some part of him was aware, not of how he would die, but only that he would; and that death was very near.

I remember going to the morgue to identify him. When they pulled the sheet back off his face he looked like he was sleeping; his mouth was pursed and slightly open as if he was about to take a deep breath. Dad was a great snorer. He roared his snores. Now he was silent. The doctor and the policeman who had brought me to the morgue looked at me. I nodded my head once, the way penitents do when they have received the host. Then I left him stone cold and silent for ever. I didn't feel anything, because he wasn't there. There was a corpse that looked like him, that's all, and I had to get it buried. Up until the funeral I was obsessed with the idea that I would not be able to lift his coffin. The weight of it would crush me. I thought of every way of avoiding 'the lift'. But the dead weight waited for me.

After the obsequies were over, I felt confused and angry. Confused because the coffin was so incredibly light, as if he wasn't in it, and angry because I'd been somehow sidelined. I kept asking my friends why I hadn't been there when he died. It was an irrational and stupid question, maybe because it came from a stupefied mind; a mind suddenly confronted with its own mortality. I distinctly remember my father's coffin being wheeled down the aisle of the funeral home's church. It was hoisted from its trolley to the hearse like a piece of timber for transportation. Suddenly I was breathless, angry and empty. I was terrified that they would drive him away and that would be it. All the lost years of separate lives and miscommunication weighed down on me. I know now that I was experiencing some of that same loneliness that my father's words had hinted at.

I shouldered his coffin into the grave. The unbearable lightness of it remains with me today.

When I left the graveyard I decided to leave Ireland. It was hardly a conscious thing and I told no one about it. I didn't fully understand it or where the impulse came from: I just knew it was time to go, the way my father had known it was his time to go.

It took me many more years to readjust the balance in my responses to that time and all the half-understood history that had in some inexplicable way gathered itself into my father's coffin. Part of it came in the last years of my mother's life in the early 1990s. She was ill and suffered from a rapid decline due to Alzheimer's disease. Sometimes she didn't know any of us. Sometimes she was angry and I realized that whatever else she may have forgotten, she still knew how to swear! Most times she seemed happy in her own world that none of us knew anything about.

The things she didn't remember were as telling as the weird and confused things that she did. Other people tried to fill in this surreal patchwork with their own recollections. It was an eerie kind of jigsaw haunted by unfamiliar people and places, where nothing fitted together seamlessly. The act of trying to get hold of her history so that I could fill in my own had the double effect of allowing me to jettison a lot of misunderstanding by understanding more of this dying woman.

The doctors found that she had a series of small scars on her heart which suggested that over her lifetime she had had several mini-strokes. This discovery astonished me. How did we not know? How did she cover it up? Why was she afraid to seek help? Maybe she never knew how to ask. Whatever else may have caused them, I became convinced that they were evidence of a life of hidden emotional turmoil. I don't know how I reasoned it but for me the scars on her heart spoke loudly about the missing parts of her history. At the end of her life I was only beginning to discover my mother and that in its turn helped me to unearth incidents in my own childhood that took me by surprise. I was beginning to understand how her life impacted on my own. Mother had talked about people and happenings in her past that suggested why she was the way she was. They also hinted at what drove her. The more I discovered, the more a feeling of recognition began to stalk me. Back in my childhood I too had buried feelings of not belonging. I could feel them again, vibrating in the world my mother's regression had thrown up.

My mother was the eldest daughter of nine siblings and it seems she was expected to spend a lot of her own childhood looking after the others. Her own father, my grandfather, the man who never knew my name, appears to have expected much of her in the way of service and gave back little in the way of affection. He was a great churchgoer and no doubt had a very Victorian view of what children should and should not do. I got the feeling that my mother was more of a servant than a daughter. If she had a dislike of men who were abusive to women, my grandfather had instilled it in her by his neglect. It was obviously something that he never saw, or felt the need to make good, as the years passed. My mother's relationship with her own mother was also ambiguous; although she constantly visited her and nursed her until she died, I rarely witnessed any affection when they were together. 'Duty' would have been a more appropriate word.

In those last few years as she retreated into the progressive deterioration of Alzheimer's disease Mother only remembered the house she grew up in. She never recalled her life in Evolina Street. She had flashing recollections of our last home and all she used to say about my father was that 'he went away one day and never came back and good luck to him!'

His passing seemed to have little effect on her. There were no tears, no sadness, no grieving. I put it down to shock and my mother's steely resolve never to show any emotion. But I didn't know then what I was learning now: as a child, she had received little in the way of emotional nurturing. Her childhood was very short with a squad of siblings to look after. As a young woman she became self-reliant very quickly because she had to. Even if she had had someone to turn to, she would not have known how to. There were other things she said which meant nothing to me. I didn't know the people she spoke of. Many were mentioned with obvious distaste; other things made her laugh. Sometimes she laughed quietly to herself about something none of us knew anything about. Often when someone, particularly a man, was introduced whom she should have known she would stare at them in a long, withering silence. Most times she didn't like to be touched and rarely acknowledged it if she was.

The fact that she remembered very little about living in Evolina Street amazed me. She might recall other things that happened during the years we lived there but, living in that house in that street was something she had little recall of. It was when I was puzzling over this and trying to piece together other people's memory of that time that I was made aware of my own lack of knowledge. I was greatly concerned about why my mother had so easily forgotten my father. The way she spoke of him, it was as if she had simply 'let him go'. Generally her memory could be prompted about him but she was dismissive too, as if she didn't want to be bothered by the effort. I was surprised at this, given their bitter quarrels combined with the fact that they had grown up a railway bank apart and had known each other as teenagers. Trying to rebuild this picture of my mother's past, I was beginning to find a woman whose life history was filled with hurt and rejection. It was also a picture of survival, for she had refused to surrender to the pain. Mother was strong, defiant and angry at injustice because that was the way her life had been.

I found myself looking at this woman who had to be reminded who I was, realizing that there was so much that I didn't know that the bits and pieces of history I gleaned from other relatives were a revelation. Her own quirky flashes of the past sometimes threw me completely. Her own mother having tattoos on her body, and my uncle having been sent to Borstal with, it seems, his father's approval, were the least of them. My mother had never talked about her childhood even though I pestered her frequently, and now I was discovering it piece by fractured piece. The weight of the things she had endured and kept to herself for a lifetime amazed and frightened me. Mother was forever trying to help others and solve their problems, yet she had built a defensive wall around herself for the whole of her life.

When we moved to our new house, Mother became pregnant again after almost ten years. It began to dawn on me that it was about nine months after the birth that the rows had begun. Maybe this was the key to my mother's madness, and the reason she remembered nothing of our previous home. The new baby must have disinterred deep, unresolved feelings about the child who died. The child that she never saw nor held. The child that was taken away from her and buried, and she was never told where. My father was the only contact with that child and maybe when she saw him hold and nurse the new one the hurt unleashed itself in the way that it did. Pain, long buried comes out like poison. Maybe too, that was why she was never demonstrably affectionate with us. She never knew affection and was afraid of it. It would breach that protective wall. With so much despair to unload, she only knew how to shout and scream at the person who was closest to her. She could only throw it in his face disguised as something else.

My father's response was to stay away from home. In any case, Friday nights were sacrosanct for the working man in Belfast. They all gathered in their local: the ritual was obligatory. I'm sure my father didn't understand what was going on in my mother's inner life. None of us did. She was a closed book with a lock on it. The camaraderie of the pub, the companionship of friends and its ambient embrace became his substitute for the absence of affection at home. He steeled himself with alcohol. It put a distance between him and the torment he was coming home to. Most times I pitied him. He was not able for her, and she had no way of explaining herself. The rage and the pain was too great. The key had been long since lost.

My mother died a tiny frail creature curled up in the foetal position, childlike, in a world of her own, away from the burdensome one she had carried silently inside herself for so long. This is how I remember her dying. It is not how I remember her living. If under the spell of Alzheimer's she forgot a lot of things, visiting her in those last few weeks I remembered the stories she shared with the handful of neighbours who came and went. Occasionally I would hear them talking, usually about their husbands or money. They were funny stories. I loved to listen because laughing was not something my mother did often.

There was the story of the man who had bought a suit from a friend for five shillings only to find when he arrived home that the bottom had been burnt out of the trousers with a hot iron. The friend who had sold him the suit had drunk the five shillings as soon as the unfortunate purchaser turned the corner. His wife scolded him for his stupidity and his poor choice of friends. The next day, while her husband was sulking around the house, she and a friend took the suit to the pawn. The pawnbroker only ever checked the cuffs of the jacket and trousers to ensure that they weren't frayed and he paid the women twenty-two shillings for the suit. Out of sympathy, the wife bought her husband a cheap pair of trousers for a few shillings and told him she had given the suit to the ragman and borrowed the money for the new trousers. Her gullible husband believed her, thought she was a saint, and put two shillings extra in her housekeeping money the next week. These stories were better than the *Keystone Cops* or *Abbot & Costello*. There was a sense of slapstick and idiot buffoonery about them. But they were real, and the women who sat in our house enjoyed every minute of them. Stories poured out one after the other, and there were some that I suppose I wasn't meant to hear. Stories about infidelity. Even a story about a woman having a sudden miscarriage in the scullery and panicking about cleaning up 'the mess' before her husband came home. 'Should have left the mess to him who made it!' I heard one of the women declare.

One of these neighbours had a daughter who had married and gone off to live in the country and would call to see my mother when she visited her own. Every time she came she ended up crying. But it was angry crying. I always went into my bedroom next to the living room. The walls of our house were not made to be sound-proof, and I could hear the girl's anguished complaints. 'Should have never married him. He's forever down in that mission hall hallelujahing with the rest of them. And every night he is down on his knees asking Jesus to save me and make me a good and obedient wife. Christ Jesus, it's saving I need all right, saving from the likes of him!' When she was angry she was fine but then the sobbing started: 'If I could only get away from him. I get sick just sitting in the same room as him. Sometimes I feel I'm dying down there.' My mother would sit and listen, waiting until the girl was so choked up with desperation that she could hardly speak. Then she inter-rupted, her words calm but forceful. 'Now you listen to me. You don't have to put up with any of that. You're not a prisoner in that house. You may be married to him but he doesn't own you. You just tell him, he might be married to Jesus, but you're not. He can keep all his Jesus talk to himself. Remind him that he wasn't like that when you married him and you don't have to put up with it just because you have a ring on your finger.'

Mother was not a tea and sympathy woman. She gave advice like a command, like the secular equivalent of a female Moses. Her first commandment might be, Thou shall not do what others tell you to do; her second, Thou shall only do that which is pleasing unto thyself and the others can go and frig themselves if they don't like it! Once when a neighbour told her of a cousin who had 'turned' – had become a Catholic in order to be married and had signed 'the promises' to bring up the children in the Catholic faith – my mother was adamant, but her words made me laugh: 'Unless she married the priest and is sleeping with him she can tear up "the promises". Her children are her own and she'll have enough promises to keep with them without a priest breathing down her neck! Women need to cling to their children, not the tailcoats of clergymen.' Mother Moses was not so much a confessor as someone who heard other people's secrets. But if anyone complained about their marriage and how unhappy or unwanted they felt, she chastised them for being foolish. 'Marriage can be purdah for a woman. If you think it's a cure for loneliness you shouldn't do it!'

I thought about this during the last months of her life. The word 'purdah' had stuck with me. I think I was about fifteen at the time she said it and a woman's purdah fascinated me, whatever it might mean. I thought my mother was never lonely. Well, no more than anyone else. She never allowed herself to be: she was always doing for others or listening to others complaining. But I don't think she had a special friend, someone that she could complain to.

THE BRAHMA BULL AND THE CRINOLINE LADY

O the bricks they will bleed and the rain it will weep
And the damp Lagan fog lull the city to sleep
It's to hell with the future and live on the past
May the Lord in His mercy be kind to Belfast

THESE ARE THE CLOSING LINES OF A CONTEMPORARY POEM BY MAURICE
James Craig set to a traditional refrain that I remember from my
childhood. It has re-emerged with its new suit of words. I still
smile at the poem's implicit cynicism and its plea for God's mercy
on a city that has mauled the heart out of itself for decades. The
suffocating presence of the past and all its attendant shibboleths
hangs heavy on the city I grew up in. Sometimes that seems a long
time ago and then it doesn't. The past is like an accordion player's
moving hands pulling out and squeezing back the melody of
memory. Over the years I have come to believe that wherever we
go in the world and whatever we do or become, there is always a
reckoning. I am sure you can never truly understand the journey
you have been on or what you have become until you return to

your point of departure. So I chose to fast-forward out of my childhood. By the mid-1960s I was no longer a child. Before the decade ended and the 'Troubles' began I had left the city I grew up in. My father died suddenly when he was sixty-two. My mother lived for another twenty years. Most of that time I lived away from the city, frequently abroad, returning now and again like the proverbial prodigal son. I have gone back to the last months of my mother's life because it was then that, unknown to her, she gave me this memoir and I found and fell in love with her again.

Lots of street songs and come-all-yes have come back to me as I journeyed back across the years. I thought I had forgotten them but they have returned to me in snatches of verse and melody like signposts along the roadway. One of them is entitled 'The Raggle Taggle Gypsy'. The verse I remember runs 'What care I my house and land/What care I for my children O/I will eat the grass and drink the dew/for I'm off with the Raggle-Taggle Gypsy O.' For more years than I care to remember I have been following after that dark-haired gypsy until eventually I, too, had to come home wearied by the fancies of the gypsy dream weaver.

I moved to live in Dublin and was making frequent trips to Belfast. My father had been dead some twenty years and my mother was still living in the house in Mayflower Street. She appeared to be the tough old bird I remembered, self-sufficient, always cleaning and polishing about the house as if it might disappear if she didn't. She was less mobile now and for years she had been giving herself insulin injections for diabetes. I don't remember her ever having an ailment in her life that required the attention of a doctor. Mother was hard on doctors. In her view men knew little or nothing about women's bodies. 'It's men that make women ill. So why would I want one of them trying to tell me what is or what is not wrong with me?' she would declare if anyone suggested she see a doctor.

Her diabetes had been diagnosed when she was in hospital giving birth to my younger sister. She was fond of explaining that her hair turned grey overnight a few weeks after the baby was born. I smiled knowingly. Such transformations only occur in Greek tragedies – but as I look back on it, I do recall that at one time she was a brunette and the next she was grey. I admired her for how she coped with her diabetes. I was squeamish about such things but Mother had no such qualms. 'If a thing needs doing, just do it and don't think about it. Thinking time is a waste of doing time' was her answer when I asked her about sticking needles in herself. And thinking was a particularly male affliction: '. . . and that's why men generally die before women,' she informed me. 'Old men sit on their backsides thinking about the past until they eventually talk themselves into the grave.' I laughed at these homilies and once remarked to her that my father had only been sixty-two when he died, and was still working. 'Aye,' she answered. 'But he was thinking too much about what he would do when he retired.' 'Thinking and stress are not the same thing,' I calmly told her. Mother was not one to be put in her place so easily. 'They both come out of the same egg, and one begets the other.' With that she brought the conversation to an end. Mother had hardly mentioned my father's name since his death. One day her hair was coloured and the next it had turned grey. One day my father was alive and the next he wasn't: that was all there was to it and nothing more needed to be said on the subject.

At first I simply put it down to the process of grieving and the peculiarities of her character. It was not Mother's way to dwell on things, so I let it rest. After a while her silence irked me. It was a few months before I tried to talk to her about it. 'You don't bring that up with me,' she said. Her face was fixed and there was no trace of emotion in her voice, but there was something in the accusatory way she pronounced 'you' at the beginning of her answer. I watched her face waiting for something more. I should have known better. I resented her silence and the seeming erasure of my father's existence. What I didn't realize was that I was going through the grieving process in a similar state of submerged silence. In our separate ways we had both sealed the tomb and didn't know how to reopen it. It was as if the past thirty years had not happened. If she chose to forget it so emphatically, then where did that leave us, her children? What had the past meant? How could it be so easily buried? There were no ready-made answers. Mother had chosen to dam things up inside herself. When anyone brought up the subject of my father, her reaction was muted. She was like a tide going out; quietly and invisibly, part of her seemed to leave the room.

If Mother's memory had made huge tidal retreats, it left me stranded with my own memories. In piecing this memoir together they have come back again, as unresolved things do. They wash up again years later.

In the months after my father's death I became aware of something I had lived with all my life yet had never noticed. There were no family photos on display and there never had been. It was when I was sorting out the clothes for my father to be buried in that I found them packed away in a biscuit tin in my parents' wardrobe. There were photos of the day of their wedding. Standing outside the registry office they appeared young and handsome and happy. There were assorted photos of me and my sisters as children and a few holiday snaps. The main events of marriage and birth were recorded for posterity but there was precious little to record the years in between. The fact that there were no pictures of family or friends on the wedding day didn't strike me. I was so delighted with the relaxed atmosphere of the smiling couple that the absence of any well-wishers was irrelevant. It did feel strange to be laying out the clothes my father was to be buried in while I was looking at a picture of him on his wedding day. Suddenly I became indecisive. I wanted to ask Mother's advice about what he should wear but I didn't. Briefly I thought of writing a letter to him and placing it inside his coat pocket. I hesitated, realizing that I didn't know what to say. There were so many questions I wanted to ask that I knew would never be answered. Then I thought what if the funeral attendants found it and returned it to my mother, thinking it had mistakenly been left there? I felt foolish, vulnerable, sad and curiously angry all at once. I was afraid of what others might read even though I was unsure what I might write. What I failed to understand then was that if I was unsure and afraid to write a letter to a dead man because of what it might reveal to others, then why did I expect my mother to talk to me about things I might not have understood even if she had the words for them? I placed the photos back in the tin box thinking that at some time in the future I might talk to her about them.

However, there were two pictures hanging on the wall of the tiny living room. My father had bought both of them. They were cheap reproductions that must have been churned out in their thousands. One depicted the head and shoulders of an oriental woman. Her face was attractive in the way that some men find oriental women attractive, her ethnic face westernized in the style of a glamorous but lifeless mannequin. Her clothes were rendered in garish turquoise, green, yellow and gold: a poorly remodelled kimono emphasized the lady's feminine appeal rather than the culture which she supposedly came out of. The sallow complexion of her skin gave the impression that it had been smoothed over with some dun-coloured residue. I have seen that picture so many times over the years in car boot sales, church jumbles and junk shops that I know my father was not the only man to have been captivated by the image's questionable charm. The other picture looked as if it could have been an illustration from a children's story set in Mexico. It revealed a rickety old cart drawn by a mule which was shading itself under a tree. On the ground the carter was seated with his back to the wheel and his head resting on his knee in the attitude of sleep. A great sombrero obscured his face. The scene was highlighted by brightly coloured wild flowers in the undergrowth. The two images had nothing in common. They hung on the only two spaces on our living-room walls for as long as I remember. When I was a young man they irritated me. They were kitsch and naïve. After a while I didn't see them any more. A long time later they came back to me, demanding my attention. Now they seemed to be animate things, resonating with an importance that mocked my adolescent dismissal. Now they were no longer a piece of irritating kitsch: they were icons talking to me out of my own history.

It was many years after my father had died, when I was making visits to my mother who was nearing the end of her own life, that I sat and looked at them. Mother's age and her recurrent bouts of illness meant that she had taken to sleeping on the couch in the living room. Many evenings as she slumbered under the image of the sleeping Mexican carter I reflected on how my mother had little interest in the aesthetic appearance of things. She had never bought a picture to hang on the wall, and house plants were unheard of. Apart from her beloved brassware there was little ornamentation that I could associate exclusively with her. The décor changed and the house was painted because it needed to be painted, not from any desire to make it more pleasing. I knew my mother had worn make-up and lipstick but as I watched her sleep I couldn't remember her applying it or fussing over clothes. In her wedding photo she had looked like a forties film star. Where had it all gone? It wasn't simply age that had stolen her femininity; at some time in her life she had decided that such things were not worth the time spent on them. Her face was very old now and make-up would have made it more like a mask. Mother wasn't keen on cover-ups, partly because she 'didn't care a tuppence ha'penny toss' what people thought and probably because she was quick to see through the guise of others. Watching her in the carelessness of sleep I thought how she looked a lot like her father, and that made me think of my own.

In him, there seemed to be more of the feminine. He was the one who painted the mirrors at Christmas. It was Dad who taught me to make colourful decorations from painted newspaper. He made up stories about the injured creatures he brought home. It was Dad who bounced children on his knee and played with them like a child himself. I looked at the pictures on the wall again. They had more in common than I'd thought. They were images of a world that seemed tranquil and dreamy. A world that was exotically beautiful, though somehow inaccessible. Maybe his pictures were his dreams. Perhaps he had an unrealized wanderlust hidden inside him. Maybe he too hankered after the 'Raggle-Taggle Gypsy O'.

Mother turned in her sleep. Maybe she was aware of my thinking and was protesting a little as if saying, Your father's gone. It's me you're here to look after. The thought made me smile. Mother would never ask anyone to look after her. Even if she wanted to she wouldn't know how to. Mother was Father's opposite: her impetus was male. She was the one who got things done. Action, even frenzy, attended her. Cleanliness, tidiness, making the world better, throwing out the claptrap and making the house function – that was what mattered. I looked at the fireplace and the mantelpiece littered with gleaming brass. The fire was blazing. She had banked it up with coal and slack before she lay down. Across the room, a few feet from where she lay, a china cabinet stood. Next to the fireplace, it was the other main feature of the room. It was a hideously modern misrepresentation of art nouveau, all glass and mirrors and crammed with little bric-à-brac ornaments, the kind every house in the street was full of. Mementoes of childhood holidays that my sister and I had bought as gifts, thinking them wonderful works of art. There were animal figures and human characters which were wistful and full of sentiment, the by-product of a Victorian era that viewed the world through mawkish rose-tinted spectacles. Toby jugs, Coronation memorabilia, porcelain teacups, thimbles that had never been used, a Babycham Bambi and much more. To Mother the cabinet was little more than a dust gatherer, but for reasons known only to her, it remained where it was.

One item was always placed to the forefront of the display after its contents had their regular dust down. It was a small ceramic figure of a young girl dancing. Her arms were delicately poised in front of her as if stretching out to someone. The hands and fingers were finely wrought as though the artist had taken a lot of time to create that pleading gesture. What drew me to the figure was the exquisite lacework of her petticoats, layer upon gossamer layer of them. They were so intricate and detailed that I used to think that a thin film of liquid porcelain must have been poured over real lace and then attached to the dancer. They seemed to be floating as if the little dancer was about to fly off. Mother always referred to the little dancer as the 'Crinoline Lady'. I don't know where the figure came from. I remember it sitting on top of the small cast-iron fireplace in my parents' bedroom in our previous house. The 'Crinoline Lady' must have been packed with great care to ensure she survived the journey to our new home. Now that I think of it, the little dancer was the only vaguely feminine thing I associated with my mother. It was the only object that was clearly hers. It was special to her in a way that her brassware was not. I wondered at the 'Crinoline Lady' who was about to dance off into the air. I looked at my mother asleep and thought how she too was about to leave this world. She was the little dancer grown old and weary. Why had she looked after this little figure for so long? What special meaning did it have for her? Did she, in some part of herself, want to be a dancer and fly off? I wished I could ask her but I knew I never would. Like 'the Crinoline Lady', Mother would just look at me, silent as her statue.

A big white ornamental bull sat on the bottom shelf. It was Dad's. He called it the 'Brahma Bull' and told me that bulls like it were only found in India. This magnificent animal always looked out of place among all the other paraphernalia in the cabinet. There was a look of dismissive hauteur about it as if it regarded everything around it as of lesser significance. It wasn't really white, more a creamy colour with a long mane of thick brown hair. On the back of its neck, above its shoulders it carried what looked like a deflated hump. Short and black horns swept backwards from its head. Curiously, its ears were large elongated ovals: they protruded from its head at the top and back of its jaw. The bull's head was huge and heavy, inset with great staring eyes. When you forgot the muscularity of its bearing, it looked gentle like a deer. The bulk of the beast's body did not allow you to be taken in for long. Its legs were short and thick to carry such weight and its scrotal area almost touched the ground. Here was a creature who knew its place. The 'Brahma' would cede nothing to man or beast. Its pride of bearing flowed out of every line. The fact that the enamelling had uniformly cracked all over it did not detract from it; it simply toned down the white lustre of its coat giving it the appearance of having flecks of grey and silver hair in its hide. It aged the bull and made it more real. I knew that Dad had bought it on some outing with my mother.

What was it that had attracted him to the creature in the first place? What did my mother see in it that made her keep it safe, like the little dancer, all these years?

I took the bull out and noticed that one of its horns and ears had been broken off and glued back into place. Any other ornament would have been dispatched to the bin without a second thought but the 'Brahma' had been saved from such a fate. Mother must have sensed its importance. I smiled at the thought that maybe she had broken it accidentally while clearing out the cabinet to dust it. She must have glued it together without telling Dad. Was it a way of secretly having one over on him, or did she genuinely sense its importance to him? I would never know. I only knew that neither I nor my sisters broke the 'Brahma'. Dad had not damaged it, as he never went near the china cabinet, and he would not have made such an untidy repair. So there was only one suspect and she was saying nothing.

My ruminations about the mystery of the broken bull's ear suddenly unearthed in my memory another household artefact that had been missing for years. Dad had once brought home a small cuckoo clock and hung it in the corner of the room, over the gas meter box. The little bird stuck its head out on the half-hour and chirped once. At the hour it emerged in its full glory, cuckooing loudly. Dad said he was brought up to the sound of clocks ticking and chiming so he liked the cuckoo clock. Mother hated it. Every day when he went to adjust the timing chains, she would bristle. 'I've enough to do in the day without listening to that thing reminding me every hour,' she protested. Dad refused to hear and kept pulling the winding chains. For several months after it was brought into the house the cuckoo was allowed to sing, but no song lasts for ever. One evening Dad sat looking at the wall clock in silence and then announced that it wasn't marking the hour. No one had noticed and no one said anything. It was only to be expected: the clock was a matter of disagreement between Mother and Father so my sisters and I stayed out of it.

For a few evenings Dad worked at the clock but it was a lost cause. The chirping cuckoo refused to come out of its box and time passed unheralded in the house. Dad lost interest and after a time the clock itself disappeared. I was convinced that the failure of the bird's mechanism was an act of sabotage but I never shared my suspicions with anyone. I was no lover of the clock anyway. I suppose that as the bull made no noisy intrusions into Mother's life it was spared the fate of the cuckoo. Then I reasoned that it was more than that. The bull was powerful in its silence, the way my father could be. Perhaps Mother thought it was better left alone. Only she knew it was damaged. She, after all, must have repaired it. Maybe that was enough. It gave her an edge over the power of silence!

I had grown up in this house and had left it many years ago. During that time I had made many irregular visits, necessary ones, occasioned by illness or work needing done or the obligation of birthdays or Christmas. The bull, the ceramic dancer and even the cuckoo clock in its time had all been there but never before had I considered them with such intensity. Apart from my sleeping mother and myself, they were the other presences in the room. They radiated a life of their own, uncovering memories and feelings that surprised me. It was the same with the pictures on the walls. My dislike of them seemed irrelevant beside what they now seemed to reveal about my dad. I wondered if the appeal of the images lay in the unconscious feeling they triggered in the man, feelings of escape, longing, beauty, desire and natural harmony. The world the people in the pictures inhabited hinted at a kind of paradise.

I was thinking about these things when I remembered a film from the late 1950s. Although it had been screened on television several times I felt I had watched it with my parents. In my mind I saw them sitting together on the settee while I sat on the floor in my pyjamas in front of the fire. Dad had made rasberryade and ice-cream milkshakes. There were chocolate biscuits, crisps and a saucer full of midget gems of which Dad had insisted that the black ones be left for him. The film was called *The World of Suzie Wong*, I think. It starred William Holden as an American artist who had come to Hong Kong, or maybe it was China, in search of new inspiration. The Suzie Wong character was played by the actress Nancy Kwan who affected a dreadful Chinese accent. Her eye make-up was heavily accentuated to give her face an oriental look. Her hair was very long and unnaturally black, tied up in a chignon. Her clothes were silky and gaily coloured with embroidered flowers and animals. In the course of the film Suzie becomes the artist's model. She is innocent, playful and childishly demanding. Inevitably, the artist falls in love with this child-woman without realizing it. Several scenes towards the end of the film are backdropped with the work the artist has created, street scenes, harbour scenes, family groups and landscapes gradually giving way to more and more paintings of the model, marking his increasing infatuation. I realized the artist's paintings of his model were echoing Dad's picture of the oriental woman. Was she his Suzie Wong? Did my dad harbour a dream of going to some exotic land and living as a painter? Was the picture of the Mexican scene another manifestation of his wishful thinking?

Before he died my father had started night classes in painting and drawing. He obviously had some rudimentary talent and I knew he was anxious about how he would spend his time in retirement. Now I was beginning to think he had had this urge about painting long before retirement loomed. As a teenager I had read Somerset Maugham's novel *The Moon and Sixpence*, loosely based on the life of the artist Paul Gauguin. The book had inspired me when I read it. Here I was some thirty years later dimly conceiving my father as another Gauguin turning his back on Belfast's mean streets to run off to an exotic paradise with nothing more than a suitcase full of cheap sketching paper and an assortment of paint and brushes. I was even more convinced that the 'Raggle-Taggle Gypsy' had been whispering in my dad's ear as well as my own. I couldn't get the image out of my head of my dad, wrapped in a native sarong, staring out across some isle of Avalon with his fingers wet with paint! Mother must have tuned into my rapture. She turned and slowly began to wake. 'Oh Maurice, what are you doing here?' she asked me.

THE LONG GOODBYE

MAURICE WAS MY MOTHER'S YOUNGEST BROTHER, THE ONE WHO VISITED us at Balloo on his motorbike and sidecar. He was about twenty-five years older than me. As far as I was concerned we bore little resemblance to each other. Failure to recognize me was becoming a habit with my mother. If I wasn't Maurice, I was her youngest brother Harry. I dismissed it as the forgetfulness of age and used to tease her about it: 'You're losing your marbles, Minnie'; to which she would sometimes answer that she had a head like a sieve or complain that if she wasn't careful she would not be able to find her way home from the end of the street. Mother was not given to light-hearted self-ridicule. This forgetfulness should have registered with me. Mother probably did not want it registering with anyone: that would create a fuss, and fussing with my mother was some-thing everyone wanted to avoid. Apart from rarely recognizing me, she seemed to have lost track of her neighbours. If I mentioned any of them by name she would look blankly until I fed her some information: 'Do you not remember Ivy who lived next door to Mrs Lynn and was always complaining about Mrs Lynn's big ginger tomcat?' Then she would remember. Increasingly she would dismiss such conversations, claiming not to have seen the person for years.

Other things began happening with regularity in the house. The teapot would be left to stew on the stove for hours. The pot of potatoes and vegetables which she had prepared for her dinner would be left until they had burned dry. The stench of stewed tea, blackened potatoes and burnt metal were becoming familiar. 'Oh dear, I don't know where my head is these days,' was her usual response if anyone bantered with her about the 'burnt offerings'. Forgetfulness is one thing, but when a person stops doing familiar things you have to put it down to more than simply having got out of the habit. Mother was a great one for reading the death notices in the evening paper. Every night she would sit scanning the columns for someone she had known. Increasingly the people she mentioned had belonged to her life as a young woman or were the sons and daughters of neighbours she had known as a child. Now she stopped reading the paper, with the excuse that she could never find where she had left her glasses. She also stopped watching the news on television, which she had never missed. The radio too was permanently switched off. Silence became Mother's milieu. She took to sitting by the fire staring into it for long periods.

These changes seemed a matter of course for an elderly person living alone and so, I supposed, did the personality changes that came with them. She was becoming impatient and angry over little things. Her outbursts were laced with swearwords that came from nowhere, as if she had no time for anyone or anything and had become irritable and cynical. She was quite a handful, her moods were difficult to deal with and I had little time for what I saw as an increasingly warped view of the world. I made the mistake of seeing all these changes as separate, the usual effects of ageing. I failed to see that they represented one disparate but critical mass. What I didn't realize then, and only begin to realize now, was that if Mother's personality was changing it was because her world was changing. She was losing a meaningful relationship with the world around her as her mind slowly but surely moved on to another one. She was becoming dismissive of everything because she had less and less connection with things. At first the memory lapses were an irritation to her. As they became longer, the irritation turned into refusal to be bothered with a world that she no longer knew.

I should have recognized it when she complained about falling while out shopping. I should have known when her fridge was always full of the same two or three items. When I visited her after not having seen her for a few months and encountered her emaciated face with great dark circles round her eyes. The thin blue lips like a slit rather than a mouth, and the bony skull pushing out through the skin creating a frightening mask of a face, should have warned me. But when she couldn't remember when she had last eaten or when she had her last insulin injection I knew this was not forgetfulness. She was sick.

When I later learned she was in the mid-stage of progressive Alzheimer's disease it all added up. Her deterioration was rapid and entailed long periods in hospital where everything associated with her was prefixed with the word 'geriatric'. She was in the geriatric unit, she was being looked after by geriatric nurses, and her physician was a geriatric consultant. It was as if my mother had mutated into another life form. Most of the nursing staff were kind and tolerant of this old woman who most of the time didn't seem to know or care where she was. There were times when her demeanour was aggressive and she snapped at them for not making the bed the way she wanted it or for some other insignificant reason. At first I found it embarrassing, then I thought: how could she be anything else? Mother was a fighter. She always had to fight for things; if not for herself then for others. For all I knew, the nurses fluttering around the beds, fixing up lines, pulling curtains, raising and lowering headrests could have been the mill girls in the factory where she was charge hand and she was there again, barking out orders and keeping everyone in check.

As time passed, Mother's consciousness vacillated back to her past in a haphazard chronology. Undoubtedly in her mind she knew where she was and who she was with even if no one else did. The problem came when she was suddenly jolted back into the present. Then she was lost. Now the people talking to her in the hospital ward were not the children she had been playing with a moment ago. In this flip-flopping world of colliding realities she could find no bearing. Familiar landscapes, streets or rooms came and went without warning. There were echoes of things she knew and voices too but now the face in front of her did not fit the voice. The street she had been standing in a second ago was gone. The new reality which had imposed itself on her was intimidating and threatening. She did not know where she was or why all these strange people were talking to her, telling her things that didn't make sense.

Mother was a survivor. Her first instinct was to attack. Like the butterfly that flaps open its wings to reveal a great pair of staring eyes at its predator, she rounded on whoever was sitting with her. 'Who are you? What are you doing talking to me?' They were not questions, they were orders to clear off! You had to talk to her gently, telling her reassuringly who you were and why she should know you. All the time her eyes were fixed on you, never once moving away. It was hard to meet that deadly stare. After a few moments her face would soften as she began to recognize you. Then she might suddenly ask, 'Where did Sally go?' No one knew where Sally was or even who she was because Sally was a figment of her imagination.

Sometimes there was more than defence in her responses. Once, a social worker was visiting her to assess her for whatever specialist assistance he deemed she might require. He sat with a clipboard of questions talking to her as if he had already decided she was incapable of answering. 'Can you tell me your name?' Mother stared blankly at him. He noted something on his board. 'Do you know what day it is?' his voice asked vacantly. Mother kept looking at him as if he wasn't there. 'Do you know what year it is?' Again she made no response. The man made some more notes then sat quietly looking at her. 'Do you know who that lady is?' he asked, pointing to my sister. He was noting Mother's continued silence when she stretched out her arm and tapped on his notepad with her index finger. 'Listen you here to me,' she began. 'If you don't know my name, what are you doing sitting there talking to me? And if you don't know what day it is, how are you going to know where you're going tomorrow? As for what year it is, all you need to know is that I am a lot older and smarter than you!' I could hear the anger rising in her voice. Her eyes never left his face. The man had dealt with 'cranky' patients before and he attempted to calm her. 'Now I wasn't trying to upset you. I just wanted to ask you a few wee questions.' There was a note of professional insincerity in his voice as if he was talking to a troublesome child. It was a fatal error. Mother's rising anger settled into contempt. Her finger tapped again on his notepad. 'If you don't know my name, what's that written down there?' The social worker, one of the nurses who had overheard the entire conversation and my sisters and I knew there was no answer. All of us smiled, for different reasons. 'Well I think I'll just be going now, but I would like to come back in a couple of weeks to talk to you again,' he said rising to leave. 'You just do what you like, son,' she answered dismissively. There was nothing affectionate in her use of the word 'son'. The man knew it and forced another weak smile as he left the ward. Part of me was proud of my mother's pluck. I knew that even as he was leaving he would be noting the aggressive response as indicative of the patient's mental decline.

In the later stages of her 'decline' Mother was less and less inclined to deal with reality. The past became her refuge. It was a past that I knew little about and my sisters knew only a fraction of. This new world that leached out from the never-never land that Alzheimer's induced, fascinated me. I was discovering a woman whom I'd had only the faintest glimpse of as I was growing up. All the people and places that spilled out of her confused memory impacted on me in a way that I was ill prepared for. I experienced my own roller-coaster of emotions – mostly confusion, sometimes resentment; even guilt and anger were there. In a strange way Mother's world was pulling me into itself.

She seemed to spend most of her time in the years leading up to her twenties, a period of her life that was a closed book to me. She had never talked about that time. Under the spell of Alzheimer's she was off down the backstreets of her youth as if everything was yesterday; as if the present, her illness, the last forty years – and even us, her family – were a dream of half-remembered things that was rapidly evaporating. Everything after that was a struggle to remember. Sometimes she pretended to remember, to avoid the struggle. What remained were like fragments of an old faded cine film. Lots of times the reel of memory came to a flickering stop, only to restart again several years later. These slippages and loops didn't seem to bother her. When my sister produced a hastily put together album of family photos she eyed it with detachment. It was as if she was looking at someone else's history. When she discovered some yellowing snapshots of the street she grew up in or a group shot of my grandparents and their neighbours she would light up. She studied them and would smile or tut-tut in remonstration. Occasionally her lips moved as if she was talking to the people in the picture. Days later, she would be talking about them in the present tense, relating conversations she had with them only a few hours previously. She complained about having to 'run messages' for someone called Hester. She told us she had been shopping that morning with someone we knew had been dead for over twenty years. If anyone tried to inform her of the fact she simply shook her head, treating the informant like a fool. 'Don't be ridiculous, sure I was on the bus with her this morning.' Time had distorted backwards inside my mother's head: the past was her only present. Yet her recent past, the one she shared with her children and the man she had married, was all but gone. It made me think that perhaps it was more than the past that had been erased. The woman I had grown up with and who had shaped most of my childhood was disappearing into an invisible fold in time. The impetuous, hot-blooded Mother Courage had been reduced to a bedridden, feeble old woman. Her physical deterioration had been rapid and frightening and she was oblivious to it, content to be washed away by whatever spell the past cast on her. Over the months I watched her grow smaller, until she looked like a doll.

One day after much persuasion I managed to get her into a wheelchair and wrap her in blankets before taking her for a walk in the hospital grounds. She sat silently, looking around her but taking in nothing. A few bus stops from the hospital there was a graveyard. I remembered walking through graveyards with her when I was a child. She would be pushing the pram with my baby sister in it. Now here I was pushing her like an infant and trying not to think about the graveyard down the road. Her hands were long and claw-like. The flesh had fallen off them and her veins looked like they were about to burst through her skin. She was tiny in the swathe of blankets and I found myself talking to her as if she was a child.

The hospital was built on the edge of the city. From the grounds you could still see a vista of fields and hills. My mother had grown up only a few miles from where we were standing and would have been familiar with the area. It was numbingly cold but I didn't want to go back inside. 'Are you cold, Mum?' I asked. 'I'm all right,' she answered in a noncommittal way. I pointed to a small hillock, known locally as 'The Moat'. 'Do you remember the Moat, Mum? We used to come here and roll Easter eggs down it and then roll down ourselves after them.' Mother's face remained impassive. 'I banged my head once and Dad said that I was lucky, I had got another egg for nothing. That night I insisted on going to bed with a bandage on my head so that I could look like a pirate.' I was rambling but I was caught between the desperate need to keep her with me and the novelty of the memory. 'You threatened to bring out the witch's box from the glory hole if the swelling hadn't disappeared in the morning.' I paused for a moment, intrigued by the clarity of the incident. 'You know, you had me so scared that I prayed to God to take the swelling away but leave me a black eye so that I could wear an eye patch like a real pirate. Then you wouldn't think I was acting it just to get off school.'

At that moment I felt that a whole bag of memories had been poured into my head and I wanted to talk about them all. Prefixing the stories with the words. 'Do you remember' or 'I never told you this but . . .' was pointless. She couldn't remember or care. I pushed the wheelchair onwards until I found the bus shelter. Quickly I ran us into it, out of the biting wind. We were alone there and I stood watching the hospital visitors come and go from their cars. I wanted to tell her about all those secret journeys I had taken on the weekends. That was pointless too: my words would simply be blown away in the wind. So we waited in silence until that became more unbearable than the cold. As we entered the hospital again we had to pass the kitchens where the evening meal was being made. There was a slightly pungent aroma of boiled ham, chicken and over-cooked vegetables. 'This place smells of cats' piss,' Mother declared, shaking her head in disgust.

I left the hospital clutching the collar of my overcoat as it flapped around me. Passing the bus shelter, I thought of Mr Robins's pigeon loft. Mother and I must have looked like a couple of lost birds taking refuge from the storm while we tried to get our bearings. As I stood there in the freezing cold, memories had arrived in my head the way Mr Robins's birds exploded into their loft as they returned from flight. Incidents long buried beat about my head like birds looking for their perch. There was a sense of urgency about them. I needed to talk to my mother about them, but I didn't. Instead, everything just fell at my feet and was blown into the corner with the leaves that were trapped there or else were caught up in the wind's turbulence and blown away across the fields. They say that most homing birds lose their way because of the effect of elec-trical storms. The massive discharge of electrical energy short-circuits the creatures' intuitive navigational skills. Usually after a few days' rest their autopilot kicks in and they find their way home. In my mother's case that autopilot mechanism was fused beyond repair. Wherever home was for her it was very different from the one I remembered. I walked away more cold and empty inside than the inclemency of the weather could make me. Somewhere in that big grey box of a building, my mother was roosting.

On my way into the city to catch the train home I had to pass through the graveyard where Mother's parents were interred. I had passed by it so many times it hardly made any impression on me. Mother would not be buried here but with my father several miles away in another cemetery. She had little recall of her life with him. In her head she lived in a time before he came on the scene, a time when she lived at home with her parents, though they never seemed to play a great part of it. Grandmother made short appearances in this time-shifted world but my grandfather was pushed well back into the shadows. If he did briefly show up, Mother's demeanour changed markedly. It was another mystery the veil of Alzheimer's left hanging in the air. There was a chilling irony here. Mother was to be buried with the man she had lived with for most of her life, but who had disappeared almost entirely off her intellectual and emotional radar. Now in her confused present, she was back living in her parents' world and with her father – the man she had little or no time for before her mind slipped its time lines.

For ten months Mother resided in the hospital. It was obvious that she was not going to leave. My younger sister worked there and spent all her free time with her. I was able to keep abreast of what was going on by phone. It was a one-way street which Mother was disappearing down by the day. My sister's calls informed me where Mother had been that day or who had been to visit her. Mother had been no further than the ward toilet – and all her visitors were ghosts.

These ghosts fascinated me. I knew so little about my parents' childhood or adolescence. For years I had pestered them with questions, but evasion and silence was what I got in return. I was always fobbed of with statements like, 'Well, I'll tell you about that tomorrow' or, 'It's so long ago I can't really remember.' Over the years I gave up enquiring. Now I didn't have to ask questions. Alzheimer's had opened Pandora's box and all manner of things came pouring out. Of course lots of it didn't make sense and there was little order to it. It was like a jigsaw with missing parts: you had to imagine them and then put the imaginary pieces into the vacant spots.

What I found myself discovering was a lonely child who had

to grow up fast. This child observed the world acutely and kept it at arm's length. She had learned that it could be a hard place. The adults in her world were barely affectionate and she learned not to be hurt by their unkindness or neglect. As the eldest daughter she was left to look after her brothers and sisters. Often she referred to her mother as 'sitting there like Lady Muck'. There was little resentment in the reference, but it said enough. I had only ever been in my grandparents' home a few times as a child. It certainly was a cut above the others in the street. Granny McLean was a small woman but she had an air about her. She was used to having people fetch and carry. Despite her stature I was half afraid of her. Many years later, when I first read about the Queen of Hearts in *Alice in Wonderland*, I thought of Granny McLean. Grandfather was a remote authority figure. He had his own business employing several men, owned several properties and no doubt had his fingers in more pies than anyone knew about. He was the quintessential Victorian puritan father figure. He had sired nine surviving children but knew little about fathering! The maxim, 'children should be seen and not heard' was one he took to heart. When he entered the house everything went quiet.

As this picture began to unfold through Mother's disordered revelations it was becoming clear why she had found it difficult to express affection in her own life. The young woman who was forever defending others was compensating for all those years she had felt unloved and alone. There had been skeletons hidden away in my mother's cupboard. She left them there unseen by the rest of us all her life and now the alchemy of Alzheimer's was dragging them out into the light. However, they had not been quiet in their hiding place. I began to sense that those mini-strokes and the scar tissue on her heart were more than physical. They were the symptoms of psychological pain. Something that began early in her life and which she carried quietly inside herself until it erupted.

I was receiving regular updates on my mother's condition and would make the trip from Dublin to Belfast to visit her. My sisters and I would tell each other the latest event in Mother's world. It was as if she had decided to give us each separate parts of her jigsaw to piece together. By this stage Mother never recognized us as her immediate family. Instead she saw us as her brothers and sisters. Even when we did finally get her to accept who we were it lasted only for a matter of minutes. She was not totally incognizant of the world about her. She once made the remark about the other patients with her: 'See those auld decrepits there, they're all dying and they haven't the sense to give up.' It was a telling statement. She was dying herself and wasn't ready to give up. I wondered what was going on inside her head. I was never sure what she knew about her condition but sensed that she understood she was near the end. As the scars on her heart testified, Mother never looked for sympathy. Neither was she much good at confession. Touching her vulnerability had always made her angry and the more anyone probed, the angrier she became. I knew it. I had been served up many helpings of it.

Years before we were aware of her illness, I used to visit her. It was obvious she was ageing but not from that insidious senility that was already sending out its spores. I would joke with her about her relationship with my dad or with us, her kids. Mother always smiled weakly, knowing that my humour was only a guise. When I became serious and threw up some unpleasant incident or probed her about her feelings she retreated into her shell. If I was persistent she would become defensive, then angry. Sometimes the anger was almost volcanic. Even as an adult I was still looking for evidence of emotional attachment, affection – any sign of connectedness.

I wanted to feel her loneliness, for that too was a sign of having been connected. I wanted to understand how she felt about my father. Did she really love him? Did she ever tell him? Why did she hardly ever mention him? I pursued her with questions. In the end she rounded on me. It was exactly like the rows she and my father used to have. It was obvious that my insistent questions had led us both into territory that neither of us knew how to negotiate.

I studied her as she lay asleep. She was small and bony. Illness had wasted her so that her flesh looked like it had been carelessly dropped over her frame. I thought about the scaldy chicks in the pigeon house and how incredibly light they were to lift. Where had all her fierce energy gone? Where was the fight? I remembered what she had said about the other patients who hadn't the sense to give up. Had she already made that choice and decided to keep it to herself? I was stunned by the discovery that my mother had had mini-strokes, but now that it had sunk in, it disturbed me. What had caused them? Evidently they were the result of some series of emotional traumas, but what were these and when did they happen? The questions weighed me down but the last one landed like a sledgehammer. Was I responsible?

I thought back to those evenings; the tension between us had been very raw. Resentment and anger, misunderstanding and desperation had fuelled our exchanges. At times it was like two wild animals fighting over the same kill. I told myself I needed Mother to come out of her protective shell to admit to feelings of love and loss. Maybe hidden away behind all the angry words was the fact that what we were both fighting for was the ownership of my father's affection. Perhaps each of us thought the other was less deserving. Yet when I thought about it, I realized my father was not really the issue and our rows about him were bruising evasions of something else. Beneath all the accusation and recriminations was a desperate need for acknowledgement, affection and an affirmation of belonging. Back then, neither of us wanted to admit any vulnerability and right now I was drowning in it.

'No wonder you have scars on your heart,' I said quietly to her recumbent body. I couldn't tell if she heard me and even if she had, could she understand? I thought of the two fighting animals exhaustedly eyeing one another. I was feeling guilty. I wanted her to open her eyes and see me. It was then I realized I was only a few years younger than my father had been when my parents were caught up in their own whirlwind. I had been a child then and had metaphorically walked away from their world. Sometimes, in the tell-tale way that Alzheimer's announces itself, Mother would call me 'Jack', before her senses reordered themselves. So maybe I was 'Jack' when we fought over his memory. I didn't know whether the idea comforted me a little or confused me. It was my father who declared 'There's a want in him' when Mother expressed anxiety about my 'comings and goings,' as she called them. It was beginning to dawn on me that Mother and I wanted the same things. We both had a lonely childhood: happy in our own world, we never learned to share our emotions or ask for anything. Now here I was at her bedside agonizing over the past while she had retreated into hers.

Listening to my mother's ramblings about her childhood broke open the vista to my own and in so doing pushed down the barrier and the distance that had grown up between us. I had understood things as a child and had unconsciously carried that childish understanding into my adulthood. Only fools believe the umbilical cord is ever truly severed. I was beginning to learn the fallacy of that. Something still connected us and I was desperately trying to reel it in while the tide of her life was fast flowing out. It came as no surprise that when the doctor looking after her called my sisters and me into the family room, it was to confirm what we already knew. I hardly heard it. I watched his mouth form the words: advanced age, chronic diabetes, severely weakened heart, advanced Alzheimer's, poor respiratory capacity. The list went on. But it didn't matter. Only the final phrase 'end stage situation' struck home. It sounded like a term from a space monitoring facility. 'The craft is at end stage situation, landing at minus sixty seconds.' What he really said was that continually stabilizing or resuscitating Mother would only delay the inevitable. It was putting a great strain on an already exhausted body. It was time to let go. There was nothing more I could reel in. She was outward bound, swimming toward the Great Sargasso Sea. I could hear Dad's voice in my ear when we were on the fishing boat out of Groomsport harbour: 'Let her go, son!'

'We have a special facility in the hospital for people in your mother's condition. We call it a Care Pathway for the Dying. To explain it simply, it's a special unit where the patient is monitored closely and, if you like, "eased" through that final doorway. You understand what I am saying?' The doctor sounded as if he was reading from a prepared script. We all did. He was asking our permission to change her medication from one which would bring her back from the brink to one which would provide an easier passage out of life. My sisters and I looked at one another. Elaine, whose years working in the hospital meant that she knew precisely what this Pathway for the Dying entailed, answered for us all. 'We need to talk about this.' 'Of course.' The doctor nodded and stopped as he was about to go out the door. 'She's an incredibly tough woman, your mother. Time outruns us all and she's very tired now,' he said quietly. He looked at me. 'I read your book. Now I know where your strength came from.' Then he pulled the door after him.

We knew there was nothing to discuss. The burden of Mother's dying was wearing us all down. 'It basically means instructing the doctor to cease all medication except painkillers or anything else to help her through the last stages,' Elaine outlined. I heard the words 'Not for resus'. I thought of the blue letters and numbers stamped on the carcasses hanging in the butcher's shop that first evening we came to look at our new home. 'Call it medical ethics or hospital protocol but it requires the next of kin to give the go-ahead,' Elaine continued. I took a deep breath and exhaled loudly. It's not like throwing a fish back in the water, is it? I wanted to say but I kept it to myself. Instead, a line from a hymn I used to hear children singing in the gospel hall near our house was suddenly in my head. I could hear the words 'You in your small corner and I in mine'. 'OK,' I said, suddenly standing up. 'There isn't really any option here.' I turned to my sisters. Both were quiet. 'We all have to agree on this.' It was like one of those secret oaths you swear with your friends when you are a child. We decided to take some time to consider what we were about to do.

It didn't take long. We stood in the hospital corridor with the doctor and confirmed our decision to 'let her go'. He nodded sympathetically and said 'Leave things with me' as he walked off. The starchy white housecoat stuck out at the back and swayed as he walked. He looked a bit like a giant seagull as he rounded the end of the corridor and disappeared. A few people passed by, then they too were gone. The corridor was stuffy. The heating had dried up the air and I could smell lunch wafting up from the kitchens. 'Cats' piss!' I said, walking off in the opposite direction from the doctor. What a smell to die in, I was thinking.

'How long does this "pathway" process take?' I asked my sister as we sat in the hospital canteen. 'Usually about forty-eight hours. It rarely goes beyond three days.' I leaned across the table. 'Does anyone ever change their mind?' Elaine looked at me, puzzled for a moment. 'There's hardly enough time for that,' she answered.

Later that day, on the bus journey back home I tried to remember some of the bus trips I had secretly taken as a child but all I could think about was the 'journey' I had sent my mother on. I mouthed the words the doctor had used: the 'Pathway for the Dying'. I looked at the passengers on the bus. I remembered how on my own furtive journeys I sometimes imagined the people travelling with me were really dead. They all sat unmoving, staring out the window like mannequins. They never spoke. They got on and off the bus in silence. The words kept repeating themselves, the 'Pathway for the Dying'. It sounded in my head like some ancient esoteric treatise! God, I hope they don't call us in to pray over her, I thought in a flash of panic. 'Don't worry, Mum I won't let any holy men near you,' I said. I continued talking to myself, only to realize that I was talking to her. 'I never knew where I was going when I took those mysterious bus rides. I wasn't a bit afraid. Once I found an injured bird. It was some kind of hawk or hunting bird. It had talons and a hooked beak and really small piercing eyes. I wanted to bring it home but I knew you would be very angry. I thought Mr Robins would be able to fix it. But then you would have known about my secret excursions and about me keeping my dinner money.' The subject of the dinner money forced another confession out of me about the stolen pennies for the gas meter. I was feeling a bit unnerved. It was as if someone had shaken out the contents of my memory and I was having to explain a lot of things I wasn't prepared for. The bus had to pass near to where Mother had grown up. Quickly I determined to get off. I was interested less in finding her childhood than in trying to get away from the guilty embarrassments of my own. To my astonishment, part of me was beginning to believe that in some impossible way, the things that were in my head were floating across space and time into my mother's head. I was feeling shame and fear, not the way a child does, the way an adult does! I walked through a couple of streets until I came to the railway embankment where she would have played and where I wanted to think she courted my dad. There wasn't much of it left. I walked along the ridge of what remained. I had played here as a child, usually to get away from the foreboding atmosphere of my grandparents' home. A few times I came here with my parents to collect blackberries. There were other times when I came here alone determined to walk the disused track until I reached its terminus. O God, I thought. Where's the terminus for Minnie? There was no answer so I left the question behind on the empty embankment.

Two or three days, even a week, was much too short for what I was hurriedly planning. It seemed more meaningful than pacing out the time in a hospital corridor. I decided to go back to where I had grown up. Visiting my ill mother had unearthed large tracts of my childhood. The confirmation of her passing and my putting her on the 'Pathway' made going back an imperative. 'Going back' and 'letting go' were somehow the same thing in my excited state.

Duncairn Gardens was still there; so were the trees that lined it. Evolina Street was gone. The whole area had been redeveloped. Streets had been knocked down and rebuilt in a different config-uration. The original names had been replaced. I recognized all of them except Evolina. It had gone for good. The tiny, four-classroom school was gone and so was St Barnabas church. The 'Donkey' picture house had long since been demolished and replaced with a section of new housing. All the citadels of my childhood had been bulldozed into oblivion. I hurried up to the waterworks. No one was poling model boats. The little sun hut where the old men brought their dogs had been removed; even the swans had gone. Half a mile away in Alexandra Park I confronted the same loss.

Half of the parkland that I remembered had been swallowed up by new urban developments. There was no stream for catching 'spricks' in. The big tree with its rope swing where I had learned to fly was no longer there. Even the lake where I had watched my father swim was choked with weeds. The whole place looked like it had been abandoned. I walked towards the city centre. Clifton House was still there, whilst everything around it had gone or been replaced. The Co-op building remained but was now part of Belfast's Art College complex. The offloading yards and the animal pens at the docks were now an industrial enterprise site. There was no point in going to Smithfield Market, as it had mysteriously been gutted by fire a long time ago. There was nothing left but the weight of memory. Here I was trudging through the disappeared backstreets of my childhood just as my mother had gone back to hers! I would never have found half of those memories if I hadn't had to piece together the lost vignettes that her rambling dementia had uncovered. But memory was not enough. With so much of the physical landscape of the past gone, I needed a marker, something that confirmed it wasn't all an illusion, or a makey-up story that I had concocted in an effort to make sense of Mother's fractured past.

Then I remembered the Indian Chief. The big Red Indian chief exploded into my head, obliterating everything else. The memory was making me breathless. It was one of those Saturdays when I was supposed to go to the Cartoon Cinema with my dad. The night before, I had been playing in my imaginary world and Dad had remarked that he wasn't sure whether I was a cowboy or an Indian. Then he told me that he would take me to meet a big Indian chief the next day. That night I couldn't sleep. I was restless with fear and expectation. Here I was, half a century later experiencing the same emotions, only this time I was fearful that I wouldn't be able to find him again.

I remember my father walking me hand in hand through the great sombre mill house and grain stores that made up Belfast's dockland. Not far from these had been the commercial offices of the shippers and importers. The buildings were copies of the classical era, full of Corinthian columns and plinths and all sorts of ornate stonework. Their bulk and weight seemed awesome to my seven-year-old mind. I was glad of my father's reassuring hand but I was still intimidated about going to see the chieftain. 'You have to be very respectful, he is very old.' Dad's voice was serious but there was a lightness in it. He, at least, seemed happy to be visiting the Indian. 'What's his name?' I asked. 'Thunder Eagle,' he answered without the slightest hesitation. On we walked through the empty streets with the tall buildings dwarfing us. The name of the Indian chief was so grand that I was too afraid to ask any more questions. I was trying to imagine what Thunder Eagle would look like and what I would do if he spoke to me in Indian! Suddenly, we stopped. 'You see, up there,' my father said, pointing to a great stone face that looked out from the side of an arched gateway. I looked at the huge face becoming bigger as Dad hoisted me on to his shoulders. Though I was now eight feet tall the face still stared down at me. The warrior's head was massive.

I could almost see it again as I had then. I had to find it. I knew that it would still be there. However long it took, I had to find it.

The streets were thronged as I walked down Royal Avenue retracing my steps from over forty years ago. It was September. The autumn sun was bright, with a distinct chill in the air. Early shoppers were mingling with lunchtime office workers and shop assistants scuttling in and out of various bars and cafés. The sense of bustle did not dispel my anxiety. Had my old Indian been bulldozed out of existence like so many other parts of the city? The Albert Clock, Belfast's poor attempt to replicate Big Ben was leaning to the right as it always had done. I crossed the road to check. Sure enough, the famous old clock was doing just that: leaning. It struck two o'clock. Time was running out, I thought, for me, my mother, and perhaps even Thunder Eagle. The leaning clock might have to suffice as the memorial I was looking for. It had metaphoric significance, if nothing else. Time was askew. Time was off balance, like the sense of time in my mother's head and my own desperate reclamation of the past. But something in me was not convinced. The clock was a marker, not a memorial. I knew I was near the place where I had met the Indian. If I could home in on that walk with my dad I would find him.

I stumbled through the streets scanning every building. Redevelopment had not clawed its way into the area. These old buildings were constructed to last. Finally I thought I had found it. The giant reddish brown façade was now sadly dilapidated and beyond repair. My eyes scanned it. There was the Ethiopian's head surrounded by pomegranates. He had flat lips, a flat nose and huge ears with earrings that a gymnast could swing from. Beside him was an Indian, but not a Red Indian; pineapples, grapes and pumpkins surrounded him. He had black eyes and huge flowing whiskers. His lips were pursed in a kiss. There was an Eastern sultan beside him crowned with a majestic turban. I had forgotten about all these faces and was remembering them as my eye danced urgently towards my Indian chief. His head-dress of feathers pressed back into the stone as though a wind was blowing through them. He had a long nose and set mouth. His eyes were huge and soft. I looked at them, half realizing why after all these years I had remembered his face rather than the others. I studied Thunder Eagle for some minutes while he studied me. As I walked away I could only think how imponderable, yet accepting the chieftain appeared. He was all knowing and all embracing, as if he had seen it all before.

I left Thunder Eagle and the city thinking how little remained of that part of it that I and my mother shared. At the end of her life I was rediscovering her the way I had rediscovered my old stone Indian, only now we were making our own separate journeys, life-times apart but still umbilically connected. The disappearing city made me question how far imaginatively and emotionally I had travelled from it. As a young man I had chosen to leave the city exhausted by its troubled history and its antagonistic incapacity to move away from its myopic concerns. I was beginning to under-stand that I had done the same thing as a child with my own troubled family and had unconsciously carried those childhood resolutions into my adult life. Slowly I was realizing that only the city of my childhood was lost.

I had walked off into the world with the understanding of a child. I had gone in search of something I was only now becoming aware of. A sense of belonging. A place that could be a home. Somewhere amongst a people that would nurture me and perhaps satisfy what my father had called 'the want in me'. Piecing together the picture book of my childhood had revealed things about my manhood years that were forcing me to ask difficult questions. Had the trajectory of my life been settled in those early years and had I carried this 'lost boy' inside myself for all those years? Here I was back in the city I had so determinedly walked away from. In this vigil journey I was learning that I only needed to open myself to my own history to find some of the answers that may have created that 'want' and ultimately made me the gypsy chaser I had become. The vague deadline that the doctor had drawn up and which had started my mother down her 'Pathway' had also set me on my own. The word 'deadline' made me smile to myself. I walked off through the city hardly aware of my surroundings.

A few hours later I sat in the Crown Bar, a renowned watering hole in the city. It had been an exhausting day in too many ways. I was glad of the refuge. Inside the Crown's baroque interior I was pondering whether I had really understood what I had left behind. I have a love/hate relationship with the city. I know that underbelly of vibrant colourful life, the coarse, savage humour, the passionate camaraderie and the ugly bigotry and blindness. I had come back to it like the prodigal son, with the knowledge that all those things had been part of my past. I thought I had broken free of its snares but no one is ever entirely free of the past. The past is said to haunt us with good reason. If history is seen to threaten our sense of ourselves, then we withdraw and the poison of self-doubt will fester and create monsters. If it does not create monsters it cripples and maims our sympathetic grasp of reality. It was this understanding which drove me away in the first place and now it was bringing me back.

I listened half-heartedly to the animated conversations around me, grateful to be able to eavesdrop on them and relieve myself of my introspection. Everywhere the talk overflowed with fabulous obscenities and unbridled language. In the past few months Mother had found an outrageous capacity to swear. I had got over my embarrassment and secretly enjoyed it, the way I enjoyed the verbal enthusiasms of the drinkers. It reminded me of the aggressive graffiti I had grown up with. I hadn't seen much of it as I trudged the backstreets that day. Mother could swear a hundred times better than those pathetic slogans and she could have silenced the intoxicated punters in the pub. Maybe Alzheimer's had released a part of her that had got buried inside her and she couldn't care two flying frigs how it came out or who it offended. I left the pub thinking about my prodigal return. One thing was for sure: I would not be eating the 'fatted calf' on my own. The feast table was full of ghosts all gabbling away and telling me their stories. For the next three nights I talked through some of these 'stories' with my sisters while we sat waiting for the inevitable. It was all in vain. Mother had decided to take her time along the 'Pathway'. Wherever she was going it would have to wait until she was ready to go there.

As I drove home to Dublin I discovered a new piece of graffiti emblazoned on a wall that enclosed a different hospital from the one I had spent the last three nights in. It asked starkly 'Is there life before death?' It was a profoundly sarcastic and exquisite mockery of all the years of chaos and killing that had engulfed the city. I laughed at it and thought how relevant it was to my own concerns about my mother who was also mocking the 'deadline' that had been set for her.

She continued to mock us all for weeks. The doctor simply shrugged at her resistance. 'I've always believed that, in spite of all medical science, people really choose their own time to go, and Minnie is living proof of that!' he explained. But it didn't explain anything. Mother's body had contracted into a foetal position. All her muscle tissue had wasted and foreshortened. Her legs and knees were pulled up towards her chin and her arms were folded across her chest so that her clawed hands rested on her shoulders, yet her complexion was unblemished and shone like a young girl's. I thought of the little statue in the china cabinet. I leaned over, brushing the hair from her face and kissed her gently. 'This is some song and dance you have been leading us on.' For a moment her eyes opened and she looked directly into mine. It wasn't a look that I had seen before. I had become used to telling her mood from her eyes. They could be penetrating and aggressive; at other times they were inquisitive or unsure. This time they were incredibly passive. I felt there was something urgent she wanted to say and only her eyes could tell it. As if they alone were safe from the confusion in her head. I stroked her head reassuringly as she watched me.

My sister touched an ice cube to her lips and she sucked at it greedily. 'She can hear everything you say. She knows exactly what's going on, don't you?' she informed me while clearly talking to my mother as well. Later we sat together in the hospital café, talking. 'She can't speak much, but you know Minnie – she didn't have to say things for you to know exactly what she wanted.' I smiled in agreement, thinking to myself that I would rather have had the words. Now neither of us had them.

Over the last few weeks I had fretted and agonized over what I should say to her before she finally left the earth. Night after night I tossed and sweated, dreamed and screamed about her and at her. Many of those nights I found myself sitting on the number 77 bus with her. She was wearing beautiful earrings which seemed to hypnotize me. It was one of those old 1950s buses with an open platform from which you got on and off. We were sitting on the end seat near the platform and I was terrified of falling on to the road and being run over by another vehicle. Every time I looked at her earrings I felt safe. 'Don't worry, you won't fall off, I'll look after you,' I heard her say, and again I felt unafraid. Her gloved hands patted my knee and her arm enclosed me. 'Where are we going?' I always asked and her answer was always the same. 'Don't you fret, we'll be there soon and then you'll see.' We never did arrive though the dream replayed itself for weeks. At times I woke up exhausted. In some of my dreams we had been arguing. I was asking questions that she refused to answer. I became angry and the argument grew so bitter that I woke up. I cursed her for hanging on so long and then I couldn't get back to sleep. Like a child, I was afraid that the curse would turn back on me.

Watching her lying there, all folded up like a piece of origami, I could feel that curse inch its way back to me. She emitted little animal grunts as she laboured through her breathing. 'I have to go now,' I said, running my fingers down her cheek. Her eyes blinked rapidly like a dreamer's then rolled open for a few seconds to reveal that penetrating stare. I knew she was looking at me from somewhere very far away. Whatever strength remained in her was concentrated in her eyes; then they blinked shut again. When I was a child and was leaving the house to play outside she used to call after me, 'Don't go where I can't see you!' I wanted to think that that's what she might have been saying. There was such intensity in her eyes. They were bright and clear as if they were lit up from the inside. Whatever those eyes were trying to say they were not speaking to the child in me.

Over a cup of coffee in the hospital café my sisters and I tried to gauge where Mother was on her 'Pathway'. She had everyone confused. She should have passed away weeks ago. Even the doctors were baffled and could offer no explanation. My sister made the joking remark, 'She's very stubborn, Brian . . . just like you!' I raised my eyes and smiled weakly. 'You know what she was like: once she got something in her head nothing could change it. God help anybody that tried,' she continued. 'Don't I know it. I still have scars from all the arguments we had,' I responded, trying to appear resigned. My sister looked at me for a long moment before answering, 'But Brian, that was only with you!' I squirmed. In the past weeks I had been discovering many things, and some of them I didn't care to confront. I had to leave. The following day was my birthday and my sons had prepared a 'surprise' party for me. I had to be home for that. I rushed away from the hospital with my sister's words still in my ears. I arrived at the railway station with over an hour to spare. It was only a short walk from where I had found my Indian chief. I decided to visit him again.

His great ancient head stared out across the city. Those imponderable eyes had seen so much. If he could speak, he could tell a thousand tales. I wanted to believe that his stone eyes mirrored those blue crystals that stared out of my mother's face. It was fanciful thinking, but fanciful thinking was what I needed. Inside my head I began talking to the chief. A flood of garbled words and recollections spilled out. For weeks I had been swallowed up in a sea of history. At times I found myself washed up on strange shores where I shivered, lost and confused before the sea dragged me back into itself. Sometimes it surprised and amused me. I had been treading water too long. I needed to get past history. Thunder Eagle's huge face looked down on me. His big stone eyes had the habit of changing each time I looked at them. At least, I imagined they did. Maybe that's what connected them with my mother's staring eyes: they were both lit up from the inside, in different ways. Thunder Eagle seemed to be saying that the only way to get past history was to make peace with it before it was too late. That charge on my conscience was not one that sat easy with me. It would have to wait. I had a train to catch.

The numbing rhythm of the train, the landscape I knew so well flicking past, and my own weariness all combined to produce a feeling of lethargy. I was planning how I might feign surprise at my party. I considered how I might intrigue my children about my visit to the Red Indian chief the way my father had done. The dilemma that the stone warrior had set me was still floating around in my head, but I was feeling too listless to deal with it. I looked around at the other travellers. My attention was drawn to a passenger sitting a few seats in front of me. She was in her early twenties and had a large bird cage on the seat beside her. Inside, a green budgie hopped backwards and forwards from one perch to another while its owner made noises through her pursed lips to entertain it. I studied the pair with some amusement, glad of the distraction.

I thought of the sick budgie we had in our home in Evolina Street, and how Mother held it in her cupped hands close to the fire to revive it. She set it on a newspaper on the hearth where it lay quiet and still. It was dead but she didn't want us to know. Because birds in the house always unnerved her she would even leave the room when Dad took it out of the cage to clean it. That night she held it so tenderly, repeating its name softly, 'Joey, Joey, Joey, Joey. Poor Joey, poor, poor Joey.' It sounded as if she was chirping to the bird. Out of nowhere, it suddenly came to me how only a few hours ago I had kissed her. It was a spontaneous thing. I couldn't remember the last time I had kissed her or when she had kissed me. I had stroked her face and forehead as I was leaving; that, too, was an intuitive act.

Maybe Thunder Eagle wasn't telling me what I needed to do after all. Maybe he was confirming that I had already done it and I should stop agonizing over history. His great stone face had emerged out of history to befriend me again after all these years. Here he was beside me riding the Dublin train with a budgie and a young woman mouthing bird talk. He was closer to me now than on all those other occasions I had stood in the empty street looking up at him. He was telling me things and I felt close to the moment when Mother blinked her eyes. He seemed to be saying that it was time to acknowledge the past because it is always with you. Mourn what's been lost, and leave it lost. Validate the pain that may have been caused to you and confess the pain you may have been the author of. It is only by letting one erase the other that you can mend whatever may be broken. Restoring the broken relationship meant 'letting go'. The phrase was like an old echo. That's what I was waiting for my mother to do, and maybe that was also what she was waiting for me to do.

I was becoming stupefied by all this heady thinking. I was

beginning to think of those wise old Indian chiefs in the Saturday matinées. They stood wrapped in blankets and war bonnets. The peace pipe carved with animal heads and adorned with feathers lay across their arms. They spoke with great solemnity and wisdom. But the words in my head did not come from flickering images in the 'Donkey' picture house. They came from Thunder Eagle – and he was set in stone! The train rattled on, bringing me back to that train hurtling past me on that small spit of a beach that my long walk had brought me to. The people in the carriages stared out blankly. I waved to them and a few waved back. For a split second I imagined Mother waving back at me. Then it was gone again, leaving me unnerved and unsure. I looked out on the sea and the coast of north County Dublin.

The next day I was sitting at home waiting for the birthday cake to be ceremonially paraded into the room accompanied by an enthusiastic chorus of 'Happy Birthday'. The phone rang and Elaine's voice calmly announced, 'She's gone.' 'How was it ?' I asked. 'Slipped away in her sleep, it seems.' 'Are you OK?' 'Yes, I'm OK.' 'Does Brenda know?' 'Yes, I rang her already.' 'Is she OK?' 'Yes, she's OK.' The questions and answers came automatically. 'I'll come up,' I suggested. 'No need, she's not going anywhere. Tomorrow will do.' 'OK, I'll call Brenda about funeral arrangements and we can all meet tomorrow.' 'OK, I'll see you tomorrow. Oh, by the way, happy birthday!' I put the phone down. I had never heard so many OKs in so short a conversation.

We had our little party. I made a big fuss of blowing out candles, opening presents, hugging and kissing and being greatly delighted at the whole affair. After the excitement had all died down and the kids had gone off to play somewhere I quietly informed my wife, 'I have to go up tomorrow.' She looked at me knowingly. 'She died some time this afternoon.' I explained what my sister had said about

305

my mother not going anywhere. I smiled. 'She's just gone on the biggest journey of her life and we have just had a goodbye party without even knowing it.'

The fact that Mother chose to die on the anniversary of my birth never registered with me. I did recall the doctor talking about people choosing their own time to go. If that was the case, she had left me plenty to think about. What preoccupied me was the last image I had of her lying snuggled up in that foetal position. She would have to be buried like that. I could imagine the morticians gently manoeuvring her scrunched-up body into the coffin.

A few years before she died I had visited a museum in Arica, a small town on the border between Chile and Peru. The museum's curators had recreated a burial tomb they had discovered many years previously in the Andean foothills. Behind a hermetically sealed glass screen several mummified corpses were on display. All the bodies had been buried in the foetal position. One of the remains was that of a woman. Two things intrigued me about the body. One was the beautiful earrings she was still wearing. They were made from sea shells, a strange thing to find in the mountains. The other was the small basket which had been laid beside her. There was something wrapped in cloth inside it. The notes accompanying this ancient tableau explained that the basket contained the body of a very young child. The two corpses were evidently mother and child. Whether the mother had died at the time of giving birth was not known, but they had been reunited in death and the afterlife. I am not sure if it was some unconscious need for comfort or some-thing to fill the void now that she was gone that brought the visit to the tomb of the Indian woman and her child back to me. Implicitly, it had something to do with my preoccupation with my own and my mother's childhood. Maybe it was her way of telling me that she was reunited with the stillborn child she had carried inside herself for all those years. I was sure it also had something to do with mending the broken relationship that the chief had whispered to me about.

When I went back to sort out the funeral arrangements I visited the Indian a few times. He still captivated me. He was certainly a memorial to my childhood, but his remoteness was too profound to be a memorial to my mother. I can hear her now shouting at me, 'You needn't bother yourself thinking you can put some bloody Red Indian on my grave. You just keep all your fancy notions to yourself. Do you hear me!' For Minnie I needed something more recent. Something that rang out of the streets of my childhood and hers. Something that was human and that spoke about love and longing and the joy of having lived.

As a young boy I had enjoyed skipping. I loved the ritual of the moving ropes, the dance-like steps and the songs that accompanied them. One in particular has stayed with me. I always associate it with my mother. It's called, 'I'll Tell My Ma'. The last two verses go like this:

> Albert Mooney says he loves her,
> All the boys are fighting for her
> They rap at the door, they ring at the bell
> Saying, O my true love are you well
>
> Out she comes as white as snow
> Rings on her fingers, bells on her toes.
> Ould Jenny Murray says she'll die
> If she doesn't get the fella with the roving eye!
>
> Let the wind and the rain and the hail blow high
> And the snow come tumbling from the sky

307

I'll Tell Me Ma

She's as sweet as apple pie
She'll get her own lad by and by.

When she gets a lad of her own
She won't tell her ma when she gets home.
Let them all come as they will
For it's Albert Mooney she loves still.

Wherever my ma flew off to, I like to think it was with rings on
her fingers and bells on her toes. That's what we do with birds so
that we can locate them in the dark, and hear them when they fly
back to us in the night.

ACKNOWLEDGEMENTS

Grateful acknowledgement are due to David Higham Associates for the use of lines from 'Ballad to a Traditional Refrain' by Maurice James Craig, and to A.P. Watt Ltd for permission to quote from 'An Irish Airman Foresees His Death' by W.B. Yeats.

Special thanks are also due to the following: Maurice Hayes for his wonderfully erudite lecture dedicated to the memory of John Malone, my former headmaster, and entitled 'Why Can't They Be Like Us'; Thompson Steele, former teacher from my schooldays, who supplied me with much background material in publications from the East Belfast Historical Society. I would also like to acknowledge the publishers and contributors of the *Belfast Magazine*, particularly Terry O'Neill, Joe Baker and Harry Johnston.

To David Hammond I am indebted in a special way, most memorably for the evening in his home when he sang me back to my childhood. Davy was a collector of many things but his songs were better than any archive film footage. Thank you my old friend, even though you are gone from us I can still hear the melodies.

Gerry McLaughlin is another old friend and I am grateful to him for finding and collecting material in the library when I was unable to get there.

Thanks to the Central Library and also especially the Linen Hall Library, especially the Chief Librarian John Gray.

There are many people whom I met, sometimes by intention

and sometimes by chance, and their own memories had the effect of reminding me of things I had forgotten and things, sometimes, I might have preferred not to remember. To all of them I am most grateful.

Finally to my editor, Robin Robertson who waited for the book, and to Clare Reihill who gave me the title after I thought the book was done. Between them they sent me back and took me, in the lines of Van Morrison, way, way, way, way back.

Brian Keenan